Social change

By the same author

Political Manipulation and Administrative Power (1979)
Political Culture in Israel (1977)

Social change

The advent and maturation
of modern society

Eva Etzioni-Halevy

Routledge & Kegan Paul
London, Boston and Henley

First published in 1981
by Routledge & Kegan Paul Ltd
39 Store Street,
London WC1E 7DD,
9 Park Street,
Boston, Mass. 02108, USA and
Broadway House,
Newtown Road,
Henley-on-Thames,
Oxon RG9 1EN
Set in Press Roman by
Hope Services
Abingdon, Oxon
and printed in Great Britain by
Redwood Burn Ltd
Trowbridge & Esher

British Library Cataloguing in Publication Data

Etzioni-Halevy, Eva
Social change
1. Social change
I. Title
301.24   HM101   80-41727

ISBN 0-7100-0767-1
ISBN 0-7100-0768-X Pbk

To my son Oren, with love

Contents

Preface

A Chinese proverb supposedly says that, 'To prophesy is extremely difficult — especially with respect to the future.'[1] It is perhaps not quite as difficult, but still far from easy to 'prophesy' with respect to the past and the present. That is to say, it is not easy to work out a coherent pattern and make sense of past and recent occurrences. Social life as we know it today bears little resemblance to what it was a few hundred years ago. What is the nature of this transition (currently referred to as modernization)? How did it come about and what has it brought in its wake? Quite a bit of sociological knowledge has accumulated on this subject; but not enough has been done to extract a coherent pattern from it.

There are a great many theories and a wide array of empirical data, but not enough has been done to integrate each and bring them together. There are many texts on sociological theory and even on the theory of social change, but for the most part they are not focused specifically on the advent and maturation of modern society, and no general outline of these processes can be seen. There is an abundance of relevant research findings, but most of them are fragmentary and dispersed in a multitude of books and journals; there is a lack of general texts which piece them together and present them systematically in conjunction with the pertinent theories. Also, many of the empirical analyses are written by scholars for scholars, using technical jargon and presupposing an extensive knowledge of quantitative research methods. There is a sparsity of texts in which these analyses are presented simply, clearly, and concisely, so that they can be appreciated not only by professionals, but also by students, amateur scholars, and the general public. This book is designed to fill these voids.

Most, if not all, textbooks in sociology are written from the point of view of one theoretical perspective — as a rule either 'mainstream' or Marxist. This book endeavours to present both viewpoints as objectively as possible, to confront them with the type of empirical data that (one may hope), will be regarded as unbiased by the representatives of both, and to remain as balanced as possible in its conclusions. In previous analyses I have adopted a non-Marxist framework and in one of them (Etzioni-Halevy, 1979) have taken issue with the Marxist point of view. However, it is precisely because of this that I have made a special attempt in this book to avoid as far as possible an anti-Marxist bias. As is well known, in the social sciences it is not humanly possible to be wholly objective, but at least the attempt can be made, and it should be left to the reader to assess the degree of its success.

The advent and maturation of modern society, although more narrowly focused than social change in general, is still a very broad subject. No single work can cover all its aspects. With regret, many highly relevant and eminently interesting topics had to be excluded. For instance, the demographic transition, urbanization, the growth and proliferation of large-scale organizations, changes in race and ethnic relations, changes in the family, and changes in the position of women in society, had to be largely or wholly omitted. I hope that there will be another opportunity to make up for this. In the meantime, this book focuses on what seem to be the cardinal aspects of society, and those that have figured most prominently in the various theories: the economy, the class structure, the political structure, and the structure of education, as they changed throughout the process of modernization and up to the present.

Also, it proved impossible to include all societies that have undergone or are undergoing modernization. A choice between societies had to be made and it fell on our own, that is, Western, capitalist societies. Some theories of modernization and development refer to Western societies in particular, others deal with these processes in general, wherever they occur, or else try to establish the relationship between modernization in Western and non-Western countries. This book presents all types, because they are logically interconnected. But the empirical analysis is focused on modernization and subsequent changes in Western societies only. The assumption is that despite several differences among them, these societies have enough in common and are sufficiently different from others, to warrant their presentation as a distinctive type of society, where distinctive types of transformations have taken place. The main purpose of this book is to identify these transformations. On a lighter note, the book includes a chapter on the search for alternative social formations, and examines the extent to which this search may eventually lead to further changes in capitalist societies.

A few years ago I co-edited a book of readings on social change:

A. Etzioni and E. Etzioni-Halevy (eds) (1973), *Social Change* (2nd edn), New York, Basic Books. Many of the references in the present work are to readings in that volume. The two books may thus be used in conjunction with each other. However, the perspectives of the two books are not identical and some readers may prefer to use one without the other. It is hoped that each of them makes its own, independent contribution to the understanding of modernization and modern life.

Eva Etzioni-Halevy

Acknowledgments

This book was written at the Department of Sociology, Faculty of Arts, The Australian National University. I am greatly indebted to the head of this department, Professor J. Zubrzycki and my colleagues there for the support they have given me in writing this book by easing my teaching and administrative duties while it was in progress. I am also most grateful for their personal encouragement.

I would like to express my deepest gratitude to Dr M. Alexander, Mr A. Ashbolt, Professor L. Broom, Dr C. Forster, Dr Z. Halevy, Dr J. Higley, Dr A. Hopkins, and Dr S. Mugford, for reading parts of the manuscript and for their most valuable and helpful comments. Special thanks are due to Dr W. D. Rubinstein, on whom I inflicted almost all chapters of the book, who read them with unfailing patience, who corrected several historical inaccuracies, and whose comments were an invaluable help. The revisions undertaken on the strength of all these criticisms greatly improved the manuscript, but I must claim sole responsibility for whatever shortcomings remain.

Finally I would like to thank Connie Wilsack and Mrs Penelope Hope for their outstanding work in editing the text, and Mrs Sandra Kruck and Mrs Ettie Oakman for their patience in deciphering my illegible handwriting and for their excellent work in typing the manuscript.

The author and publishers are grateful to the following: McGraw Hill, for permission to reprint the extract from p. 311 of G.Lenski and J. Lenski, *Human Societies*, 1978; MacGibbon & Kee, for permission to reprint a table from p. 38 of W. L. Guttsman, *The British Political Elite*, 1963; the American Philosophical Society, for permission to reprint a table from O. Ashenfelter, 'What is Involuntary Unemployment?', *Proceedings of the American Philosophical Society*, vol. 122, June 1978, no. 3, pp. 135–8; Professor S. H. Cohn, for permission to reprint a table from p. 7 of his book, *Economic Development in the Soviet Union*, 1970; Oxford University Press, for permission to reprint a table from p. 8 of H. Chenery *et al., Redistribution with Growth*, 1974; Prentice-Hall, for permission to reprint a table from p. 172 of

R. Heilbroner, *The Making of Economic Society*, 1962. The tables from *Social Change in the Twentieth Century* by D. Chirot, © 1977 by Harcourt Brace Jovanovich, Inc. Reprinted by permission of the publisher. Robert D. Putnam, *The Comparative Study of Political Elites*, © 1976 p. 187–88. Reprinted by permission of Prentice-Hall, Inc., Englewood Cliffs, New Jersey.

Introduction

An anecdote popular among sociologists tells of an expedition of three scholars: a physicist, a geologist, and an economist, stranded in a remote desert. The only food they had left was a can of beans — but nothing with which to open it. The physicist suggested that his glasses be used as lenses through which the sun's rays would be focused on the can, and a hole would be pierced in it. The geologist proposed that a sharp rock be used to achieve the same effect. And the economist said: 'First, let's assume a can opener . . . .' The idea, of course, is that economists are accused (especially by sociologists) of basing their models on unwarranted assumptions. Having been told this anecdote, some economists retaliated by wondering aloud what a sociologist would have suggested if he/she had the bad luck to be included in the expedition. They decided that it was impossible to come up with an answer, but one thing they held to be certain: had two sociologists been present, they would have come up with different and probably contradictory suggestions. Had a third sociologist been included, his opinion would have differed substantially from those of his two colleagues. Indeed, it cannot be denied that there is a grain of truth in this view: there are almost as many sociologies as there are sociologists.

For this reason, a book such as this cannot simply draw on a well-established and integrated body of sociological theory in order to map out the advent and maturation of modern society. Throughout the hundred and fifty-plus years of its existence, sociology has produced a multitude of (partly consistent and partly contradictory) theories on this subject. The first task, therefore, is to introduce some semblance of order into this maze.

Classifying theories on the advent and maturation of modern society

For this purpose, and at the risk of superficiality, the relevant theories have been classified as follows:

1

(1) *Classical theories* — the theories of sociology's nineteenth-century founding fathers, including Auguste Comte, Herbert Spencer, Karl Marx, Ferdinand Tönnies, Emile Durkheim, Max Weber and others. Although these theories differ widely, there are some common themes which run through all of them — foremost among these, their deep concern with the transition from pre-modern to modern society, or with what we now call modernization.

These classical theories have influenced contemporary sociology and following this line of influence the latter may be divided into two broad schools of thought: 'mainstream' and Marxist theories.

(2) *'Mainstream' theories* — these are of mixed theoretical ancestry. They have been influenced by practically all classical sociologists, particularly by Weber, Durkheim and Marx, and are customarily subdivided into more narrowly defined groups of theories. Of these there are two which have included a special interest in the development of modern society — structural-functionalism, and the power and conflict school.[1]

Structural-functionalism was most heavily influenced by Durkheim and Weber, and also by an earlier version of functionalism in anthropology.[2] It views society as shaped by a multiplicity of causal factors and as a system of interrelated elements. It puts major emphasis on values, consensus, and integration, and on the way in which the various elements in the system fit in with each other and contribute or 'fulfil a function' for the whole. So much so, that it has been accused of having little or nothing to say on social change. In contrast to anthropological functionalism, however (and perhaps partly in response to this criticism), structural-functionalism has made a substantial contribution to the analysis of modernization, and to the analysis of the further developments that have taken place in society as a result of modernization.

Structural-functionalism has also been criticized for ignoring power, coercion and conflict. These concepts form the main focus of the power and conflict school. This school emphasizes that power causes conflict, which causes change, and that the nature of the change depends largely on the nature of the conflict; it has applied this conception chiefly to the analysis of modernization and modern society. The power and conflict school has been greatly influenced by Marx; but it has been affected no less by Weber and other classical theorists. Also, this school is critical of some of Marx's tenets and accepts them only after introducing far-reaching revisions into them. Therefore it must be kept strictly apart from the other main group of contemporary theories

—which is also concerned with power and conflict, but whose theoretical lineage runs exclusively from Marx himself, and which accepts Marx's theory in its totality.

(3) *Marxist theories* — among all classical sociologists Marx stands out as a category all by himself, for he was the only one who fathered an entire (and highly influential) school of thought, which also did him the honour of naming itself after him.[3] Several classical sociologists put forward concepts and insights which filtered through into contemporary ('mainstream') sociology, but their concepts were frequently modified, revised, lifted out of their original theoretical context and re-woven into new analytical frameworks. Marx, however, stands out in that he alone had his theoretical framework adopted as a complete entity by an important, contemporary school of thought. This school includes orthodox Marxists who accept only minor deviations (if any) from Marx's original framework and various neo-Marxists who advocate slight modifications without questioning Marx's general framework. Also, they all support Marx's major concern with the rise and development of modern, capitalist society, although some broaden this concern and juxtapose the development of capitalist society with the under-development of the third world.

Theories versus empirical data on the advent and maturation of modern society

Guided by this classification, the analysis confronts the two contemporary schools of thought with empirical data on modernization and the subsequent changes in modern societies. As is well known, the empirical testing of sociological theories is wrought with great difficulties. Some of their tenets are highly abstract and generalized, and therefore not subject to direct empirical testing. Also, some of the data required to test these tenets are not available, or may be subject to conflicting interpretations in line with the interpreter's own theoretical affinities. This does not mean that the attempt to bring together theories and data should be abandoned, but merely that expectations must be scaled down: theories may be confronted with data, but they may not be conclusively tested by them.

Hence, those who expect the empirical evidence to lend unqualified support to one theoretical stream and unequivocally to negate the other are apt to be disappointed. After all, if the weight of the evidence were so clearly on one side, the proponents of the rival school of thought would not have constructed their models in the first place or – once constructed – would have abandoned the task a long time ago. Therefore this analysis – perhaps by necessity no less than by choice – attempts to steer its way between the two opposing schools of thought, maintaining a balanced and as objective a stand as possible.

In this context the reader must not be misled by the label 'mainstream', which has been given to the non-Marxist school of thought. This merely stems from the fact that for some time this school has been dominating the sociological scene and the label it acquired at that time has been retained even now. For lack of a better term it has been adopted here also. It is true that Marxists have proposed the name 'bourgeois sociology', but this has been rejected, for even by their own admission Marxist sociologists are no less 'bourgeois' in their social backgrounds and in their social positions, and derive no lesser benefits from the bourgeois system than do their rivals.

What can an analysis which confronts both 'mainstream' and Marxist theories with actual data on modernization and modernity hope to accomplish? It cannot 'prove' or refute either of the schools of thought. But it may bring out the shortcomings or sift out the most fruitful elements of each. Kant is supposed to have said at one time that he was not so much afraid of being refuted as he was of being misunderstood. It is hoped that this analysis will at least avoid such a misunderstanding of the major theories, and perhaps even lead to their better understanding. However, the main focus here is not sociology but society. Its main purpose is thus to lead to an eclectic, but wider, understanding of modernization and modern society.

Plan of the book

The plan of the book follows the logic of this exposition. The first, and shorter part of the book contains a general analysis of the main sociological theories as classified here. Classical theories of modernization are examined in chapter 1; 'mainstream' sociological theories of modernization, development and modernity, are dealt with in chapter 2; Marxist theories concerned with the same topics are presented in chapter 3; this chapter also includes a short section in which the theories are set beside comparative empirical data. But the main emphasis in the first part of the book is theoretical.

In the second and more substantial part, the emphasis shifts towards a more concrete and detailed analysis of modernization and recent changes in Western, capitalist societies.[4] Here the analysis is divided into social spheres: the economy (chapter 4); the class structure (chapter 5); the political structure (chapters 6 and 7); and the educational system (chapter 8). The discussion of each sphere opens with the presentation of a number of criteria for comparing this sphere in pre-modern and modern societies, for tracing the changes from one to the other and the changes in modern societies themselves. There follows an account of the main tenets of the two rival schools of thought with regard to the respective social areas and of the actual developments that have taken place, so far as this can be ascertained from historical and empirical data. The theories are then evaluated in the light of these data and some concrete conclusions are drawn. These conclusions point to certain problems which, on their part, have given rise to a continued search for social alternatives. These alternatives are discussed in Part 3 (chapter 9). Finally, in the conclusion the threads of the analysis are drawn together and some more general conclusions are presented.

Part I

This part presents a general discussion of classical and contemporary theories of the advent and maturation of modern society. It includes both theories of modernization in the West and theories of modernization in general — pertaining to Western capitalist as well as to non-Western countries. There follows a short section in which the theories are confronted with comparative empirical data.

1 · The advent of modern society in classical sociology

The transformation which culminated in the industrial revolution, is usually considered as the most significant change human society has undergone since the neolithic revolution[1] some seven to ten thousand years ago. Not surprisingly, this transformation has been a major concern of sociology ever since the discipline's inception. The term 'modernization'[2] and analysis known as 'modernization theory' is a relatively new product of the twentieth century. But fascination with the great transition as such dates back to the nineteenth century and its analysis is the crux of what came to be known as classical sociological theory.

The nature of the transition

The first classical theories were global, evolutionary schemes attempting to map the design of human history from the beginning to the end of time. They were closely followed by theoretical schemes which presented pre-modern and modern society as polar dichotomies and focused directly on the transition from one to the other. They were also followed by other global theories which presented social change, i.e., human history as a series of never ending cycles. Yet even behind the most encompassing theories (of both the evolutionary and the cyclical type) lurked a special concern with that part of human history which, close to their own time, had transformed society beyond all recognition: the collapse of the old regime and the advent of modern industrial society.

Global evolutionary theories
This special concern with the nature of the transition is clearly evident in the theories of the early evolutionists such as Auguste Comte and Herbert Spencer.[3] Both these theorists devised paradigms setting out the general laws of evolution, but in both the emergence of modern

industrial society figures as the most crucial part of this ascent, and modern society itself figures as a distinct type of society. In large part, then, the global schemes were designed to explore this distinctiveness and to discover what series of transformations have led up to it.

Auguste Comte (1778-1857)[4]

For Comte, social evolution (which culminated in the development of civilized Europe) was the inevitable product of intellectual evolution and specifically the cumulative development and successive rationalization of human thought. This evolution has had to pass through three stages: the theological, the metaphysical, and the positive. The theological stage was one in which all phenomena were explained by supernatural powers (such as demons, spirits and gods), in which knowledge was limited and fantasy rather than reason ruled. This was also the stage in which priests dominated and military men ruled — encouraging warfare and conquest. The theological stage of intellectual development was thus the basis of militarism as a form of social organization. Historically, it tallied roughly with antiquity.

Next, came the metaphysical stage, in which all phenomena were explained by abstract ideas. It was an advance on the previous stage since it entailed more disciplined and rational thought processes, but its weakness lay in the fact that in it, each phenomenon was explained by a parallel concept, so that little was achieved in the way of clarification. Inexplicably, this stage of intellectual development formed the basis for a judicial-legalistic social structure, in which wars of conquest were abandoned in favour of fortifications and defence. Historically, this stage was roughly commensurate with the Middle Ages.

Last comes the positive stage in which, for the first time, phenomena are explained in terms of scientific principles and laws based on empirical observation. Historically, it coincides largely with the modern era. The special importance of this stage is that it (and it alone) enables man to exert control over nature. Thus not only is it the first stage in which scientific thought is predominant, but it is also the first stage in which such thought forms the basis of a technologically advanced industrial society. It is further unique in that it alone leads to the progressive abandonment of war and to a successively more peaceful social organization.[5]

Herbert Spencer (1820-1903)[6]

Like Comte, Spencer's concept of social change was a universal process of evolution, but while Comte saw this evolution as based primarily on the advance in human thought, Spencer emphasized the analogy with the biological organism and conceived evolution in terms of growth, differentiation and reintegration. Like the evolution of the organism, the evolution of society is expressed first in an increase of size, and as is the case in the organism, this increase leads to a growing differentiation, or distinctiveness of parts. Both in the organism and in society this differentiation of structure is accompanied by a specialization of function. Simple structures that fulfil a variety of functions evolve into differentiated structures that fulfil distinct functions. As the parts become increasingly dissimilar, they also become increasingly dependent on each other. The small, simple organism can easily be divided into parts, each of which then continues its unperturbed existence; but for the large, complex organism, division signals death.

So it is with society. Small, simple, hunting tribes (as they existed in the distant past), where division of labour was minimal, could easily be divided and the separated parts continued as before. Indeed, this happened repeatedly when resources were scarce. As society becomes more complex however, and the division of labour more elaborate, each part increasingly depends for its survival on an exchange with other parts. If a modern city such as London or Manchester were to be cut off from its surrounding rural areas it would soon cease to function. Hence complex societies are more differentiated, but also more closely integrated than their simpler predecessors.

Spencer's evolutionary scheme (like Comte's) covers human history — and prehistory — as a whole, but its implicit focus, too, is the great transition from pre-modern to modern society. For this evolutionary scheme also produced a typology with 'militant' and 'industrial' societies as the main types. Militant societies are based on external warfare and internal coercion; industrial societies are based on contractual relations, individual initiative, voluntary co-operation, the protection of individual rights, self-restraint, and permanent peace. Militant societies feature inheritance of positions, industrial societies feature openness of rank and movement between positions. Spencer thus attributed to industrial societies some of the features commonly associated with modernity. At the same time, he classified some non-modern societies as industrial, because they concentrated on peaceful production rather than on warfare, and he emphasized that some complex, modern societies may well contain survivals from the militant type.

Karl Marx (1818–83)[7]

Marx differed from Comte and Spencer in that he regarded society's material, economic conditions, as its basis (or infrastructure). He defined the economic realm rather broadly as encompassing the conditions and forces of exchange (for example, the structure of the market and the organization of commerce); the conditions of production (including resources and historical settings); the forces and modes of production (including scientific knowledge,[8] the means of production, capital — where relevant — and the organization of labour and ownership); and the relations of production (the relations between those who own and control the means of production and those who actually produce). He also differed from Comte and Spencer in that he saw the relations of production as the basis of the class structure — which he regarded as the most central feature of society: in practically all hitherto existing societies there were at least two classes — one that owned and controlled the means of production, and an exploited class that actually produced. Finally, he differed — especially from Comte but also from Spencer — in that he regarded the state and the realm of ideas as society's superstructure, whose shape depends to a large extent on economic conditions and class interests.

Yet Marx resembled these thinkers in that he, too, presented a global, evolutionary perspective on the overall development of man and society. According to this perspective (which he developed with his close collaborator, Friedrich Engels), the evolution of society passed through several stages. In the earliest stage, property took the form of tribal (communal) ownership and social life was an extension of the family. In the second stage, private property emerged, slavery became the dominant institution and society was divided into two main classes: citizens and slaves. This stage corresponded to the historical period of Western antiquity and was most highly developed in ancient Greece and Rome. The third stage of development was feudal. In it, the nobility, whose position was based on a complicated system of land tenure, became the main ruling class and slaves gave way to serfs as the subjected class. Historically it corresponded with the European Middle Ages.

Marx regarded oriental society, characterized by despotism and centrally controlled public works as an alternative to the Western stages of antiquity and feudalism; but his main analytical powers were focused on the West, where the next stage of development was the rise of modern capitalism. For Marx, the most distinctive features of the capitalist system are, in the first place, a ruling class — the bourgeoisie or capitalists — whose position is based on the private ownership of industrial means of production. They include in the second place a production process based on the exploitation of 'free' labour, that is, labour that is separated from the means of production. The feudal serf was attached to the land which provided his livelihood and could not be forcibly separated from it. Under capitalism, by contrast, the producer has no rights whatsoever over the means of his livelihood. He is therefore 'free' only to sell his labour on the market.

The third distinctive feature of capitalism is that it presupposes the accumulation of capital in the hands of capitalists, and that this accumulation[9] is taking place through the expropriation of surplus value[10] from labour. If the capitalist were to pay the labourer the full value of his work, there would be no surplus value and no accumulation of capital could occur. In actual fact, he retains a portion of that value and this is the source of his capital, which may be reinvested in further production and thus enable the expropriation of further surplus value from labour.

Yet another distinctive feature of capitalism is the alienation[11] it produces. In the past the peasant or craftsman invested creative efforts in his work and through it he fulfilled himself. In capitalist society work is fragmented and the worker is transformed into an appendage of the machine; his work is no longer spontaneous, but imposed on him and controlled by others. Hence work is external to him and through it he experiences nothing but misery and debasement. Also, the worker is alienated from the fruit of his labour. Once it comes into being, the commodity he produces no longer belongs to the worker; rather it confronts him as an alien being, as a power in its own right. Finally, the worker becomes alienated from the means of production and from capital. Both of these rightfully belong to the worker, for it is only the exploitation of previous work which has enabled the capitalist to acquire them. Yet they are not only separated from him, but are used as a power that stands above him and to which he must submit himself. The labourer thus becomes alienated from his work, the product of his work, the means of his work and the profit of his work.

The more the worker produces, the more productive machinery the capitalist can acquire, the more his profits grow and his enterprise expands. As a result of this expansion, accompanied by an increasingly sharp competition, each successful capitalist 'kills' many others. Thus, capital concentrates into fewer hands and the bourgeoisie pushes large parts of the hitherto propertied class into the propertyless working class. In this manner a polarization occurs, there is a growing tendency of society to split into two camps. These confront each other with hostility, waiting for the spark that will ignite the overall, final class struggle between them (see also chapter 5). The consequent demise of capitalism will be followed by the next and last two evolutionary stages: socialism and communism. Under socialism the means of production will be nationalized and a dictatorship of the proletariat will be set up. Even though this dictatorship will work for the benefit of society as a whole, it will not last. It will give way to communism, in which classes will be abolished, the state will wither away and each will work according to his ability and receive according to his needs.

Marx's main concern was thus the advent, dynamics and demise of modern capitalism. Yet, like Comte and Spencer, he believed that he had established the universal laws of evolution that had brought about this development. He saw in each evolutionary stage a prerequisite for the next and more developed one. He thus believed that all societies must eventually go through the same (or equivalent) evolutionary stages. Although different societies could pass through the same stages at different times, no one could avoid them. None could thus evade capitalism before advancing to socialism and communism. Marx (1976, p. 91) expressed this idea most forcefully in the now-famous phrase: 'The country that is more developed industrially only shows, to the less developed, the image of its own future.'

Polar dichotomies
Much less encompassing and therefore less pretentious are the theoretical schemes advanced by Tönnies, Durkheim, and Weber. These theorists seem to have abandoned the quest for general laws of evolution which universally lead to (what we now call) modernization. Instead they apply their analytical tools to this process as such. No longer do they assume that there are several evolutionary stages which culminate in the emergence of modern society. Instead they present their schemes as dichotomies of pre-modern and modern society and are concerned with the transition from one to the other.

Ferdinand Tönnies (1855–1936)[12]
For Tönnies this dichotomy is one between *Gemeinschaft* (community) and *Gesellschaft* (society). The community is characterized by long-term, close, and all-encompassing emotional ties between its members, by solidarity, harmony, and mutual trust. The character of society may be illustrated by the sign allegedly posted at the entrance to an American store: 'In God we trust. Everyone else pays cash.' In other words, it is based on mutual suspicion and mistrust. It is further characterized by transitory, impersonal, commercial relationships in which each person strives for his own advantage at the expense of others.

Not surprisingly this system leads to frequent conflict and to perpetual isolation and loneliness.

The prototype for the first pattern is the family; it is also to be found in other small groups such as the rural community and the small town. The second pattern is prevalent in the big city and the large organization. Throughout the last few centuries Western Europe has made a transition from *Gemeinschaft* to *Gesellschaft*. Though some elements of *Gemeinschaft* persist in modern *Gesellschaft*, they are merely a watered-down version of the real thing, and are already disintegrating.

Émile Durkheim (1858–1917)[13]

Durkheim's analysis, like Spencer's was concerned with the social consequences of differentiation or the division of labour.[14] But he shares with Tönnies the dichotomous view of past *vis-à-vis* present society. For Durkheim, the first pole of the dichotomy is a simple society, where there is little division of labour, all perform similar tasks, and differences between people are minimal. In this society solidarity is mechanical, that is, based on the similarity between all members and on a collective conscience (i.e., collective values) which is itself based on this similarity. The second pole in this dichotomy is modern society, characterized by a complex division of labour and much greater scope for individual development. In this society solidarity is organic, that is, based on the interdependence created by the division of labour. Relationships between people are determined by the goods and services which they require from each other, and are therefore specialized and contractual.

Although this is basically an elaboration of Spencer's idea, Durkheim differed from Spencer in recognizing that the interdependence created by the division of labour, and expressed in the contractual relationship, is an important, but not a sufficient, basis of integration in modern society. This is so since the contract cannot be self-sufficient. If it is to have any validity, it must be based on pre-contractual elements. It is only the laws and commonly accepted norms that govern the contract (but are not included in it) that make the contract possible. For instance, without the commonly accepted norm that contracts are to be honoured, they would be valueless.

Durkheim came to the further conclusion that the specific norms relating to contracts are not sufficient either, that even in modern society integration must still be based on broader norms and values. Of these Durkheim distinguished two types: collective (for example, religious or national) norms and values which form the basis of a group's or a society's solidarity, and norms relating to individual aspirations. As long as both types are generally accepted, social solidarity is strong, and individuals tend to shape their aspirations in accordance with them, and hence in accordance with the possibilities open to them. But when they are weakened, a state of anomie (or normlessness) follows. This is interconnected with the weakening or disintegration of tightly knit social units (such as families and religious groups), it leads to loneliness, to the soaring of individual aspirations beyond all chances of realization, and therefore to meaninglessness and despair. This is in fact what has happened in modern society, as evidenced by the fact that suicide rates in Europe were rising throughout the nineteenth century.

Max Weber (1864-1920)[15]

Weber's theory is similarly focused on the transition from pre-modern to modern society and on a dichotomous distinction between the two, although his concern is with modern *Western* society. He perceived this society as unique and his main interest was in describing this uniqueness and explaining its emergence. When he studied other societies, he did so mainly in order to accentuate their contrasting features and thereby to illuminate the uniqueness of the West.

For Weber, the distinctiveness of modern Western society lies in its rationality and the emergence of that society is basically a process of rationalization. It can be recognized in three related dimensions: the tendency to adapt means to ends ever more effectively; the tendency towards ever more systematic organization of reality; and the decline of myth and magic or the growing reliance on reason. More concretely, this rationalization finds expression in a variety of cultural and social spheres. It is evident, first, in the development of Western religion and especially Protestantism with its overriding emphasis on doctrine and ethics. It is further evident in the development of modern Western science. Knowledge has filled an important role in other societies as well; but the combination of theory, mathematical calculation, and systematic empirical verification which characterizes science is unique to the modern West. It is further evident in the evolution of the Western legal system. Following ancient Roman law, this legal system is more systematically organized than any other, and relies to an unusual extent on general rules rather than on precedents.[16]

Nowhere is rationalization more clearly evident, however, than in the growing importance of bureaucracy. This structure is characterized, among other things, by a hierarchy of authority, by a clear-cut division of labour which demarcates the various bureaucratic positions, and by objective impersonal rules. These and other characteristics ensure precision, speed, unambiguity and reduction of friction. Hence, bureaucracy is the most effective organization known to. mankind. Some bureaucracies, of course, existed in past societies (the Catholic church, for instance). But they were few and far between and they were limited to the area of state and religion. It is only in modern society that bureaucracies have come to proliferate and to penetrate into wider areas of social life. Also, they now approach to a much greater extent the 'pure' model of bureaucracy. Thus, the state, too, has become more rational, based as it is on a more rational bureaucracy and on a rational legal system.

Finally rationalization finds expression in the rise of capitalism and in the distinct spirit which characterizes this economic system. For, as Weber saw it, the distinctive feature of capitalism is not (as some of his contemporaries postulated) the pursuit of profit as such. 'It should be taught in the kindergarten of cultural history', admonished Weber, 'that this naïve idea of capitalism should be given up once and for all' (1958, p. 17). Nor is the most distinctive feature of modern capitalism the expropriation of surplus value from the labourer, as Marx taught. Rather, it is to be found in the principle of economic rationality: the rational acquisition of profit, with the aid of a rational organization. Concretely, this rationality is expressed in:

(a) The separation of the economic enterprise from the household. Previously, production would frequently take place at the family's premises and the accounts of the family and those of the enterprise were intermingled. The capitalist enterprise, on the other hand, is detached from the household in spatial as well as in economic and legal terms: family property and corporate property are now independent entities.

(b) This separation makes possible a rational calculation of the enterprise's intake and expenditure as well as its long-range profit.

(c) Such profit in turn, accrues from exchange in a free market, rather than from political pressure or favouritism, as frequently was the case before.

(d) The capitalist enterprise engages formally free labour (as distinct from slaves or serfs). This is important for rationality, for it absolves the employer from the obligation of looking after the general welfare of the employee and restricts it to the payment of wages. In this manner he may concentrate his efforts more fully on production.

(e) The capitalist enterprise tends to develop into a bureaucratic organization—whose rationality has been discussed.

The rationality of the capitalist practice was at first promoted and complemented by the rationality of the capitalist spirit, with which many new entrepreneurs and many of their workers were endowed. This spirit of capitalism was characterized by Weber as being the polar opposite of the traditional ethic, with which some other producers and workers still identified. While the traditional ethic implies an inherent resistance to change, the spirit of capitalism entails an enthusiasm for new and improved methods of organization and production. While the traditional ethic calls for only moderate exertion and accepts work merely to maintain a customary standard of living, the spirit of capitalism extols strenuous work as a 'calling', as a means of self-realization as well as a path to success. While the traditional ethic sanctions indulgence, the spirit of capitalism includes the stringent injunction to refrain from idleness and from enjoying the fruit of one's labour, that is, to refrain from wasting both time and money. In other words, it puts major emphasis on asceticism.[17]

Weber was well aware of the fact that his conception of rationality raises some insoluble problems. He admitted that what may be rational as a means to the realization of one end, may well be irrational from the viewpoint of another end. Thus, the entrepreneur, embodying the spirit of capitalism, was highly rational and highly irrational at one and the same time. He was rational because he employed the most effective methods to lead him to success, but he was also irrational because he would not permit himself to enjoy the benefits of that success.

Although Weber thus recognized the problem of 'the irrationality of rationality', he did not feel that it invalidated his view of modernization in the West as basically a transition from an emphasis on myth, magic, and tradition, to an emphasis on rationality, achievement, and improvement. Like Tönnies and Durkheim, Weber thus saw past and modern society as polar opposites, and the advent of the one as tantamount to the decline of the other.

Global cyclical theories

In the meantime, other sociological theories came to the fore which once more endeavoured to embrace the totality of human history. However, the propagators of these theories — foremost among them Vilfredo Pareto (1848–1923) and Gaetano Mosca (1858–1941), did not see history as a succession of evolutionary stages. Rather, they viewed it as a never-ending series of repetitious cycles which lead nowhere except to the recurrence of yet another cycle. By the very nature of their models, therefore, these theorists could not attribute the same degree of significance to the emergence of modern society as the evolutionists or 'polar dichotomists'. None the less, many of their analyses dealt with this process. Events directly connected with it (such as the French Revolution or the development of modern bureaucracy) figured most prominently in their writings, if only to illustrate the general principle that despite these massive transformations — some, and perhaps the most crucial aspects of society, have remained basically as they were before.

In a way it is surprising that the same social reality and human history could have been perceived as evolutionary stages or basic transformations by some theorists and as repetitive cycles by others. The reason for this divergence is that the 'cyclical' theorists focused on a particular aspect of society and history: the dynamics of political power. Both Pareto and Mosca saw all societies as divided into a minority that wields such power and therefore rules, and a majority that wields no such power and is therefore ruled. Both saw the dynamics of change as the replacement of one ruling group (referred to by Pareto as a governing elite) by another, and the replacement of that by yet another one.[18] The advent of modern society thus merely brought about yet another such cycle of replacements and new elites which rule just as previous elites did before. It is as if Pareto and Mosca had conveyed the message that (to paraphrase a popular saying) pre-modern society was characterized by the domination of man by man, and in modern society it is precisely the other way around (see also chapter 6).

Explaining the transition

The theorists who attributed more significance to the transition to modern society also made a certain effort to explain it. Comte considered the development of all (including modern) societies as based on the evolution of ideas and on the successive rationalization of human thought. Spencer accounted for evolution (and therefore for what we now call modernization as well) by a multiplicity of internal and external factors such as soil and climate, population size and density, technology, economic factors, warfare and commercial contacts with other societies. Tönnies emphasized trade as a stimulus to modernization. Durkheim saw the transition from simple to advanced society as a result of the pressure of population growth and density. But it was left to Marx and Weber to work out elaborate theories of the transformation, and particularly the rise of capitalism.

Marx's explanation

In contrast to other classical sociologists, Marx saw material conditions or economic factors not only as the basis of society, but also as the prime mover of history. He defined the economic sphere rather broadly (see above), and hence he cannot be accused of narrow determinism; but he did not assign any independent causal role to other social spheres. Since he held such a broad view of the economic sphere, he considered the possibility of contradictions within it, and he assigned special importance to such contradictions in causing social change. Thus, the relations of production develop from the forces of production. Nevertheless, they are not always in harmony with them: the forces of production develop constantly, while the relations of production sometimes stagnate. When this happens, the stagnation obstructs the further development of the forces of production. It is this contradiction which leads to the revolutionary and most far-reaching social transformations.

This is so since changes in the forces and relations of production, and especially the contradictions between them, lead to changes in society's class structure and class struggles as well, and these, in turn, are important propellants of dialectic social change. The major social classes (those who own and control the means of production and those who actually produce) are in constant opposition to each other and the antagonism between them permeates all of human history. When the disjunction between the forces and the relations of production occurs, however, class consciousness is heightened and the class struggle comes to a head. It culminates in a revolution, and a new class structure, and through it a totally new social order emerges. The economic factors, as mediated by class struggle, are thus the major sources of social change. Other factors, such as the state, and the realm of ideas have a certain impact. They may accelerate change or retard it; they may act back and effect certain changes in the economic factors; but *ultimately* the economic factors account for change.

Like all social change, the rise of modern capitalism, too, can be accounted for by economic factors and class conflict. According to Marx, modern capitalism proper dates from the sixteenth century, but its roots are to be sought in medieval society. The earliest cause of the rise of capitalism is the emergence of the medieval cities where an embryonic form of the capitalist economy and the capitalist class structure developed. Next in chronological order came the expansion of the markets following the discovery and colonization of America, the rounding of the Cape and the opening of China and India to

European trade. This opening of markets created a greatly increased demand for industrial products, and hence gave an unprecedented impulse to both commerce and industry.

One of the major prerequisites for the development of capitalism is the primitive (i.e., original) accumulation of capital that was to be invested in the creation of the new capitalist enterprises. This was achieved, in part, by importing precious metals from the newly discovered territories. This alone, however, would not have sufficed. For the accumulation of capital, workers who are 'free' from the ownership of the means of production are required. Hence people had to be separated from their traditional property. This was accomplished through the technological progress of agriculture which made it possible to reduce the size of the land and the number of hands needed for cultivation. Consequently the fifteenth and sixteenth centuries saw the conversion of much agricultural land into pastures (required for wool exports). This led to the expulsion of masses of peasants from the land and their flocking into the cities as 'free' labourers.

The increased demands of the world market and the accumulation of capital meant that the feudal mode, in which production was monopolized by guilds, became inadequate. To meet the new needs, the manufacturing system took its place and production was thereby increased; but eventually even manufacture no longer sufficed to meet the demands of the world market. It was then that steam and machinery revolutionized industrial production; the place of manufacture was taken by large-scale industry. The result was an increase in production beyond anything that humanity had known before.

As the forces of production developed and industrialization proceeded, old, feudal relations of production were no longer adequate to contain them. 'They had to be burst asunder; they were burst asunder' (Marx and Engels, 1973, p. 34). Totally new, capitalist, relations of production developed. Through these developments, the emergent bourgeoisie could no longer be contained in the old order either. It vied for supremacy with the feudal nobility and became the new ruling class. Concomitantly, the newly created proletariat replaced the medieval serfs as the new subjected class – thus the new social order of capitalism was created.

Once it came into being, however, capitalism did not become a stable system. For not only does it create a polarization of classes and thus sharpen the confrontation between them, it also creates some self-destructive contradictions which continually intensify this class confrontation, and will eventually bring it to fruition. The constantly evolving forces of industrial production lead to an enormous increase in production. 'The bourgeoisie during its rule of scarce one hundred years has created more massive and more colossal productive forces than have all preceding generations together' (Marx and Engels, 1973, p. 34). At the same time the expropriation of surplus value from the proletariat reduces the capacity of most of the population to consume. This leads to the recurring crises of overproduction which increasingly threaten the very existence of capitalism.

Also, the concentration of capital in fewer hands and the consequent growth of economic enterprises leads to the banding together of ever-increasing numbers of workers throughout the production process. At the same time, the control of production remains in private hands. There is thus a growing contradiction between the increasingly socialized nature of production and the persistent private control over that production. This is yet another exigency which hastens capitalism to its inevitable doom. By overthrowing capitalism, the workers have nothing to lose but their chains. This fact, together with the deepening crises of capitalism will lead to the aggravation of the class struggle and eventually to the revolution which will usher in the socialist, and later the communist, society.

Weber's explanation
Marx's explanation of the rise of capitalism has been considered as most powerful.[19] The only problem with that explanation is that it emphasizes economic factors to the almost total exclusion of anything else. Weber, on his part, viewed social change as caused not only by economic factors, but by values and ideas as well. Weber did not belittle the importance of economic factors as sources of social change as is sometimes claimed. Indeed, interpreters who make this claim thereby show a lamentable ignorance of some of Weber's writings. For in his most famous work, *The Protestant Ethic and the Spirit of Capitalism*, Weber indeed emphasized the importance of religious doctrines and ethical precepts, yet in his less famous *General Economic History* he emphasized economic factors no less than values and ideas.

In this latter book Weber explained the role of economic factors as sources for the development of capitalism much in the vein of Marx himself. His analysis of the expansion of the markets, the transformation of arable land into pastures and the expulsion of peasants from the land differed little from that of Marx. In addition, he stressed the importance of the new methods for coal extraction and for the smelting of iron which gave such an enormous thrust to the development of industry. This analysis, however, brought Weber little fame, because it adds only marginally to what Marx had already said so well. In addition, Weber pointed to the role of the modern national state, in making rational, capitalist activity possible, but this analysis too did not earn him great recognition.

Weber's most distinctive, and therefore most famous, contribution lies in the claim he made that economic factors, however important (and even in conjunction with political factors), cannot bear the whole burden of explaining the advent of modern capitalism; values must be taken into account as well. He assigned special importance to ascetic, achievement-oriented values which encourage entrepreneurs to work hard and at the same time to refrain from enjoying the fruit of their labour. These are values which encourage entrepreneurs to make profits and not to expend them on consumption, but rather to re-invest them so as to make additional profits. This distinctive set of values, Weber christened the spirit of capitalism (see above). They were part of capitalism itself, but at the same time they also had a most crucial role in encouraging the original accumulation of capital without which the capitalist system could not have come about.

Marx and Weber thus agree (as any observer must) that the accumulation of capital was a major prerequisite for the development of capitalism. But Marx believed that this accumulation came about chiefly through the expropriation of the peasants and the exploitation of the labourers, while Weber thought that it materialized through the dedication and self-denial of the entrepreneurs, or the capitalists, as well. This raises the question of what made the capitalists embrace such unusual devotion to work and readiness for self-denial.

Weber's reply was that it originated in the Protestant ethic which found its purest expression in the doctrine of sixteenth-century Calvinism. On the face of it, this doctrine does not seem to promote economic activity; certainly it includes no overt attempt to encourage such activity. Inadvertently it has, nevertheless, had this effect. Most important in this respect is the Calvinist doctrine of predestination. The Almighty in His infinite but incomprehensible wisdom has pre-ordained a certain part of mankind for salvation and condemned the rest to everlasting damnation. No one knows why some and not others are among the chosen ones and no one can do anything to change his own fate. At first glance, this would seem to be a fatalistic doctrine which encourages passivity: since there is nothing anyone can do to change his fate, why bother to do anything at all? This doctrine, however, also holds that the Almighty has given man a sign by which he can tell whether he is among the elect: worldly success. Those successful in this world may be confident of success in the next world as well. Despite being a doctrine of predestination, the practical implications of the Calvinist doctrine are thus that God helps those who help themselves.

This doctrine must have aroused acute anxiety for the true believer, but at the same time it also provided him with the means of allaying that anxiety: to make enormous efforts in the achievement of worldly, economic success. Combined with this latent encouragement of exertion for economic success there is in the Calvinist doctrine a strong emphasis on asceticism, on abstaining from the worldly pleasures which success would have made possible. This, of course, is precisely the combination of values required for the accumulation of capital.

The connection between religious doctrine and the accumulation of capital becomes even more evident in seventeenth-century English Puritanism. Analysing some influential Puritan writings, Weber shows that they include explicit injunctions for hard work in a calling and even for the accumulation of wealth. These are coupled with injunctions to refrain from expending that wealth, and also to refrain from wasting the time which could be used for the accumulation of more wealth.

The spirit of capitalism, which found its most prominent expression in the eighteenth century, is clearly the outgrowth of this ethic. Indeed, it is nothing but the Puritan ethic from which the religious basis has been removed. Dedication to work, the acquisition of wealth and the saving of time and money now figure as moral rather than as religious injunctions.

The whole chain of influence, as Weber conceived it, should now be clear; the Calvinist doctrine inspired the Puritan ethic; together they gave rise to the spirit of capitalism, which exerted a crucial influence on the development of capitalism itself. But how does one know that this was indeed the case? There are three ways in which Weber attempts to prove his point. First, he shows that Protestant countries developed to a greater extent than Catholic ones. England, the Netherlands, and the United States (especially the New England region) developed to a greater extent than did Spain, Portugal, and Italy. The latter had been the pioneers of capitalism at the beginning of the modern era, but despite this lead they were overtaken by the Protestant countries, where the true, rational type of capitalism made the greatest strides forward.

Second, Weber tries to demonstrate that wherever the Protestant ethic and the spirit of capitalism prevailed, they preceded (rather than trailed behind) the development of capitalism. For instance, in the eighteenth century the spirit of capitalism was clearly predominant in the New England region of the United States, while the region itself was but sparsely developed. Only later, after the spirit of capitalism had left its mark, did this become one of the most highly developed regions of the United States. Finally, Weber attempts to show that some oriental countries, especially China and India, enjoyed economic conditions that were no less favourable to the development of capitalism than were those in the West. In both commerce was well developed, and in India some initial accumulation of capital took place yet capitalism did not develop in these countries. This was so chiefly because the ethics of their respective religions (which were themselves propped up by dominant class interests) were not encouraging for economic development. The Chinese, Confucian ethic was this-worldly, but emphasized acceptance, harmony, rather than active mastery of the world. Hinduism emphasized asceticism, but was other-worldly; it called for withdrawal rather than for active participation in this world.

Many volumes have been written both in criticism and in defence of the Weber thesis. It has been claimed, among other things, that Catholicism, no less than Protestantism, has developed a work and achievement ethic; that it was budding capitalism which gave rise to the Protestant ethic (rather than the other way around); that both capitalism and Protestantism have independently sprung from the same conditions − thus neither gave rise to the other; or conversely that each has influenced the other equally. The most forceful criticism seems to be that in any society there is always a variety of free-floating ideas. From among these, those that are most appropriate for the economic structure and/or the interests of the ruling class are chosen and become dominant. The Protestant ethic was successful in Europe precisely because it was so well suited to the needs of developing capitalism and because it supported the activities of the developing entrepreneurial class. Despite its forcefulness, however, this criticism still leaves unanswered the question of why the Protestant ethic was not adopted by the entrepreneurial classes of Spain, Portugal and Italy, even though capitalism was more developed there when Protestantism made its debut, and why this early capitalism shrivelled there.

It seems, then, that the Protestant ethic cannot be denied some causal influence on the spirit of capitalism which, in turn, must have played a certain role in the development of capitalism, but it is at present not possible (and probably never will be possible) to know how decisive this role was, just as it is impossible to assess the weight of economic factors in this development. Both Marx and Weber have thus had important insights into the development of capitalism and neither has been invalidated by the other.

Evaluating the transition

The insights of Marx, Weber, and other founding fathers into the transition to modern society have been deeply influenced by the intellectual and social-historical context in which sociology began.

The controversy in European thought

Thus it has been claimed (Nisbet, 1967; Zeitlin, 1968) that sociology as a discipline was born in the context of a controversy between a pro-modern and a pro-traditional view in European thought. Modernism (that is, the affirmation of modernity) was characteristic of seventeenth-century philosophy and of eighteenth-century Enlightenment ideas. It affirmed progress, reason, science, and individual liberty. The essence of society was believed to be in self-sufficient, rational, free individuals and in the state, which was seen as the best guarantee of their freedom. The intermediary groups and traditional institutions (such as the family, guilds, organized religion and religious communities) were disparaged because they were seen as hampering this freedom.[20]

This emphasis on rational individualism was continued in the nineteenth century, for instance in the philosophical tradition known as Utilitarianism,[21] but much of nineteenth-century thought may be seen as a reaction against it. This new conservative and romantic thought reasserted the importance of tradition and traditional social groups. Such groups were now seen as counterbalancing the power of the state, and therefore as promoting rather than subduing individual liberty. They were also regarded as important because they fostered stable values, social solidarity and integration. At the same time, there was a distrust of modernization, which was regarded as causing the loss of such communities, moral breakdown, social disorder, loneliness and alienation.[22] As Nisbet (1953, p. 3), paraphrasing some famous words by Marx — put it: 'A spectre is haunting the modern mind, the spectre of insecurity . . . personal alienation and cultural disintegration.'

This fear, and the conservative reaction that it called forth was not only the result of intellectual reasoning, but also a response to certain traumatic occurrences at the end of the eighteenth and the beginning of the nineteenth century — especially the collapse of the old regime, the French Revolution and the industrial revolution. The French Revolution not only engendered social disorder by its very occurrence, but also produced legislation which had a disruptive impact on the family, on guilds and on religion.[23] The industrial revolution (attendant upon the rise of capitalism) brought dislocation and uprooting of men from the soil. This too, led to the disintegration of traditionally secure communities, the rise of an impersonal environment, the deterioration of the quality of life and hence to demoralization.

The ambivalence in sociology

It is these crises which brought about the conservative refutation of what was seen as the naïve optimism of the Enlightenment, and it is against the background of this controversy that sociology emerged. Indeed, according to Nisbet (1967), what classical sociology has done is to lift these debates out of their ideological context and turn them into conceptual and theoretical frameworks. Thus, many of the founding fathers combined both Enlightenment and conservative ideas in their theories and showed a deep-seated ambivalence towards modernization. Some of them were able to resolve this ambivalence by emphasizing either the positive or the negative side of the change, but most were caught up in the dilemma and did not resolve it one way or the other.

Spencer, for instance, sided predominantly with modernity. Like the Enlightenment thinkers, he believed in progress, and he saw progress as inextricably linked with evolution. He saw the emergence of an industrial state as leading to a greater emphasis on individual rights, to a less repressive[24] and a more peaceful type of society. He hoped that after the perfection of the industrial state an even better era, primarily devoted to the development of man's ethical nature would arrive. Towards the end of his life he became discontented with the build-up of armaments, armed conflicts, imperialist expansion and increased state control, which became evident in modern and (especially British) society at the time, but mostly his theory implies the affirmation of modernity.

Tönnies came close to the other extreme by siding predominantly with tradition. He recognized that without the transition from *Gemeinschaft* to *Gesellschaft* liberalism, individualism and other worthwhile aspects of modern society could not have come about. He further recognized that the city — the prototype of *Gesellschaft* — was also the seat of culture and science, but this recognition was outweighed by his blatant idealization of, and nostalgia for, the communal way of life. Community spells loyalty, honour, friendship. *Gesellschaft* spells egoism, conflict and distrust. In the community each cares for the others; in the *Gesellschaft* it is everyone for himself. Hence Tönnies's deep concern for the loss of community and his apprehension for the rise of modern society. The Nazis subsequently vulgarized his (and similar) ideas by sanctifying the racially and nationally based community. This was not what Tönnies had in mind, and he is not to be blamed for the misuse of his ideas. Yet his basic allegiance with traditional community branded him as a predominantly conservative thinker.[25]

Other classical sociologists remained more ambivalent with regard to modernization. This is clearly evident in Comte and Durkheim's theories: both were influenced to some extent by the Enlightenment, but they were more deeply influenced by nineteenth-century conservatism. Both believed in social progress, but they were also concerned with social order, consensus and cohesion. Both welcomed some aspects of modernization, but they also had a deep regard for traditional communities and associations which had fulfilled such an important role in pre-modern society, and were therefore greatly distressed by their dissolution.

Comte, like Spencer, saw human history as a process of linear ascent in which evolution was intertwined with progress, and he regarded the transition to the positive-industrial stage (that is, modernization) as the peak of this ascent. None the less, he also showed a strong admiration for medieval society, in which social order had been assured by strongly knit traditional associations and, especially, the family. He was appalled by the breakdown of social order and the excessive individualism caused by the disintegration of such associations, and he called for the restoration of social order through their resurrection. Following this dual line of thought, he presented the blueprint for a new and superior social order which derives from the positivist stage, but is also reminiscent of medieval society. In it, science replaces religion, but many social institutions remain largely as they were in that society. He sought to effect a synthesis between tradition and modernity in this way.

The same two-sided approach is evident in Durkheim. He regarded the transition from simple to modern society as progress, i.e., as an advance to a higher social type and to a more elevated culture, marked by less repression, more flexibility and more scope for individuality. Yet he did not see such individuality as leading to greater individual happiness. On the contrary, he saw individual well-being as anchored in the social solidarity and common values of the traditional groups and associations. Hence his concern over the weakening or disintegration of such associations in modern Europe. This process may have given greater scope to individual self-expression, but it has also led to growing anomie — a state of moral confusion and social disturbance which results in individual loneliness, anxiety, and despair. For Durkheim, there was thus a paradox built into modernization: the more society advances, the more individual happiness recedes. As he saw it, the only effective remedy to this paradox was in the renewed strengthening of small-scale associations, through which individuals would regain their sense of community without forgoing the advantages of modern life.

A two-sided approach is also evident in Marx's evaluation of the rise of modern capitalism. On the one hand, this development liberated the traditional subjected class from the oppression of feudalism, but on the other hand, it led to the formation of a new exploited class through particularly ruthless devices of expropriation (Marx, 1976, p. 875):

the historical movement which changes the producers into wage-labourers appears, on the one hand, as their emancipation from serfdom . . . and it is this aspect of the movement which alone exists for our bourgeois historians. But, on the other hand, these newly-freed men became sellers of themselves only after they had been robbed of all their own means of production, and all the guarantees of existence afforded by the old feudal arrangements. And this history, the history of their expropriation, is written in the annals of mankind in letters of blood and fire.

Marx saw modern capitalism as exceedingly oppressive and as evoking an unprecedented degree of alienation, but he did not have much use for the traditional institutions and associations of pre-modern society either. Certainly he did not see the solution to alienation in their revival. He was basically an heir of the Enlightenment in his staunch belief in progress and he did not see such progress as resulting from a return to the past. Rather, Marx pinned his hopes on the future, and he saw the evils caused by capitalism as the labour pains preceding the delivery of a new world. Just as slavery had to pave the way for feudalism and feudalism was necessary for the development of capitalism, so capitalism is the prerequisite for socialism and communism. Despite its oppressiveness, the transition to capitalism must thus be welcomed, for without it these next two stages would not be possible.

Weber was less optimistic, but equally ambivalent, in his approach to the transition to modernity. On the one hand he saw its most central process — rationalization — as liberating mankind from the rigidities and superstitions of the past and as leading it towards more effective ways of doing things. On the other hand he did not see it as holding out the promise of a brighter future. As rationalization proceeds even further it is apt to become self-defeating, for it will lead to the domination of the bureaucratic way of life. Weber regarded the bureaucratic structure as technically superior to all other forms of organization, but he mistrusted bureaucracy's overemphasis on order and organization, and he did not cherish the prospect of bureaucratic values dominating the totality of social life. In contrast to Durkheim, he thus did not fear the loneliness caused by disorganization, but the emptiness caused by over-organization, and he expressed his misgivings in the following words (Weber, 1958, p. 182): 'of the last stage of this cultural development, it might well be truly said: "Specialists without spirit, sensualists without heart; this nullity imagines that it has attained a level of civilization never before achieved".'

In contrast to Marx, Weber did not see socialism – which might follow capitalism – as an effective cure to those ills. On the contrary, it might even intensify them by increasing the mastery of bureaucracy. He thus did not foresee a solution to what he regarded as the tragic paradox of rationalization: its turning from a liberating force in the past to a regimenting force in the future; and by bringing to light this paradox, Weber became a notable representative of the two-sided or ambivalent approach to modernization which permeated so much of classical sociology.

From classical to contemporary sociology

Nineteenth-century classical sociology advanced some global schemes relating to human history as a whole. As sociology developed, it became increasingly aware of its own limitations and therefore wary of such grand schemes. Such paradigms began to appear as too pretentious; the attempt to map out history as a whole was abandoned and the task of predicting the future was relegated to futurologists. Some of the classical theories were also criticized for their one-sidedness: Comte, Durkheim and Weber for overemphasizing ideas and values,[26] and Marx for over-emphasizing economic forces. Some classical sociologists (especially Comte, Tönnies and Durkheim) were further criticized for their sociological conservatism – and especially for idealizing the past.[27] Also, with the hindsight of the twentieth century and its two world wars it seemed easy to ridicule those nineteenth-century theories which had foreseen the imminent cessation of warfare, and the pacification of society.

None the less, it has been recognized that all classical theories had been inspired by the issue of the transition to modern society and that they had made a major contribution to our understanding of it. This is shown by the fact that many of the concepts which they devised for the analysis of this transition have found their way (either directly or indirectly) into contemporary theories of modernization and development, becoming a cornerstone for some and a bone of contention for others.

The redeeming feature of Comte's theory was his conception of the rationalization of human thought which comes to fruition with the positive stage, that is, with modernity. This concept of rationalization recurs and is further developed by Weber, and forms one of his main contributions. The strong point of Spencer's theory lay in his conception of differentiation tempered by reintegration — which recurs (with some variations) in Durkheim's writings. Durkheim's main contribution lay in his conception of anomie as an affliction of modern society. Tönnies's distinction between community and society has been severely criticized among other things for under-playing the importance of communal elements in modern society, but his model, too, has made a useful contribution to contemporary understanding of modernization. Weber's contribution, however, was undoubtedly more outstanding: not only his idea of rationalization, but also his distinction between the stability oriented traditional ethic and the modern spirit of flexibility, change, and achievement, has become one of the main pillars of contemporary sociological analysis; so too has the conception of a polar dichotomy between tradition and modernity contained in Weber's as well as in Tönnies's and Durkheim's models. All these conceptions and insights have filtered through into contemporary 'mainstream' sociology and its offshoot modernization theory, which will be our concern in chapter 2.

No classical sociologist, however, has been as influential (or as controversial) as Marx. Much of contemporary 'mainstream' sociology developed out of this controversy, as a revision or refutation of Marx's framework. He was also the founding father of the rival school of thought — Marxism, neo-Marxism and dependency theory. He thus fathered a divergent framework for the analysis of contemporary development — which will be our concern in chapter 3.

32   *The advent of modern society in classical sociology*

Selected readings

Etzioni, A., and Etzioni-Halevy, E. (eds) (1973), *Social Change* (2nd edn), New York, Basic Books, chs 1, 2, 4, 5, 6, 7, 8, 9, 22.
Marx, K. (1976), *Capital* (trans. B.Fowkes), Harmondsworth, Penguin.
Nisbet, R. A. (1967), *The Sociological Tradition*, London, Heinemann.
Weber, M. (1958), *The Protestant Ethic and the Spirit of Capitalism* (trans. T. Parsons), New York, Charles Scribner's Sons.
Zeitlin, I. M. (1968), *Ideology and the Development of Sociological Theory*, Englewood Cliffs, N. J., Prentice-Hall.

2 · The advent of modern society in contemporary sociology (A): 'mainstream' and modernization theory

Like classical sociology, contemporary sociology developed in the context of some traumatic events, including the rise of fascism and nazism, the two world wars and the Cold War between the Western and communist blocs. The new 'mainstream' sociological thought of the first half and towards the middle of the twentieth century had little to contribute to the analysis of the two wars, but it did address itself to the interpretation of fascism and nazism and endeavoured to place these phenomena in the broader context of modernization in the West.

From the middle of the century and onwards sociology was greatly influenced by the Cold War. At that time the Western and the communist blocs were engaged in a strenuous competition, among other things for the allegiance of what came to be known as the 'third world' or the developing countries. Hence, to a much greater extent than before, politicians and intellectuals alike came to focus on the problems facing these countries. With this general shift in intellectual climate, sociology similarly shifted from concern with modernization in the West to an interest in modernization in general, including third world countries. 'Mainstream' sociologists (as well as other social scientists engaged in the analysis of modernization) now no longer accepted the assumption of Weber and like-minded thinkers that what had happened in the West was unique. Instead, they suggested that modernization was feasible in the third world as well and that there were some common features to modernization everywhere.

The main themes of 'mainstream' and modernization theory

This shift from concern with modernization in the West to modernization as a general phenomenon is shown in various aspects of 'mainstream' theory. It is evident, for instance, in one of its main themes – the analysis of strain, anomie, and disorganization.

33

Strain, anomie and disorganization

Many 'mainstream' sociologists of the twentieth century inherited Tönnies' and Durkheim's concern with the moral breakdown and social disintegration which followed the loss of traditional communities – a phenomenon which Durkheim had termed anomie. To this was added the structural-functionalists' concern with social strain. The concept of strain (defined as a discrepancy between two or more elements of the social system)[1] was developed by the two leading figures of structural-functionalism – Talcott Parsons and Robert Merton. It grows out of this school's basic assumptions, namely that the social system is made up of interrelated elements, and that as long as these are mutually compatible and fulfil positive functions for each other, the social system is relatively stable; but when two or more patterns are discrepant, or incompatible, the equilibrium of the social system is upset and this may result in social change (Parsons, 1951, 1973; Merton, 1957a).

At first, anomie and strain were seen as afflicting mainly Western societies. Among other things they were seen as accounting for the rise of fascism and nazism in some of these societies. Karl Mannheim – a German sociologist and a refugee from nazism – and Talcott Parsons – an American structural-functionalist – converged on this point. They held that the collapse of the old order, replaced by modern 'mass' society, had led to the loss of traditional community and the weakening of commonly accepted values. The traditional values and beliefs which had directed the life of men throughout the ages lost their binding power and nothing came to take their place. This led to unrealistic and unfulfillable desires and a state of perpetual social crisis. It also left multitudes of individuals in a state of moral confusion, social insecurity and emotional anxiety, which proved a fertile ground for the rise of totalitarianism. In their search for a new sense of security, masses of confused individuals were led to pin their hopes on charismatic leaders who held out the promise of restoring the lost paradise of moral certitude and social solidarity. These leaders then led their followers towards fascism and nazism with its renewed emphasis on community – except that now it was a nationalist-racial community, under the auspices of a totalitarian regime.

To this Parsons added an analysis relating specifically to the rise of nazism in Germany. According to him, an important factor in this development was the strain or incompatibility which developed between the Germany family and the German occupational structure. The German family was traditionally a patriarchal and authoritarian unit in which the father was the undisputed ruler over both wife and children. In earlier times, the family was also the production unit so that the father could dominate both units.

Towards the end of the nineteenth century, however, when Germany underwent massive industrialization and bureaucratization, production was separated from the family and vested in large-scale organizations. Following the German tradition, these came to be highly authoritarian as well. This meant that German men, especially of the lower middle class and of the working class (and those were the majority), still exerted unlimited rule in their own homes, but at the same time were subordinate and *subject* to unlimited rule by others — in their work. This social strain brought about increasing frustration for increasing numbers of German men who were looking for a new regime in which their self-esteem could be redeemed. For a while it seemed that they had found this redemption in nazism (Mannheim, 1946, 1950; Parsons, 1954, chs 5 and 6).

However, fascism and nazism (occurring in only a minority of European countries) were merely the most extreme reactions to strain and anomie which were general features of all modern, Western societies. All these societies were afflicted by internal discrepancies, a general state of social disorganization, individual loneliness, and insatiable desires, and this led to increasing rates of social deviance. This last point was developed, for instance, by Merton. Combining Durkheim's conception of anomie with the contemporary conception of strain, Merton defines anomie as a discrepancy between culturally prescribed goals and socially acceptable means for their attainment. Such a discrepancy is evident in modern, especially American, society. Here, there is a great stress on the goal of success without an equivalent stress on institutionalized means. Once a person is successful, the question of the means he employed to achieve this success becomes secondary.

Also, a strong and constant pressure to attain a high level of success is exerted on everyone, but the lower classes do not have equal access to the legitimate means (for example, higher education) for attaining such success. They are thus under great pressure to attempt to succeed through illegitimate means, that is, through deviance. Such deviance may include crime, or else alcoholism, drug addiction, mental illness or suicide, by those who cannot cope with the pressure; or even rebellion by those who attempt to solve the problem by undermining the social order and establishing a new one (Merton, 1957b).[2]

Many analyses followed those of Durkheim, Parsons and Merton, and developed the theme of strain and anomie in modern, Western societies. At the same time, another perspective was advanced. Several sociologists (including Parsons himself) now emphasized that strain and anomie were part of modernization in general, and were by no means peculiar to the West. In all modernizing societies discrepancies between more traditional and more modern structures are likely. Frequently, the traditional family structures and the traditional values no longer fit the modernizing occupational structures. Frequently, old values are abandoned before new ones are adopted and there is a moral vacuum, that is, anomie. The authority of traditional leaders is often questioned and new elites do not immediately attain the same degree of authority as their forerunners. This, as well as a general process of differentiation (see below), tends to produce disorganization and disturbances in practically all modernizing and newly modern societies. At the same time, anomie is not necessarily a permanent phenomenon. The early disorganization may well be counterbalanced later on by new mechanisms of integration such as newly legitimate political organizations and, eventually, even newly accepted common values.

The polarity of tradition and modernity

Although the new modernization theory no longer accepted Weber's conception that modernization in the West was unique, it still adopted (and even elaborated) his, Tönnies's and Durkheim's dichotomous view of tradition versus modernity. Tradition (whether in the West or in the third world) was still seen as anchored in *Gemeinschaft* type of relations and as uniformly stable, and modernity as anchored in *Gesellschaft*-type relations, as complex and dynamic. Accordingly, tradition had to be shattered or at least weakened before modernization could get under way.

This polar conception is evident for instance in W. W. Rostow's famous economic theory of takeoff into self-sustained growth. Rostow identified five stages of economic development or modernization. The initial stage is a traditional, stable, mainly agricultural society. While it persists, substantial economic development is unlikely.[3] It is in the next stage that the preconditions for such development appear. This second stage entails a change of ideas and attitudes towards economic progress, at least in part of the society, and the emergence of an enterprising elite (private or public) that is not only willing to take risks in the pursuit of profit, but is also willing to reinvest a high proportion of that profit in production.

Next comes the most crucial stage, that of economic takeoff, which despite its brevity (only two or three decades) brings about a dramatic increase in the rate of investment, so that real *per capita* output rises substantially, and there is a drastic change in methods of production.

Thus, takeoff requires that a high proportion of the increment to real income be ploughed back to further productive investment. This stage is decisive in that it lifts the economy from its traditiónal position into productivity, and ensures subsequent self-generating continuous growth. The next stage, the drive to maturity, is one in which this tendency for self-sustained economic growth is realized. It is followed by the fifth and final stage, in which economic growth continues despite high mass consumption.

Although Rostow identifies three intermediary stages of economic development (one of which is crucial for its continuity), he still sees such development as basically a transition between two poles, from rigid tradition to constantly changing modernity. In the Western countries, this transition took place in the nineteenth century; in those non-Western countries (for example, Argentina, Turkey, China) in which there was the same transformation it has been a twentieth-century phenomenon (Rostow, 1973).

The same polar concept of modernization appeared in sociological theory too, where it was part of structural-functionalism. Thus Parsons was concerned not only with strain and anomie, but also developed a scheme for the analysis of modernization, whose conception of tradition and modernity was not dissimilar to that of Rostow. Parsons's scheme was subsequently elaborated and applied specifically to developing countries, (for example, Hoselitz, 1964), and came to be widely accepted amongst many 'mainstream' theorists of modernization.

In an attempt to integrate Tönnies's and Weber's perspectives on tradition and modernity, Parsons (1951) lists five choices, or 'pattern variables' (as they have come to be known), around which, he postulates, both social action and social institutions revolve.

(*a*) *Affectivity vs affective neutrality*. Do people maximize their immediate gratification (affectivity), or are they willing to forgo present gratification for possibly greater advantages in the future?

(*b*) *Diffuseness vs specifity*.   Is one's relationship with others to be all-inclusive (diffuse), or confined to limited areas only?

(*c*) *Collectivism vs individualism*. Does the collectivity of which one is part take precedence over one's own individual goals and aspirations (collectivism), or is it the reverse?

(*d*) *Particularism vs universalism*. Are others to be treated according to one's personal relationship with them (particularism), or are they to be dealt with according to some objective, impersonal criteria?

(*e*) *Ascription vs achievement*. Are persons to be judged by their descent, or other qualities with which they are endowed by no effort of their own (ascription) or are they to be judged – and do they judge themselves – by their achievements?[4]

Modernization entails a shift in the prevalent choices. In traditional societies, the emphasis is on immediate gratification (affectivity). This does not lead to disciplined exertion or to effective planning for the future; instead, it encourages current consumption. Affective neutrality, the willingness to renounce immediate gratification, is found more frequently in modern society, especially in the middle classes, where it promotes individual success as well as saving, reinvestment, and economic growth. Presumably, therefore, it is less crucial at a later stage of modernization, when society can afford a higher level of consumption.

In traditional society the family dominates the social scene, and local communities are small and intimate. Hence the stress is on all-encompassing (diffuse) relationships, on the common goals of the family or the community (collectivism) and on personal relations as criteria for the allocation of benefits (particularism). In modern society, where kinship is less dominant, where there are fewer small communities and social structures are generally larger and more complex, the emphasis is on segmented (specific) relationships, on the advancement of individual goals (individualism), and on the allocation of benefits by objective (universalist) criteria. Finally, many pre-modern societies are relatively closed, which means that social positions in them are determined largely by descent and family background (ascription). In contrast, modern society is much more open, giving much greater scope for achievement, while ascription serves mainly as a springboard for such achievement.

Neo-evolutionism: differentiation and reintegration

Having adopted some of the classical sociologists' polar dichotomy between tradition and modernity, 'mainstream' sociologists reached back once more and introduced some of their evolutionary perspectives as well. In this manner what is known as neo-evolutionism emerged. Since Parsons, the progenitor of structural-functionalism, became the leading figure of neo-evolutionism as well, and since the basic concepts of structure and function were common to both, the two theoretical perspectives merged, and a composite theory of modernization became predominant.

Parsons opened one of his early books with the statement: 'Spencer is dead. But who killed him and how?' The reply he offered was that Spencer had been the victim of the vengeance of the jealous god, evolution, in this case the evolution of scientific theory (Parsons, 1949,

p. 3). In other words, Spencer believed in evolution, and it was indeed the evolution of sociology which has taken us past Spencer. It is ironical, however, that Parsons should have made this quip, since Spencer's central idea — that of evolution as a process of differentiation *cum* reintegration — subsequently found its way into Parsons's own writings and into those of other neo-evolutionists as well, and has become one of their central concepts.

According to Parsons, social evolution proceeds through the successive differentiation of social sub-systems. First, the political, cultural and judicial sub-systems gradually become distinct and autonomous. This in itself is not a process of modernization, but rather a prelude and a prerequisite for it. Modernization occurs when the economy, and the technology on which it is based, become fully differentiated and autonomous from other parts of society. In pre-modern society, economic activity is embedded in the social matrix of kinship and status systems, and is thus held in check by other commitments. The separation of economic activity from such commitments brings about its liberation and increases its rationality. Frequently such separation of institutional spheres leads to disturbances; but eventually it produces a new type of integration and a more effective adaptation of society to its environment (Parsons, 1966).

Neil Smelser, a close collaborator of Parsons, similarly conceives of modernization in terms of differentiation and reintegration. He sees differentiation as a transition from multi-functional to uni-functional social structures, as illustrated by the transformation of the family. In pre-modern society the family is concerned with production and consumption, with basic socialization and further education, and in some cases with religious and political activities. With modernization, most of these functions are severed from the family. Production is taken over by separate economic enterprises, a large part of education is vested in formal organizations such as schools, universities, and youth movements, political functions are assumed by national, state, and local authorities, and religious functions by the church. Thus the family is left with only consumption and primary socialization as its chief contributions to society.[5] Smelser put somewhat more emphasis on disturbances that may disrupt the modernization process, but he too envisages new integrative mechanisms which counteract these tendencies. Such integrative mechanisms may not be universally successful, but in many cases they are, so that differentiation may eventually result in newly integrated societies (Smelser, 1973).

The convergence towards modernity

The societies developing from this process of differentiation and re-integration — many modernization theorists have presumed — would inevitably become modern, that is, take on the characteristics of the now modern societies. In S. N. Eisenstadt's (1973b, p. 15) words: 'Behind the theory there loomed a conviction of the inevitability of progress toward modernity, be it political development or industrialization.' Although the possibility of unsuccessful modernization was not overlooked, and although the great diversity of transitional societies was recognized, numerous modernization theorists implicitly assumed that such lack of success would be temporary and that the diversity of transitional societies would disappear as the end-stage of modernization was reached. This point may be reached by different societies at different times, but eventually there would be a general convergence and the following common features would appear: an industrialized market economy with continuous economic growth built into it; a proliferation of large-scale bureaucratic organizations pervading practically all spheres of life; a high rate of literacy and a continuous spread of formal education; an unprecedented reduction in inequality and growing rates of social mobility; a low birth rate balanced by a low death rate; urbanization; the declining influence of religion; the structural ability to absorb continuous change; a value system with special emphasis on universalism and achievement (see above), and participatory democracy,[6] or something very much like it.[7]

It was further argued that there are certain individual traits that fit in with such modern institutional patterns. These include emancipation from traditional authorities and social networks, openness to new experience, flexibility or willingness to change, an active attitude towards nature and society, strong ambitions and high aspirations, and a distinct time conception with stress on punctuality (Inkeles, 1973).[8]

Power and conflict in modern society

These ideas, which were propounded by structural-functionalists and like-minded thinkers, dominated the sociological scene around the middle of the century. From the end of the 1950s and onwards, structural-functionalism lost its pre-eminence; it became merely one of several alternative perspectives, while other points of view came to the fore. Not all of these were concerned with modernization and modern life, but one — the power and conflict school — made this its major concern. This school was much less prolific than structural-functionalism and, besides, it reverted to a focus on Western societies. Nevertheless, it made a strong impact on the sociological scene.

The power and conflict school rejected the structural-functional emphasis on values, consensus, and integration. Instead it adopted Marx's concepts as points of departure, but introduced far-reaching revisions, combining them with Weberian perspectives and with elitist outlooks derived from Pareto and Mosca. One outstanding representative of this school is Ralf Dahrendorf. Dahrendorf (1959) follows Marx in viewing society as divided into classes and in viewing class conflict as central to society, but he maintains that Marx had conceived these too narrowly. The basic factor in both is not necessarily the private ownership of the means of production by one class, but rather the power which one class wields over the other. The ownership of the means of production is merely one instance of the more general principle of power. Such ownership may be abolished, but not power. And since it is power which gives rise to class conflict, such conflict cannot be abolished either. Conflict, in turn, gives rise to social change; hence change is also a continuous presence in society.

However, class conflicts can differ and so can the changes they produce. When various types of conflicts are superimposed on each other, when social mobility from one class to another is blocked, when the subjected class suffers both absolute and relative material deprivation, and when there is no regulation of conflict, conflict will erupt; it will be both intense and violent, and bring about sudden and far-reaching revolutionary social change. But when various types of class conflicts are separated from each other, when the rates of mobility are high, when there is little material deprivation of the subjugated class, and when class conflict becomes institutionalized − it is less intense and violent, and the change it produces is more moderate and gradual.

The first situation is that which prevailed throughout most of the nineteenth century, that is, in Marx's time, and Marx's analysis was indeed appropriate for it. At that time, the distinguishing feature of capitalism was the principle of private property which implies the fusion of ownership and control of the economic enterprise. This meant that the conflict between those who owned the means of production and those who did not coincided with the conflict between those who had power and those who had none. In this particular instance, then, Marx was right in equating class conflict with conflict over the means of production.

This also meant that the conflict of interests over power and that over property were superimposed on each other. In addition, those who lacked power, the working class, also suffered severe economic deprivation, they had little chance of raising themselves out of their misery, and they could realistically expect that both they and their offspring would spend the rest of their lives under the existing dismal conditions. Also, there was no channelling of conflict as workers were prevented from organizing and from giving voice to their claims through collective bargaining. Grievances could thus be vented only through violence. For all these reasons, conflict, whenever it occurred, was indeed both intense and violent, and the situation did indeed have the potential of revolution built into it, as Marx had envisaged.

Since then, however, 'the participants, issues and patterns have changed and the pleasing simplicity of Marx's view of society has become a nonsensical construction' (Dahrendorf, 1959, p. 57). Today, capitalist enterprises have developed into joint stock companies, and this has led to a differentiation of ownership and control: ownership is dispersed among a large number of shareholders, and control is concentrated in the hands of a few managers and directors. The power-holders are thus no longer those who enjoy the highest economic rewards and power and property conflicts no longer coincide. Also, the economic deprivation of those who lack power and the degree of inequality between them and the dominant class has lessened, and the chances of mobility have increased. Hence the parties' involvement in any conflict is becoming milder. At the same time, the waging of such conflict has become regulated by mutually acceptable 'rules of the game', including those governing workers' organization, strikes, industrial arbitration and elections. Class and industrial conflict has thus become less intense, violence has been practically eliminated and revolution no longer looms.

In his single-mindedness, Marx believed that revolution was the only solution to the problems of capitalism. Marx was mistaken. The revolution which Marx predicted would indeed have been imminent were it not for the adaptations that capitalism has been able to make, and with which Marx failed to reckon. Indeed, Marx displayed a certain, characteristic naïvety when he expressed the belief that capitalism would be unable to cope with the conflicts and contradictions created by its own structure. In actual fact it was precisely the capitalist system's flexibility that has transformed the social order, and has brought about a new society. This society is still industrial, but because of the decomposition of ownership and control it no longer adheres to the principle of private property. It is therefore no longer capitalist; it might rightly be referred to as a post-capitalist society.

Power and elites in modern society

Another theorist who is considered as a representative of the power and conflict school, is C. Wright Mills, although he focused on power more than on conflict. In contrast to Dahrendorf, who employed Marx's division of society into classes, Mills stressed society's partition into elites and masses, and, following the elitist viewpoint, he did not believe in the ability of the masses to organize for concerted conflict with the elites. He has still been included in the power and conflict school because of his critical and radical stand and because of the impression one gains that he would have greatly welcomed such conflict if only it were feasible.

Mills saw modern, and especially American, society as dominated by a power elite which manipulates the masses into accepting its rule. This elite consists of the upper political, military, and economic personnel whose power is derived from their key positions in their respective institutional structures. Ownership and control of the means of production is thus only one source of power. Those who derive their power in this manner are only one of the three dominant groups, and not necessarily always the most powerful among the three. The middle levels of power such as congressmen and trade union leaders are dominated by the power elite and have little influence of their own. Modernization and more recent changes have led to a greater concentration of power in the hands of the elites and to greater political impotence and apathy on the part of the masses (Mills, 1959a; 1973).

Another theorist who is sometimes included in the power and conflict school is Raymond Aron. This scholar attempts to combine an economic-class perspective with a political-elite analysis, but his affinities lie clearly with a (modified) elitist point of view. For him, the economic realm has to do with equality as against inequality, the political realm with power as against freedom. Of the two values, equality and freedom, he gives first preference to the second. Hence he is concerned with the political order to a greater extent than with the economic order. From an economic point of view, Western and communist societies tend to converge. Both are industrial societies with similar structures of technology and production, both proclaim an egalitarian ethic and both have, in fact, a non-egalitarian reality. But their political values and their forms of implementing them differ widely. By comparison with communist societies, Western societies are characterized by a much greater dispersion of power.

In principle, to be sure, power is universal. Aron agrees with Mills and other elitists that in any society few (the elites) determine the lives of many (the masses). In modern society this power of the elites over the life and death of millions is expanded beyond measure by thermonuclear armaments. But, contrary to Mills, he holds that in the West this tendency is moderated because power is attached to well-defined and limited spheres of action and because it is fought over by many claimants. A completely unified elite means the end of freedom; a totally disunified elite means the end of the state. Freedom prevails in the intermediate regions, and Western societies have been more successful than communist ones in maintaining this balance. Also, Western societies have been suspicious of rulers and hence have been stingy in granting them the authority to rule, and the system has had many checks on power. In spite of growing centralization, Western societies have remained democracies because these checks, designed to guarantee individual rights, have survived well into the twentieth century (Aron, 1968, 1978).[9]

The coming of the post-industrial society

The concern with recent changes and with the resultant character of modern Western societies, has also been expressed by Daniel Bell. This scholar was – in his own way – influenced by Marx, but his even greater affinity with 'mainstream' sociology, places him squarely within this school of thought. While Dahrendorf wrote of the emergence of the post-capitaist (but still industrial) society, Bell (1973) announced the coming of the post-industrial society. According to Bell this society represents the culmination of tendencies which began to appear in nineteenth-century industrial society, but the changes since then are so far-reaching as to warrant the conclusion that a new type of society has come into being. So far this society has evolved fully only in the United States, but other Western countries are well on their way towards the same post-industrial stage.

While the development of capitalism was combined with a process of industrialization in which industrial production came to the centre of socio-economic life, the more recent change is one in which the importance of knowledge has come to the fore. The most distinctive feature of the new society thus lies in its crystallization around the acquisition, organization, control and implementation of knowledge. For Marx, the central axis around which capitalist, industrial society revolved was the exploitation of labour. For Bell, the central axis around which the post-industrial society revolves is the 'exploitation' of knowledge.

It might be argued that knowledge forms an essential part of *any* economic process, and that no production can take place without a certain know-how. But because of the development of science, the knowledge that came to be crucial for Western society is distinctive: it is abstract, theoretical knowledge, especially that pertaining to multi-variate systems, rather than the common-sense knowledge utilized in most other societies. Moreover, knowledge has come to occupy a more central place in post-industrial society than it did in any other or previous societies. In industrial society knowledge was of course important, but the central problems were nevertheless those of the accumulation of capital, investment, and production. Only in the post-industrial society have these problems dropped into the background and permitted knowledge to emerge as the central axis of society.

Also, in the industrial, capitalist society, a considerable proportion of the workforce was engaged in industrial production, a large part of it in unskilled work of the mechanical, assembly-line type. Hence aliena-tion — as conceived by Marx — characterized the relationship of the worker to his work. Since then, however, there has been a growth of the service and white-collar sectors relative to the manufacturing sector. This implies that fewer people are working with things; more and more are working either with symbols or with other people — in either case, a less alienating type of work. Moreover, within the remaining general category of productive workers, the percentage of unskilled labour has been decreasing while the percentage of skilled labour has been increas-ing. So today only an insignificant minority of the workforce is engaged in production of a mechanical type, and certainly this is no longer the prototype of the work situation. Like Marx's concept of alienation, the bewildered little man in the grip of the impersonal all-powerful machine, immortalized in Charlie Chaplin's famous film *Modern Times,* is a symbol of industrial society only. Today, both are nothing but period pieces.[10]

The post-industrial society further differs from its capitalist–industrial predecessor in that public choice rather than individual demand becomes the arbiter of services. This is a society which multiplies the definition of rights (such as the rights of the poor, of women, of minorities, of students, of homosexuals, of children), and translates them into claims on the community. It also increases the aspirations of various groups for material goods, education, health, and for a general upgrading of the quality of life. All this increases the need for public decision-making and government intervention, not only in the economy but in a whole variety of areas. In a sense, then, post-industrial society is characterized by communalism — in contrast to the individualism which characterizes capitalist–industrial society.

A somewhat similar view on the advent of post-industrial society

has been expressed by Alain Touraine (1971). Like Bell, Touraine
views contemporary Western society as knowledge-centred, as governed
by the systematic application of theoretically-based technical knowledge to economic and social ends. Whereas the industrial society focused
on the factory as the main source of commodities, the post-industrial
society focuses on the university as the main source of theoretical
knowledge. Unlike Bell, however, Touraine holds that alienation did
not vanish with the decline of the industrial society, merely that its
nature became significantly altered. In industrial society, alienation
centred chiefly on the production process; in post-industrial society,
this type of alienation is merely a sideline to the much more encompassing alienation that results from subordination to technocratic
control. This is why the antagonisms bred by this new form of society
tend to find their most acute expression at the universities — the
centres for the creation and dissemination of technocratic knowledge.[11]

Although Touraine thus resembles Bell in his conception of the post-
industrial society, his conception of alienation in this society is more
akin to neo-Marxist views. In a sense, his theory may be regarded as an
attempt to bridge the gap between 'mainstream' sociology and such
neo-Marxist conceptions (these will be discussed in the following
chapter).

Explaining modernization

While some theorists focused on developments in Western societies,
modernization (it will be recalled) was now no longer thought to be
peculiar to the West. Nevertheless, it could not be denied that the West
had enjoyed a headstart over other parts of the world in producing it,
and that some third world countries had been more successful in the
same feat while others were lagging behind. How could these differences
be explained?

Initially there was (especially among economists) a strong tendency
to assert the primacy of economic factors, chiefly capital formation, as
initiators of modernization and development. This conception was
applied to third world countries and Western governments were therefore urged to accelerate financial aid to these countries. However, this
viewpoint was subsequently modified by a growing awareness of
the role of non-economic factors in either delaying or accelerating
modernization. This fitted in with the points of view of Parsons and
like-minded thinkers of the structural–functional school, who had

long insisted on a multi-causal analysis of social change and modernization (Parsons, 1973). At the same time, norms and values were assigned special importance and it was claimed that they could make all the difference between success and failure in economic development.

It was reported, for instance, that contrary to previous assumptions, people in some developing countries were motivated by economic incentives only to a limited extent. Hence they showed a reluctance to relinquish traditional ties and forms of organization, to enter into new, urban types of employment, and to acquire the work discipline associated with modern methods of production. It was further reported that many who engaged in industrial pursuits tended to do so only until they attained a standard of living in keeping with traditional expectations. As soon as that was reached they were inclined to abandon their jobs and return to their villages and/or their extended families (Moore, 1973). Indeed, it seemed to transpire that people in developing countries sometimes displayed values and dispositions surprisingly similar to those which Weber had previously labelled the 'traditional ethic' (see chapter 1). These dispositions were the very antithesis of the 'spirit of capitalism' which, according to Weber, had played a germinal role in the modernization of the West. These traditional values were now thought to be important in retarding modernization in some of the third world countries.

Their counterpart, the spirit of capitalism — was also analysed, and even elaborated, and broadened to include the third world situation by David McClelland. McClelland (1973) identified a certain drive that he labelled the need for achievement.[12] This drive, he claimed, emanates from what Weber referred to as the spirit of capitalism: a generalized commitment to success, not for the sake of material pleasures but for the intrinsic satisfaction of success as such.[13] And not only is it reasonable to suppose (as Weber has done) that it is this drive which leads to saving, to the accumulation of capital, to reinvestment and therefore to economic growth, but empirical research has in fact established that this is so. In his wide-ranging empirical studies, McClelland claims to have demonstrated that the prevalence of this drive in any country (Western or non-Western)[14] led to an upsurge of economic growth, some twenty to fifty years later. The opposite, however, is not the case: economic development has not brought in its wake an upsurge in the drive for achievement.

In a way, McClelland may thus claim to have substantiated Weber's basic thesis on the causal relationship between the spirit of capitalism and economic development. On the other hand, in effect he detached

Weber's spirit of capitalism from the Protestant ethic in whose context (according to Weber) it has first developed. In McClelland's view, this ethic is one possible source, but by no means the only possible source for the spirit of capitalism or the spirit of achievement. Hence, it is not surprising that the same spirit is prevalent in some non-Western, non-Protestant countries as well. In fact, at present it is more prevalent in some developing countries than it is in the West, where it was, of course, more widespread in the past. These countries are not only more successful in economic growth compared with other developing countries, but they are apt to overtake their less fortunate Western contemporaries as well.

The practical implication emerging from studies such as these is that financial aid to developing countries is not likely to prove effective unless preceded by a concerted effort to upgrade the educational system. Education is considered important because it is thought to imbue its beneficiaries with modern values and motivations, including achievement orientation, which are thought to facilitate the push towards economic development.

Another explanation for the success (or lack thereof), of modernization has been offered by Eisenstadt (1973a). Eisenstadt has focused on political modernization, whose end result he conceives of as a change-absorbing political system, with a degree of accountability of the rulers to the ruled as formally expressed in elections. He accepts the basic assumption that these traits are not necessarily confined to the West. But he no longer accepts the further assumption that they are about to gain universal acceptance in non-Western countries. Indeed, in some of those an initial advance towards such patterns was subsequently halted or disrupted.

One of Eisenstadt's major explanations for the success of modernization or lack thereof lies in the cohesiveness between the various groups and strata in a society. When such cohesiveness exists, a society's political centre is more likely to be able to cope with different groups' demands for change and to absorb such change into the system. Conversely, when basic cleavages exist among the elites and between them and various other groups in society, when basic conflicts erupt, and in the absence of overall solidarity which could bridge such conflicts, breakdowns of modernization are likely to occur. Other analyses of the same school have attributed less than fully successful modernization to inequitable landholding structures and to rampant economic inequality. The resulting frustration among the poorer elements of the population was thought to produce political turmoil, which discourages investment and diverts energy away from economic activity, and thus retards development. In the context of Western society, conflict was thought of as a change-producing element. But here, too, it was emphasized that only the regulation of conflict had produced the Western patterns of modernity as we know them today.

The various analyses thus focus on different aspects of modernization and modernity, and emphasize the role of different factors in promoting or impeding its success. Nevertheless, they have at least one assumption in common. Like their classical predecessors, they share the notion that these factors are located within the respective societies themselves. Some modernization theorists have adhered to a diffusionist approach. They hold that modernization (especially in third world countries) may be encouraged by the diffusion of values, knowledge, skills, and technology (especially from the West), while retarded modernization is the result of resistance to diffusion (Nash, 1963). But even in this approach under-development is primarily the result of some internal deficiencies in a country's social or motivational structure. Diffusion may help correct these deficiencies, but they themselves are internally generated, as is the receptiveness to diffusion or lack thereof. As Daniel Lerner (1968, p. 392) put it: 'Lifeways cannot be adopted; they must be adapted.' Even according to this view, then, modernization is greatly dependent on a country's domestic potential, including its potential to absorb and utilize the foreign (diffusionary) aid extended to it. A country that lags behind in modernization, therefore, has no one to blame but itself.

The critique of 'mainstream' and modernization theory

Since the end of the 1950s, and especially from the 1960s and onwards, structural-functionalism has come under a growing barrage of criticism. It has been criticized for the disproportional weight which it has accorded to values and consensus and for its neglect of economic factors, power, dissent and conflict. It has thus been accused of turning away from all the forces which may tear society apart and have done so, all through history. Even more so, it has been accused of being unable to cope with social change, that is, history itself. Thus Mills (1959b, pp.32-3), in his parody on one of Parsons's major books put the following words in the author's mouth. 'One point puzzles me a little . . . . How should I account for social change — that is for history? About these . . .

problems, I recommend that whenever you come upon them, you undertake empirical investigations.'

The fact that structural–functionalism has nevertheless produced a voluminous literature on at least one aspect of social change – modernization – has not appeased the critics. For the theory of modernization which grew out of structural–functionalism in conjunction with neo-evolutionism has come under an even heavier barrage of criticism. It has been variously accused of being ethnocentric, empirically invalid, theoretically unsound, ideologically biased, and ineffective policy-wise, if not downright detrimental. In short, it has been suggested that, 'Like the underdeveloped society to which it is applied, this sociology is becoming increasingly underdeveloped' (Frank, 1971, p. 2).

The critique of Westerncentrism

There is first the critique that modernization theory is ethnocentric, or as some observers put it, Westerncentric. Most classic nineteenth-century sociologists have been hesitant in welcoming modernization, expressing concern, or at least ambivalence, over the alienation, anomie and regimentation it produces. Some twentieth-century modernization theorists have also expressed concern with anomie. But most have allegedly sided uncritically with modernization, implicitly equating modernization with Westernization, and exalting the combined benefits of both for mankind as a whole. No systematic attention has been given to the thought that the advent of a non-Western social structure might not only be more feasible, but might also be more beneficial, to third world countries. The Western experience was to be uniformly emulated by these countries, which were reckoned to be lucky in having been given the opportunity to catch up so speedily without having to go through the long and tortuous historical sequel of development in the West (Hoogvelt, 1976, p. 54). As Portes (1973, p. 252) put it succinctly, 'Descriptions of modernity reflect an intellectual attitude which . . . looks confidently at itself and systematizes introspective insights into lessons for the benefit of the rest of mankind.'

The notion that a country becomes modernized to the extent that it becomes Westernized and vice versa is held by the critics to be implicit in all those models that list individualist, achievement-oriented values and participatory political structures as integral elements of modernization or modernity. It is as if they were visualizing the whole world as eventually blooming out into a multitude of achievement-oriented democracies. The view that exalts Western-style modernity as indisputably beneficial for the third world is most bluntly and un-abashedly put forward by Lerner (1965, p. 79), who writes:

> What America is . . . the modernizing Middle East seeks to become
> . . . . Those who regard this as ethnocentrism should try an exercise
> in self analysis: compare your own life with that of any Middle
> Eastern you ever knew . . . no advocate of Middle Eastern felicity
> can properly oppose the quest for things they lack because in his
> opinion Americans have too much of these same things for their
> own good.

The idea that the whole world is happily converging on to a Western (preferably American) blueprint of modernity has been challenged not only because of its ethnocentricity, but on factual grounds as well. Modernization theory has been accused of closing its eyes to the fact that modernization, let alone Westernization, is by no means a universal pattern; that many third world countries, having started out on the path of modernization, did not complete the journey, but settled down into a variety of structures that were neither traditional nor modern and most certainly had little in common with those of the West, while others most clearly chose a communist rather than a Western path to modernity.

The critique of polarity

Modernization theory has further been denounced for carrying over into the twentieth century Tönnies's and Weber's allegedly outmoded polar view of tradition versus modernity. For instance, Parsons's and his disciples' model of pattern variables (in which traditional society is characterized by diffuseness, particularism, and ascription, while modern society features specificity, universalism, and achievement orientation) has been stigmatized as a futile exercise in comparative statics. The stricture is that while two polarities are identified, little that is of value is said on how to get from one to the other, and the dynamics of the transition are thus largely disregarded. 'To develop, Hoselitz counsels, underdeveloped countries should eliminate the pattern variables of underdevelopment and adopt those of development' (Frank, 1971, p. 6). But the question still remains of how this feat is to be accomplished.

The same polar model has also been taken to task for presenting a distorted conception of reality. Frank, for instance, goes on to claim that not only is there substantial particularism in modern Western countries, but that this particularism is even exported by them to under-developed countries (although it is wrapped up in such universalist slogans as 'freedom' and 'democracy'); that in both developed and under-developed countries universalism is merely a cover-up for under-lying particularism; and that, in any case, the pattern variables are profoundly unimportant for either development or under-development.

Similarly, adds Frank, Rostow's stages of economic development (which merely represent the polarity of tradition and modernity with some intermediary stages between them) simply do not correspond to the past or present reality of the developing countries whose development they are supposed to guide; in fact, in most of these countries they have been conspicuous by their absence. While the first two stages are fictitious, the third is improbable, and the last two are therefore utopian.

In more general terms, it has been claimed that in the polar model of tradition versus modernity it is only the concept of modernity which has been fully elaborated. The concept of tradition has usually been defined by default; whatever is not modern must *ipso facto* be traditional. Thus, historical facts to the contrary, entire civilizations – in fact the majority of human civilizations – have been subsumed under the blanket term of tradition.

The assumption that tradition is necessarily an impediment to modernization and must be subdued before modernization can proceed has also been questioned. It has been argued that the mere disruption of traditional settings is more likely to lead to chaos than to modernity, and that tradition and modernity are not necessarily mutually exclusive, and may well exist beneficially side by side. It has further been pointed out that traditions differ in their flexibility and receptiveness to change. Some traditions may well support modernization by providing a source for achievement motivation, by supplying the unifying symbols that legitimize modernization and in whose name the sacrifices demanded for modernization become meaningful, and by furnishing a basis of stability and psychological security for those undergoing the vicissitudes of rapid change (Gusfield, 1973; Portes, 1973). Thus, for instance, the long-standing Jewish tradition of veneration for learning has been considered as conducive to academic achievement and therefore to success in modern Western society and a sense of belonging to traditional religious groups has been said to ease adjustment to the heterogeneity and rapid change of modern society.

But not only may tradition promote modernity, modernity may generate its own tradition. For instance, if the distinguishing feature of modernity is rationality (in Weber's terms), then this rationality undoubtedly finds expression, among other things, in the practice of replacing production methods as soon as more efficient ones become available, and in the practice (at least in the physical sciences) of discarding scientific theories as soon as superior ones evolve. Both of these unprecedented practices are by now a well-established tradition in modern society — which goes to show that rationality, far from being antithetical to tradition, may in itself be a tradition.

However, this last type of critique has been repudiated and has met with a counter-critique from the strongholds of modernization theory. Hoselitz contends that this critique invalidates neither Weber's distinction between the traditional ethic and the spirit of capitalism nor the contemporary analyses that followed in his vein. For implicit in the models of Weber and his disciples is the additional distinction between tradition and traditionalism. Tradition refers to a society's general reservoir of customs, values, and symbols that have been handed down from the past. Traditionalism, on the other hand, refers to the sanctification of such customs, values, and symbols, merely *because* they have been handed down from the past.

Tradition as such is not necessarily hostile to change, but Weber never claimed that it was. On the contrary, he demonstrated, for example, how the tradition of ancient Roman law has served as a basis for modern rational law, and how the tradition of ancient Judaism has served as one basis for the modernity-promoting Protestant ethic. What Weber had in mind, then, when he contrasted the traditional ethic with the spirit of capitalism, was traditionalism rather than merely tradition. It is this sanctification of tradition for tradition's sake which leads people to cling to their customary practices, to the rejection of change, and hence to social and economic stagnation. It is thus a sophisticated conception (rather than the simplistic dichotomy between tradition and modernity) which has been adopted and developed by twentieth-century modernization theorists.

The critique of explanations
This counter-critique, however, has not been viewed by the sceptics as exonerating modernization theory of its many faults, not the least of these being the faulty explanation it allegedly offers for the process of modernization. First, this fault is held to be evident in the differentiation model. The fact that differentiation occurs is not disputed, but the critique has been over the almost total lack of a causal explanation for this process (Smith, 1973; Hoogvelt, 1976). Even more severe are the strictures that address themselves to the causal explanations that do exist, especially the ones that seek the roots of modernization in the individual's drive for achievement and

the impediments to modernization in the opposite values and psychological constellations.

It has been claimed that these conceptions show a naïve disregard for structural factors in the process of development or under-development, a disregard that was as alien to Weber as it was to Marx, and that would not have been endorsed by him even in his wildest flight of fancy. More naïve still is the conception that McClelland's need for achievement can be deliberately fostered from abroad. It is hard to believe, writes Frank, that deeply engrained social conditions could be changed simply by admonishing people to get a hold of themselves and raise their need for achievement (Frank, 1971).

With regard to this type of explanation, it has further been suggested that what was conducive to modernization in the West, and was correctly perceived as being so by Weber, is not necessarily conducive to modernization in today's third world countries. The importance assigned to the individual drive for achievement rests on the assumption that modernization is spearheaded by a group of private entrepreneurs. Clearly there is something wrong with this assumption in the context of today's developing countries, in which development —if and when it occurs —is spearheaded by the state. What is required is not a drive for individual success on the part of entrepreneurs, but rather a single-minded determination on the part of governmental elites, coupled with a centrally monitored mass mobilization of the population for increased production and decreased consumption (to facilitate centralized savings and their use in long-term investment). Therefore, the belief that more individuals with pronounced achievement orientations will lead to speedier, more pronounced development in today's third world, is nothing but an anachronism.

However, the cardinal sin for which modernization theory is castigated is its tendency to explain both development and under-development purely in terms of internal forces working in each society. Modernization theory is accused of viewing societies as if they existed in total isolation, and of either disregarding any contact that is seen to occur, or conceptualizing it as diffusion — that gentle transmitter of universal evolution. Modernization theory is thus chastised for failing to take notice of the international power network of which both Western and non-Western societies are part. It is reprimanded for failing to recognize that modernization in the West has resulted from the advantages of a strong stand in this global system, while under-development in other parts of the world is the result of a weak position in it. It is this evasion of the role of the West in causing and perpetuating under-development that enables the adherents of this school to blame the people of under-developed countries so unjustly for their plight.[15]

The critique of the impact on policy

However, the misconception to which this last critique calls attention would not have been considered so disconcerting were it not for the effect that modernization theory has allegedly had on both developed and developing countries. By blaming third world countries for their own under-development, this theory has attached a negative stigma to these countries and transmitted a negative self-image to them. The consequent loss of self-respect which permeates the elites in these countries and filters through to the masses is anything but conducive to an improvement of the situation.

Moreover, this theory is held to have exerted a profound influence upon actual development policy. In the 1950s and 1960s, the United States and other countries showed a great deal of interest in the problems of under-development, not only because it was seen as perpetuating the misery of third world countries, but because it could eventually lead to communism. It was therefore the duty of the United States to bring salvation to these countries by helping them along the road to Western-style modernization. Today it is sometimes asked whether these were honest ideas, or cynical covers for American imperialism. There is no way to tell. But the fact remains that these ideas in some way emanated from modernization theory, that many youngsters believed the message and that many foreign aid programs were put into effect under their guidance. With the election of John Kennedy in 1960, this enthusiasm was translated into concrete action, of which the most symbolically important was the formation of the Peace Corps.

But, the critique goes on, these ideas did not work well. Since technological advance and industrialization were embraced as the hallmarks of progress, crash programs for the improvement of agricultural techniques were put into effect; these set adrift a proletariat which flocked to the towns, causing over-urbanization, the development of slums, and unemployment. Following the theories on the importance of modern values and the education designed to instill them, much money went into the formal education of people who became over-qualified and for whom no appropriate jobs were available. This caused an exodus to developed countries where job prospects were better, or else gave rise to discontent and political fermentation. Also, World Bank loans were tied to the emergence of Western-type, i.e., capitalist, institutions, which discouraged alternative (and perhaps more advantageous) development (Portes, 1973; Foster-Carter 1974; Hoog-velt, 1976, Chirot, 1977).

Moreover, it is claimed, modernization theory has come to serve as an ideological cover for capitalist imperialism. In Frank's words (1971, p. 55) it is 'the emperor's clothes which have served to hide his naked imperialism'. In line with this, some even see the Vietnam War as the indirect result of these ideas. Frank, in the aforementioned essay, even goes as far as to assert that on behalf of achievement-oriented universalism some modernization theorists have become devoted propagators of escalation in Vietnam, 'from napalming the South to bombing the North and beyond' (p. 9).

Other critiques

It should be left to the reader to judge whether the Vietnam War and its escalation are indeed a logical outgrowth of modernization theory. But some other critiques of that theory were certainly well taken, as were the critiques aimed at the power and conflict school. It has been claimed, for instance, that by neglecting the elements which have been emphasized by structural-functionalism, namely values, consensus, and integration, this school has shown itself to be no less one-sided. It has been further asserted that not all change results from conflict, and that the power and conflict school has not been able to cope with any other type of change. Dahrendorf, a leading figure in this school of thought, has been further taken to task for presenting power differences as a dichotomy when in fact they are a hierarchy and therefore cannot form the basis of class conflict. Finally, he has been criticized for over-magnifying the changes that have occurred in Western society since the development of classical capitalism in the nineteenth century.

The same critique has also been levelled at Bell, and the novelty of the post-industrial society as he depicted it has been questioned, for instance, by Giddens (1973, p. 262):

Modern technique may be staggering in its scale . . . but there is nothing which is specifically new in the application of 'theoretical knowledge' to productive technique. Indeed, as Weber stressed above all, rationality of technique . . . is the primary factor which from the beginning has distinguished industrialism from all preceding forms of social order.

In response to the various critiques, modernization theory has developed some new perspectives in recent years. The previous idea of universal convergence on a Western type of modernity has been relegated to the background; greater emphasis has been put on the structural variety of different (modern and non-modern) societies, and on the continued viability of the latter. It has been stressed that under the impact of Western influence, some traditional societies may well develop a new but not necessarily modern stand, and that such societies are not necessarily transitory but may develop their own mechanisms of stability (for example, Riggs, 1966). It has also been clarified that modernization might well occur in some spheres but not in others, and that partially modernized societies might well persist no less than wholly modern ones (Nettl and Robertson, 1968). Further, the continuity between tradition and modernity has been highlighted; development has come to be regarded as the unfolding of the traditional forces inherent in a society and as contingent on the type of tradition which preceded it (Eisenstadt, 1973b). Finally, explanations of modernization have been putting more stress, for instance, on the role of modernizing elites, rather than on the value orientations with which society as a whole is suffused (Eisenstadt, 1973b). But the most radical divergence from the previous paradigm has come about in Marxism, neo-Marxism, and dependency theory — which will be our concern in the following chapter.

Selected readings

Bell, D. (1973), *The Coming of the Post-Industrial Society*, New York, Basic Books.
Dahrendorf, R. (1959), *Class and Class Conflict in Industrial Society*, Stanford University Press.
Etzioni, A., and Etzioni-Halevy, E. (eds), (1973), *Social Change* (2nd edn), New York, Basic Books, chs 10, 12, 13, 14, 18, 26, 27, 28, 30, 31, 32, 38.
Merton, R. K. (1957), 'Social structure and anomie', in *Social Theory and Social Structure* (rev. edn), New York, Free Press, pp. 131–60.
Mills, C. W. (1959), *The Power Elite*, New York, Oxford University Press.

3 · The advent of modern society in contemporary sociology (B): Marxist, neo-Marxist and dependency theory

Marxism has been a highly influential trend of Western thought from Marx's time onwards; but in sociology it has been relegated to the margins and it did not regain respectability and come to the forefront again until the 1960s and 1970s. At that time previous Marxist thinkers gained new fame in sociological circles, and new Marxist perspectives were developed. Some of these have been concerned with the internal development of Western capitalism, others with its external connections and its place in an overall world system.

Marxist perspectives on Western capitalism[1]

Theorists of the first type have applied Marx's conceptual tools to the development of Western capitalism after his time. In this endeavour they have been led to divergent conclusions. Some believe that these developments have confounded Marx's prognoses on the contradictions and conflicts of capitalism that must inevitably lead to the proletarian revolution. Indeed, they see the forces and relations of production of late or mature capitalism as reinforcing capitalism rather than undermining it. Others see mature capitalism as still beset by major contradictions and crises which are apt to bring about its downfall.

The hegemony of Western capitalism

According to the first view, the capitalist ruling class has succeeded in establishing social order and stabilizing the system by inculcating in the subordinate class beliefs and attitudes that serve to legitimize that system. Antonio Gramsci developed the theory of hegemony, whereby the dominant class has obtained a large degree of consent from the subjected class and can therefore reduce the amount of coercion needed to repress it. The mechanisms for eliciting such consent have been various cultural institutions and associations which have been disseminating the ideology of the ruling class. In this, the bourgeoisie has been aided

58

by secondary classes and this alliance has created a formidable barrier to working-class opposition.

The failure of the working class to develop class consciousness and revolutionary opposition was also one of the major ·concerns of the Institute for Social Research, established in Frankfurt in 1923. Scholars of this institute (which went into exile in the United States after Hitler came to power) attempted to synthesize Marxism with psychoanalysis and with the analysis of culture and ideology. Accordingly, they attributed the subjugation of the working class to psychological mechanisms for adapting to subordinate status under conditions of material affluence and mass culture.

The most influential figure of the Frankfurt School was Herbert Marcuse.[2] As Marcuse (1964) sees it, capitalist society is characterized by repression in the guise of freedom; by a capacity to make people identify with the system that has been forced upon them; by alienation that is so pervasive that people are no longer aware of it. It is further characterized by a capacity to absorb and contain opposition, especially of the working class, so that this opposition no longer has the capacity to bring about social change.

This is accomplished through various devices:

(a) Technological rule: the abundance created by developing technology looks deceptively as if it is made for the benefit of all. Thus it erodes the will of the exploited to replace the system.

(b) Tolerance of limited freedom: freedom of expression and organization are allowed, as long as the alternatives they advocate are within the confines of the present system. People may choose between various parties and between various commercial products but the differences between them are minimal. By being able to choose between limited alternatives people gain the illusion of freedom; limited freedom thus turns into an instrument of repression.

(c) Commercial advertising: by extolling the virtues of consumption advertising induces people to want what the system is capable of offering. Social control is thus anchored in false and artificially created needs. The system creates the same needs amongst the working class and fulfils them too. It thus incorporates this class into the mass consumer society and this, too, dulls its desire for revolt.

(d) Mass culture: previously, culture was alienated from the establishment and formed a channel of protest. Today it has turned into mass culture, it has lost its critical dimensions and it too, is structured so as to perpetuate the system.

(e) Sex: formerly, sexual repression led to personal frustration which could be channelled into political action. Today's total permissiveness, on the other hand, releases discontent and thereby promotes conformity.

Thus, Western capitalism gives people everything except the freedom to participate in the central decisions concerning their own lives. Instead of granting people this true freedom, the system bestows on them all that makes slavery pleasant.

Louis Althusser, a very influential figure, especially in European Marxism, maintains a similar line of thought on capitalist hegemony, although he is not led to the same degree of pessimism on the possibility of opposition and change. Althusser sees ideology as an indispensable tool of social order, in that it instills the illusion of liberty, the better to ensure submission to necessity. Accordingly, ideological control is exercised by the capitalist state through special apparatuses. Althusser distinguishes between the repressive state apparatuses, which function primarily by threat of violence (including the government, the army, the police, the courts, the prison system), and the ideological state apparatuses, which function mainly through ideological control (such as the church, education, the family, parties, and cultural institutions). Repressive measures by themselves are not sufficient. Control through the ideological institutions too, is essential for the perpetuation of ruling-class power. Through these apparatuses workers are taught what is necessary for production as well as acceptance of ruling-class dominance, and members of the ruling class are taught how to control workers without antagonizing them (Althusser, 1971; see also chapter 8).

The contradictions and crises of Western capitalism

It would seem to follow from this view that capitalism has not only entrenched itself, but stabilized itself as well. Some Marxists, however, hold that capitalism is still beset by contradictions and crises that preclude such stability. Paul Baran and Paul Sweezy (1966), for instance, hold that present-day capitalism produces an ever-increasing economic surplus,[3] but still fails to provide the consumption and investment outlets for the absorption of that surplus and, hence, for the smooth working of the system. Left to its own devices, it would sink deeper and deeper into chronic crises and depressions.

These crises are countered by artificial devices to absorb the surplus. First, various artificial ways are developed to stimulate consumption, for instance, through advertising, by encouraging spurious and unnecessary innovations, and the belief that only the newest is the best. Other parts of the surplus are absorbed through taxation and through government spending, which in turn increases demand. Thus, taxation, which has traditionally been opposed by businessmen, is actually in their interest. From being primarily a mechanism for transferring income it has become in large measure a mechanism for creating income for them by bringing idle capital into production. This strategy has mitigated the crises but has not overcome them, and today, as in Marx's day, capitalism is still a self-contradictory system.

Just as capitalism's economic contradictions still prevail, so does alienation. Work is still as dehumanizing as it ever was. Men are still being imprisoned in the narrow cells provided for them by the division of labour, their faculties stunted and their minds diminished. They are increasingly engaged in producing useless, wasteful or even destructive products, and their work is therefore increasingly meaningless. Asked whether he liked his job, one of John Updike's characters replied, 'Hell, it wouldn't be a job if I liked it.' In capitalist society, all but a tiny minority of particularly lucky workers would probably agree. What is even worse, all this has had a deteriorating effect on the general quality of life, including family relations. These, then, constitute some of the necessary costs of capitalist production. However, 'what should be crystal clear is that an economic system in which such costs are socially necessary has long ceased to be a socially necessary economic system' (Baran and Sweezy, 1966, p. 144).

A complementary and even more extreme view has been expressed by Harry Braverman (1975). According to this view, the development of capitalism constantly degrades and cheapens labour, and erodes the workers' autonomy. This is accomplished by denying them the capacity to organize work for themselves, by the diminution of skilled labour and the consequent creation of an expanding mass of interchangeable and easily replaceable workers. The innovations introduced into industry are specifically designed to concentrate knowledge and managerial control at the top, and to reduce whatever capacity for creativity and control still rests with the workers.

Thus, the main development has not been the upgrading of skill among workers, as some analysts have claimed, but rather a more profound split between knowledge and productive activity and the creation of an expanding mass of unskilled workers. There has been a rapid growth of white-collar and service occupations, but many of them are not much different from unskilled labour. All this has had profound implications for the quality of human existence and this cannot be compensated for by consumer goods. This degradation of work does not lead to false contentment, but rather to the potential of upheavals in the future.

The conflict-generating potential of Western capitalism has also been emphasized by Jurgen Habermas. This thinker is usually considered as the leading inheritor of the Frankfurt School legacy in recent years, but contrary to Marcuse – the former leading figure of the Frankfurt School – he does not regard late capitalism as a system in which contradictions and crises have been manipulated out of existence. In his view they are still very much in evidence. One source of crisis is in the contradictions of the capitalist state. In late capitalism the state is required to manage the economic system, but is deprived of the managerial capacities which could have made such management effective.

A second source of crisis is the problem of legitimation. The acceptance of the system depends not only on its capacity to supply material goods, but also on its ability to convince the people that the actions of authority are justifiable and valid. Such legitimation is always in question in a system of class domination and this holds for late capitalism as well. A third source of crisis lies in the problem of individual identity.[4] The traditional supports for personal identity (such as the family and the church), derive from pre-capitalist culture, and they are declining as capitalism evolves. New sources of support cannot be deliberately brought into being and this creates potential identity crises. Thus there are fundamental contradictions in the capitalist state, culture, and socialization that increase the likelihood of class consciousness and a demand for emancipation (Habermas, 1975).

In a similar vein, J. O'Connor (1973), writes about the contradictions created by the capitalist state. He argues that the state is responsible for legitimizing capitalism through the distribution of concessions to the working class in the form of welfare, social security, etc. However, the expenses involved in these concessions outstrip the revenues, thus precipitating a fiscal crisis of the capitalist state (see also chapter 4).

Recent changes in Western capitalism

Whether they perceive Western capitalism as having stabilized itself or whether they perceive it as still beset by destructive contradictions, there is one point on which Marxists and neo-Marxists generally agree: since the nineteenth century, that is, since Marx's time, capitalism has not changed fundamentally. The developments in Western society that are given so much weight by 'mainstream' sociologists are seen by Marxists as minor, reflecting changes of detail rather than essence. They have not affected the most basic elements of the capitalist mode of production (the organization of labour and capital) nor the relations connected therewith (exploitation *via* expropriation of surplus value).

The changes that did occur were in the area of the concentration and centralization of economic enterprises. A growing tendency towards monopoly or oligopoly,[5] and specific forms of national and international organization that accompany this, are seen to reflect an alteration of capitalist society, but not its most basic economic elements or their arrangement.The mega-corporation remains within the framework of private property, and its behaviour has not changed in any substantive way. The separation of ownership and control which has attended the process of economic concentration has not made much difference either, since the managerial class has the same interests and values as the capitalist class. Other changes concern economic growth and development. These, however, have been halted in recent years and economic recession has set in (see chapter 4).

Also, equality, equality of opportunity, and mobility have not increased substantially. Moreover, the issues of equality of opportunity and mobility are seen by some Marxists as false issues. If the class structure is a system of slots, mobility merely means more persons (or their offspring) swapped from one slot to another. The spaces and their relation to each other remain as they were. The bourgeois is a bourgeois by virtue of what he owns – no matter what his origins. The basic point is, therefore, that equality has not been increasing and the various social classes have not shown any signs of converging. Thus the objective basis of class conflict has not disappeared and, according to some Marxists at least, it still has the potential of flaring up (see chapter 5). Finally, the ruling class still holds on to its ascendancy over the state and still affects its policies so as to promote its own interests (see chapters 6 and 7). The changes that have occurred since the nineteenth century, therefore, have not replaced capitalism. The present era is not a new epoch of development; it is merely the further development of capitalism.

Marxist perspectives on the world system: dependency theory

While many Marxists and neo-Marxists have devoted their analytical efforts to Western capitalism as such, several have maintained that this system cannot be analysed in isolation, and must be seen in the wider context of a world system. Only in this context can the most distinctive features of capitalism, including its unusual degree of economic growth and development, be explained. Proponents of this view, which came to be known as dependency theory, maintain that 'mainstream' modernization theory's greatest fallacy has been its tendency to see development in the Western, capitalist world and under-development in the third world in isolation. Instead, they should be seen in conjunction with each other. It is the contact between the West and the third world which has brought development to the former and under-development to the latter.

The third world countries became under-developed not because of the persistence of traditional social patterns, but because they were brought into the orbit of capitalism. Concomitantly, the Western countries evolved into capitalist powers not only through the expropriation of surplus value from their own labouring classes, but also through the extraction of economic surplus from the third world countries, by distorting agricultural production, exhausting raw materials, exploiting their cheap labour and by generally restructuring their economies in line with Western (rather than third world) needs. In this manner an international system of stratification has been created in which the West (also referred to as the 'metropolis', the 'centre', or the 'core') has acted as a global ruling class, while the third world (also referred to as the 'satellites' or the 'periphery'), has come to fulfil the role of an internationally exploited class.

This perspective, of course, is not entirely new. In a sense, it was first opened up by Marx himself when he showed how the discovery of the new world and the commencement of trade with the Far East affected the development of capitalism (see chapter 1). It was also foreshadowed by Lenin, who revealed the crucial importance of imperialism for the development of capitalism. But Marx and the early Marxists did not develop a systematic conception of the effects of Western capitalism on the third world. Marx was convinced that eventually the non-Western countries, including the colonies, would come to, or would be forced to, adopt a capitalist mode of production before they could attain socialism, but he did not explain how this was to come about.[6] Both Marx and early Marxists showed great interest in imperialism, but they focused mainly on its implications for the imperialists. It remained for neo-Marxist dependency theorists to present a systematic analysis of the consequences which it held for its victims.

Leading figures in dependency theory
The first major contribution on this count was made by Paul Baran. He

presented not only a prominent analysis of Western capitalism, but was also one of the first, if not the first, to present the ideas which came to be the core of dependency theory. Baran (1957) perceived a deep conflict of interests between the West and the third world:

Economic development in underdeveloped countries is profoundly inimical to the dominant interests in the advanced capitalist countries. Supplying many important raw materials to the industrialized countries, providing their corporations with vast profits and investment outlets, the backward world has always represented the indispensable hinterland of the highly developed capitalist West. Thus the ruling class in the United States (and elsewhere) is bitterly opposed to the industrialization of the so-called 'source-countries'. (p. 12)

The exploitation of the now under-developed countries has thus played a crucial part in the development of capitalism in the West, while it has prevented economic growth in those countries themselves. For although the intrusion of the West has accelerated the decomposition of their pre-capitalist structures, and thus established some of the basic prerequisites for the development of capitalism, it has prevented with equal force the ripening of others. By removing a large share of their economic surplus, and by a general misdirection of economic activities and resources which has led to a loss of potential surplus as well, Western intrusion has had a negative impact on their primitive accumulation of capital.

Similarly, present-day economic aid to, and investment in, developing countries is not designed to accelerate their economic development. Rather, such aid is but a bribe to their populations to refrain from overthrowing the existing system. As such, it actually hampers development, for:

Whatever small increases in national output might be attained with the help of such Western investment and charity as may be forthcoming are swamped by the rapid growth of the population, by the corruption of the local governments, by squandering of resources by the underdeveloped countries' ruling classes, and by profit withdrawals on the part of foreign investors. (p. 13)

André Gunder Frank, another outstanding figure in dependency theory, acknowledges his debt to Baran, but takes his ideas further, applying them particularly to Latin America. Like Baran, Frank believes that the West developed because it exploited the third world, and that the latter became under-developed precisely because it has aided in the development of the West. He adds that both development and under-development are the result of some internal contradictions of capitalism itself. One of these contradictions lies in that capitalism thrives on what ruins others, that is, on the expropriation of their economic surplus and on the depletion of their resources. The second contradiction lies in the polarization of the capitalist system into a metropolitan centre and peripheral satellites. Moreover, capitalism impregnates the satellites' domestic economy with the same contradiction, so that the metropolis-satellite polarization is created in them as well. This leads to a chain of metropolis-satellite relations that extends from the capitalists of the metropolis in the most developed countries to the labourers of the least developed ones. The Western capitals and their ruling classes, which are no one's satellites, act as a metropolis for the capital cities of third world countries, which act as metropoles for their countries' regional and local centres. Those, in turn, are dominated by local landowners and merchants who perform the functions of a metropolis for their own peasants, tenants, and landless workers, who are everybody's satellite and no one's metropolis. 'Thus a whole chain of constellations of metropoles and satellites relates all parts of the whole system from its metropolitan centre in Europe or the United States, to the farthest outpost in the Latin American countryside' (Frank, 1970, p. 7). Each intermediary satellite leeches its own satellites, sucking part of their economic surplus into the system. This eventually reaches the world metropolis, where it serves to enrich the bourgeoisie.

The bourgeoisie of the third world, like the bourgeoisie of the metropolis, is instrumental in extracting surplus from its own subjected classes, but because it is itself exploited by the metropolis, it is too weak to carry out the classical developmental role of the bourgeoisie in the West. It is thus nothing but a *Lumpenbourgeoisie*.

In view of this system of metropolis-satellite exploitation, it no longer makes sense to speak of the survival (in Latin America or elsewhere) of archaic institutions that have remained isolated from world history, or of feudal and semi-feudal structures that have served as obstacles to development. Nor does it make sense to speak of dual economies, in which one part has thrived because it came into contact with the West, whereas the other has lagged behind because it remained in isolation. On the contrary, the under-development of the most archaic and seemingly isolated institutions, is due to Western penetration.

That it is indeed contact with, rather than isolation from, the West which has brought about under-development, is best evidenced by the fact that many thirld world countries (for instance, in Latin America), have experienced their greatest upsurge in economic development when their ties to the West were weakest; and vice versa. It is further evidenced by the fact that the countries that have had the closest ties with the West have become the most backward economically, while those countries which have been fortunate enough to remain detached from the West, have been economically most successful – the classic case being Japan after the Meiji restoration (Frank, 1967 and 1970).

Another leading figure, Samir Amin, elaborates dependency theory, especially in application to Africa. He argues that the backwardness of the third world (the periphery), and of Africa in particular, is the outgrowth of an unequal exchange between it and the West (the centre), which in turn results from the consolidation of monopoly capitalism in the latter. This consolidation provided the institutional structures which have made it possible for the centre to export large amounts of capital to the periphery. With the aid of this capital a multitude of enterprises have been established and these have made exorbitant profits by exploiting the periphery's cheap labour reserves.

Such profits were necessary because of the fundamental contradiction of the capitalist mode of production: the tendency for the capacity to produce to rise faster than the capacity to consume. This contradiction, together with the establishment of trade unions, has made it necessary for the capitalists of the centre to increase their workers' capacity to consume by raising their wages. The rising wages, in turn, were among the factors which made for the falling rates of profit in the centre – a trend that could have been detrimental for Western capitalism had it not been countered by the rising profits from the newly established enterprises in the periphery.

The global inequality of the world system is based, therefore, upon the division between low-wage and high-wage countries. Once established, this inequality is perpetuated and increased by the operations of the world market, through which the centre distorts the economies of the peripheries to suit its own needs. It does so by imposing unequal specialization on the periphery, forcing it towards cash crops ('monetarization') and export ('extraversion'). This distortion of the traditional mode of production leads to the eviction of some of the population from the land, proletarianizing them but without creating employment for them. When a similar situation arose in Europe, new employment was available for the growing labour force, but in the countries of the third world, this economic distortion has had a retrogressive effect, casting a part of the labour force out of the productive process. It therefore hinders the takeoff into self-sustained growth, which modernization theory has so confidently predicted (Amin, 1974 and 1976).

Immanuel Wallerstein, currently perhaps the most popular figure within this school of thought, similarly attempts to explain the development of the West (the core) and the under-development of the third world (the periphery) in terms of a capitalist world system which has generated economic inflows from the former to the latter. This world system which — according to Wallerstein — developed throughout the sixteenth century, has displayed the crucial and unprecedented feature of being economically unified but politically divided. Previous world systems were in the form of world empires in which large territorial expanses, populated by different nationalities, were administered by a single political apparatus. Such empires were able to appropriate large amounts of surplus — for a time — by exacting tribute from outlying regions in return for political stability. However, in the long run, the cost (in terms of bureaucratic and military expenditures) of maintaining such stability came to outweigh the economic benefit of exploitation, and the systems were thus destined to disintegrate.

The European world system, on the other hand, has not been encumbered by an overall political entity; hence its inherent flexibility and resilience. This system alone has been capable of reaping surplus which need not be expended on the maintenance of world order; hence, it alone has been conducive to capitalist development.

An economic world system was not only conducive to capitalist development, it was indispensable for it. This was because the essential, initial accumulation of capital occurred not so much in the core countries in which capitalism actually developed, but rather in the peripheral regions, whence it was siphoned off through the mechanisms of the world system (force and monopolistic advantages in trade) for the benefit of the core. This initial accumulation of capital in the periphery was possible because there the entrepreneurial activity of landholding elites had increased productivity by organizing large-scale plantations, mines and other enterprises with low *per capita* output. 'Coerced crash-crop labour' (in other words, slavery and serfdom), which made such enterprises possible in the periphery, was therefore the critical institution for the initial development of capitalism in the core.

The landholding entrepreneurs of the periphery have been selling their products on a world market and hence have been in competition with each other. The gains in productivity that they have achieved have therefore been offset by lower prices for their products. Their increases in production have also been accompanied by increases in the number of workers employed. The economic growth they have generated has therefore remained stagnant in *per capita* terms. However, in the core, where the products of the periphery are consumed, cheaper prices have lowered the cost of living. The result, therefore, has been a growth in real *per capita* product, and hence the greater possibility of capital accumulation.[7]

In Wallerstein's view, this growing advantage of the core has brought about a tripartite system of world domination (rather than the dual system envisaged by other dependency theorists). Dominating the system have been a small number of Western core states engaged both in commercialized agriculture and in industrial production. The bottom layer of the system has been made up of peripheral states specializing in a narrow range of primary products mainly for export and consumption in the core. In between lies a group of semi-peripheral states whose system of production is intermediate – more diversified than that of the periphery, but less so than that of the core.

One of Wallerstein's main contributions thus lies in his con-ception of the semi-periphery. According to Wallerstein, in the world system of stratification, this semi-periphery has played the role which the middle class usually plays in a domestic class system: it has suffered exploitation from the rich (the core) while at the same time exploiting the poor (the periphery). And, like the domestic middle class, it has had a stabilizing effect on the system. Since those exploited in the world system are in the majority, the question arises why they have not simply overrun the exploiting minority. The answer lies in this stabiliz-ing effect of the semi-periphery. Without it the world system

would be far less politically stable, for it would mean a polarized world system. The existence of the third category means precisely that the upper stratum is not faced with the unified opposition of all others because the middle stratum is both exploited and exploiter. (Wallerstein, 1974b, p. 405)

The development of this tripartite system of exploitation has become possible through the emergence of relatively strong states within the core. These used their superior military strength and poten-tial for national mobilization to further their exploitative activities. The fact that some countries have become part of the core while others have not is largely a matter of 'a series of accidents – historical, ecological, geographic' (Wallerstein, 1974b, p. 400). But the key fact is that, given a slightly different starting point, the core countries were in a position to amass a greater economic surplus and thus create and sustain larger state (including military) machineries. Also, in the core countries the interests of the capitalist landowners and those of the merchants co-incided in favour of the state, thus leading to strong state apparatuses, while in the periphery the interests of various groups diverged, thus leading to very weak ones.

Once the world system was established, a country's position in it was decisive for its internal social structure. The core countries' advantageous position in the world system was thus crucial in enabling them to develop stronger state mechanisms, which in turn enabled them to impose their own terms on commerce in the periphery. This unequal exchange, on its part, has resulted in the appropriation of surplus from the periphery and therefore in the development of capitalism in the core. The evolution of the world system and the evolution of capitalism in the West are thus mutually interdependent (Wallerstein 1974a and 1974b).

The dynamics of dependency

In Wallerstein's view, the world system was created in the sixteenth century; Amin dates the establishment of the system somewhat later. But while dependency theorists differ on details there is a broad agreement on the dynamics of the system, made up of three consecutive stages: mercantilism, colonialism, and neo-colonialism.

The mercantilist stage lasted till about 1800. During this period, north-west Europe established itself (in Wallerstein's terms) as the core of the system; mediterranean Europe (including Spain, Portugal, and Italy), emerged as the semi-periphery, and Eastern Europe, the Western hemisphere and the greater part of the other continents became the periphery. The colonial period that followed lasted till around the middle of the twentieth century. At its peak (around 1900), the core included north-west Europe and the United States; the semi-periphery encompassed, besides the mediterranean countries, Austria-Hungary, Russia, and Japan; while the periphery was composed of the rest of the world (including Canada, Australia, and New Zealand). The neo-colonial period evolved after the Second World War, and since then the boundaries between the divisions have become somewhat blurred as the third world countries have begun to challenge Western hegemony.

Nevertheless, the core is still alive (though perhaps not so well) and it now includes, besides north-west Europe and the United States, such former peripheral and semi-peripheral countries as Canada, Australia, New Zealand, Japan and Italy, and it is shortly to be joined by Spain. Much of the remainder of the world now forms the semi-periphery, which includes, besides the communist bloc and the oil-producing countries some of the stronger Latin American states (such as Brazil and Argentina), and some 'upwardly mobile' countries (such as India and Turkey). The periphery has been shrinking, but it is still in existence and includes the weaker countries of Latin America, Asia and Africa.

During the mercantile period, exploitation took place mainly through commerce.[8] It is in this period that sustained commercial interaction between the West and other parts of the world first started, that Western supremacy in such commerce first made itself felt, and that the degenerating effect of this supremacy for non-Western countries first became noticeable. At that time, the West had little which the orient desired. But its advanced military technology forced others into trade that was little better than plunder. Monopolistic bodies of merchants were created, and the cheap prices at which they imported goods enabled the accumulation of capital. A similar result was achieved through the slave trade: African slaves were imported, for instance, to work on plantations in Brazil and the Caribbean islands. In other parts of America Indians were enslaved to work the mines. The profits of these enterprises were channelled to the West and formed a substantial increment to the Western surplus.

Trade with the West not only prevented the growth and industrialization of third world economies, but indeed had a regressive effect on them. The import of industrial products from the West led to the de-industrialization of these countries. The abandonment of traditional iron smelting in Africa and the industrial decline of India are cases in point. Even so, mercantilism did not go as far as to destroy all third world industries, and some managed to survive up to the beginning of the nineteenth century.

It was left for colonialism to complete what mercantilism had begun. This came about when exploitative commerce ceased to satisfy the appetite of the West; political domination was adopted as an additonal instrument of exploitation, thereby causing further deterioration of third world economies. This was accomplished by the following devices:

(a) *Taxation*. In order to earn enough to meet the taxes imposed by the colonial governments, villagers were forced to grow cash crops, which impaired their self-sufficiency.

(b) *The organization of production and marketing.* Giant corporations from the 'mother countries' were granted concessions for mining and production. They thereby gained a monopolistic advantage, while the third world's own ability to organize production and marketing deteriorated.

(c) *The organization of market outlets.* Finished industrial products from the mother countries were given preference on local markets, which, at the same time were 'protected' from competition by other countries. The lowering of prices for such products was the *coup de grâce* for local industries.

The colonial powers did export some of their own resources, technology, and methods of production to their colonies, but only to areas adjacent to European settlements. In all other parts of the colonial economies, backwardness was encouraged. Colonialism thus created a two-layered economy with extreme social inequality. The Westernized sector has fed parasitically on the traditional one, and those in charge of the former reaped disproportionate benefits therefrom. Such selective economic activity has also brought over-urbanization — that is, the growth of cities without matching industrialization — with attendant unemployment, undernourishment, unsanitary slums and, therefore, rising death rates.

Eventually, colonialism came to an end. Its demise was hastened not only by the anti-colonial revolts in one country after another, but also by the fact that it had become economically superfluous: once market outlets had been secured, the need for direct political control no longer existed. Hence it has been replaced by a more subtle economic colonialism.

The key to this neo-colonialism is to be found in the multi-national corporations. Since the Second World War these have proliferated and grown in size and power, so that today some two hundred of them control over half the world's output. Because of their enormous economic power, they are now the main instrument through which the West dominates the third world. This economic power has enabled them to gain access to a large quantity of raw materials and to depress their prices; it has also enabled them to take advantage of low labour costs by setting up economic concerns in third world countries and siphoning off their enormous profits. Finally, it has enabled them to preserve those countries as a market outlet (or perhaps a dumping ground) for Western industrial products. Thus neo-colonialism has stifled local production (and therefore development).

It is true that Western powers have made large capital investments in third world countries through the international corporations, not to mention the foreign aid they have been giving them. However, the surplus removed from these same countries greatly outranks both the investments made and the aid extended. Since the average rate of reward for capital investment ranges between 15 and 20 per cent, it does not take long for the profits to exceed the initial investments. This has led to growing deficits in the developing countries' balance of payments. The shortfalls have been replaced by foreign loans, which have further aggravated the situation by leading to spiralling debts and hence to further dependency.

The only way out of this vicious circle of dependency and under-development is to sever all ties with the West. But neo-colonialism is likely to be supported by puppet governments, propped up by Western power and weaponry, and by indigenous elites that retain control of whatever meagre benefits accrue to their countries from the existing state of affairs. Hence, peaceful separation from the West is most improbable. Since the puppet governments and the elites which support them are utterly dissociated from popular needs, so-called social reforms initiated or sanctioned by them have about as much likelihood of success as does peaceful separation from the West. Hence, the only alternative is emancipation from below through protest and revolution. Thus, while modernization theory regards the process of development (some disturbances notwithstanding) as basically peaceful, many neo-Marxists take sharp exception with this view. For them, the evidence from the past indicates that such massive changes as are now required have usually been anything but harmonious.

While Marx and orthodox Marxists have ascribed revolutionary potential mainly to the proletariat in industrial, capitalist societies, neo-Marxist dependency theorists now ascribe the same potential to the peasantry in developing countries (as has already become evident in China, Cuba, Vietnam, Laos, and Kampuchea). While orthodox Marxists claim that developing countries must reach a capitalist stage of develop-ment before the revolution can set in, neo-Marxists argue that this is no longer necessary. Since they are part of a world capitalist system in which they form the exploited class, they need not become internally capitalistic; for them the experience of imperialism is a sufficient precursor to revolution (O'Brien, 1975; Hoogvelt, 1976; Chirot, 1977; Baldock, 1978).

The critique of Marxist and dependency theory

While strictures of 'mainstream' and modernization theory abound, criticisms of Marxist and dependency theory are few. In part, this is probably due to the prevailing intellectual climate. Since the 1960s it has become intellectually fashionable (and admittedly all too easy) to bring into relief the many shortcomings of 'mainstream' theory, but it has become less *avant-garde* nowadays to do the same for Marxist and dependency theory.

It cannot be denied, of course, that the latter has some engaging qualities. Among other things, it shows more serious concern with inequality and it refrains from the patronizing, avuncular attitude towards the third world which has made much of modernization theory such an appropriate target for sarcasm. On the other hand it also has its flaws, and there seems to be no reason to ignore them. In dealing with Western capitalism, for instance, Marxism has failed to give due credit to the benefits which the working class has been able to obtain. It has also underestimated the value of the political rights and freedoms of citizens in Western countries, which stand out in particular in comparison with their communist counterparts. Finally, some of its adherents have followed Marx in failing to reckon with the capacity of capitalism to cope with its own problems. In other words, it has some valid points and some concise insights, but it has clearly overstated its case.

One-sidedness

The same may also be said of dependency theory. One of its basic flaws (as of so many previous theories) is its one-sidedness. Having presented a set of excellent ideas (to which the intellectual community had been oblivious), it has promptly gone on to detract from their value by failing to integrate them with previous insights of no lesser importance. Its main achievement is its convincing demonstration of the exploitative character of the capitalist world system, and of Western modernization, but it vitiates a considerable part of that achievement by turning the concept of exploitation into its almost exclusive analytical instrument. As convincing as the exploitation thesis is in itself, can it be the sole explanation of both development in the West and under-development in the third world? As the social historian W. D. Rubinstein (n.d., p. 2) wrote: 'I would only echo the opinion of the great majority of historians in saying no it cannot.'

Modernization theory may be guilty of disregarding the international balance of power which has promoted modernization in the West and discouraged it in other parts of the world. But dependency theory bears a similar (though somewhat lesser) guilt by excluding from its conceptual framework domestic factors which have worked in the same direction. Dependency theorists do not deny the role of indigenous factors (such as the strength of the state mechanism or the consolidation of monopoly capitalism in the West); a few of them have even given some attention to analysing such factors, and this is certainly more than most modernization theorists have done with regard to extraneous factors. But since dependency theorists are so fully committed to a world-system perspective, such intra-societal factors — even when analysed — remain marginal to their main conceptual framework.

In T. Skocpol's (1977, p. 1089) view, these and similar flaws in dependency theory come about because of

the 'mirror image' trap that plagues any attempt to create a new paradigm through direct polemic opposition to an old one. Social science may, as is often said, grow through polemics. But it can also stagnate through them, if innovators uncritically carry over outmoded theoretical categories (e.g., system) and if they define new ones mainly by searching for the seemingly direct opposite of the old ones (e.g., 'world system' *vis.* 'national system') . . . . The better way to proceed is to ask what new units of analysis . . . can allow one to cut into the evidence in new ways in order to investigate exactly the problems or relationships that the older approaches have neglected.

Dependency theory has not acted upon this beneficial, though retroactive advice. Consequently, it has never really offered a systematic analysis of, and has never succeeded in coming to grips with, the whole array of internal factors which may have combined with world-system factors in discouraging modernization in the third world. What weight have such factors carried? Have they included the burden of traditionalist, stability-oriented values, or have such values been totally absent or innocuous? Conversely, have achievement and change-oriented values played no role at all in the modernization of the West? If they have, why have they been omitted by dependency theory?

Values seem to be singularly neglected by dependency theorists, but other internal factors have also received only cursory attention, and hence have not always been dealt with convincingly. For instance, if one assumes with Wallerstein that the advantageous position of the West in the world system was of major importance in furthering its development, the next logical step is to ask what gave Western countries such an advantage. Wallerstein's reply is in terms of the strength of the Western states, which enabled them to gain ascendency in trade with non-Western countries. Yet in the period analysed (the sixteenth century) not all European states fitted this model. Wallerstein considered the Netherlands a core country; yet it hardly possessed a strong state. Since its government at that time was nothing but a federation of merchant oligarchies, Wallerstein doès not even try to convince us that it did. Spain, on the other hand, had an absolute monarchy, and Wallerstein stresses its strength whenever he tries to account for Western domination of the new world. But then Spain drops out of the picture and recedes from the core to the semi-periphery, even though her monarchy remains thoroughly absolutist (Skocpol, 1977, p. 1084).

Moreover, the emergence of stronger states in the Western countries is explained by these countries' greater ability to amass economic surplus and by the converging interests of the various capitalist elites. But this conception *presupposes* at least the initial emergence of capitalism in the West, and hence can hardly serve as an explanation for this emergence. Not surprisingly, therefore, Wallerstein is forced to invoke historical accidents as part of his explanation for the emergence of capitalism, which is but another way of admitting that he cannot account for the phenomenon in terms of his own world-system conceptual framework. This leads one to the conviction (if Marx's and Weber's analyses have not already done so) that intra-societal constellations can be pushed to the margins of a theoretical paradigm only to the detriment of that paradigm itself.

Mobility in the world system

The world-system paradigm seems to be on much firmer ground in its attempt to account for the perpetuation of the exploitative world system once the initial advantage of the West had been established. It is at its most convincing when it shows how this initial advantage has enabled the West to further its own development at the expense of most of the rest of the world. But even here questions arise concerning the constraining power of the world system once it was set up. Dependency theorists themselves have shown how various countries were upwardly or downwardly mobile in this global system. Yet the world-system paradigm is ill-equipped to explain such mobility. Japan's recent movement into the core (see above) has been explained by its fortunate exclusion from Western influence. But how can the changed positions of the United States, Canada, Australia and New Zealand, be accounted for? The United States, of course, shook off colonial domination rather early. But this in itself requires explanation, and it is difficult to see how such an explanation can come from the logic of the world-system paradigm. The upward mobility of Canada, Australia, and New Zealand has been explained by their ability to gain relative independence within the colonial system, because of their evolving internal power, and because of the 'capitalist potential' these countries' original settlers have brought with them from Europe (Baran, 1957, p. 141). Such an explanation is again based on concepts which are not imminent to the logic of the world-system paradigm as such.

Moreover, to substantiate its claim that the West's advantage in the world system accounts for its further economic development, dependency theory would have to show that the greatest colonial powers have also become the most highly developed ones. This, however, may prove difficult. For Britain and other European core countries were indeed major colonial powers, but the United States was not. Yet it not only became a core country, it became the very 'core of the core'. To be sure, the United States has outranked all other countries in neo-colonial penetration of the third world, but its unmatched and unprecedented economic power clearly preceded this penetration. Indeed, the American proficiency in neo-colonialism (which has manifested itself mainly in the post-war period) is clearly the *result*, rather than the cause, of this economic power.

The problematics of communist and oil-producing countries

Dependency theory thus offers no satisfactory explanation for the mobility of various countries in the world system in terms imminent to its own conceptual framework, nor has it worked out a satisfactory conception for the communist bloc's position within this framework. True, modernization theory has offered no adequate conceptualization for this group of countries either. But in the case of dependency theory, this critique is clearly more pertinent: a world-system framework in which some of the world's largest and most powerful countries have no adequate place is clearly deficient.

Some dependency theorists have classified the communist countries as part of the capitalist system's periphery or semi-periphery. But common sense tells us that the communist bloc is far too powerful in its own right, and far too incongruous with the capitalist bloc, to serve merely as an annex to it, and that it has long exceeded that marginal role. Wallerstein (1974b) has made a valiant attempt to overcome this difficulty by asserting that the communist countries are in actual fact capitalist, by virtue of forming part of a capitalist world system. Most observers remain profoundly unconvinced. They regard this simply as yet another of the various implausible assumptions that have to be made in order to preserve the internal consistency of the theoretical framework. Some dependency theorists view the communist bloc as a challenge to the capitalist world system. Yet they cannot admit it to be outside that system, for in that case the whole conception of a world system would collapse. Some of them envisage that the capitalist system will eventually be replaced by a communist one. But until this happens, the lack of an appropriate conceptual slot for the communist bloc still remains an Achilles heel of dependency theory.

Despite such deficiencies, dependency theory has made a major contribution to our understanding of development and under-development. But is it still pertinent in helping us understand the events of recent years? Hoogvelt (1976) admits that from 1973 onward, as the oil-producing countries have quadrupled their prices and have not always been willing to recycle their staggering profits back into the Western economies, the validity of dependency theory has been questioned. He holds, however, that this doubt is not really justified, since the rest of the world is still at the mercy of the capitalist centre, and, moreover, the fortunes of the Arab emirates (no less than the famine in India and Bangladesh) are still the symptoms of dependency.

And yet one cannot fail to notice that the oil-producing countries now enjoy the same monopolistic advantage over the West which, according to dependency theory, the latter has wielded over the third world for so many years; and that the Western economy seems to be no less vulnerable to such power. Similarly, one cannot but be aware that since 1973 the oil-rich countries' policies have had retrogressive effects on the Western economy, not unlike those which Western policies have had on the third world. This by no means invalidates dependency theory, but it clearly calls for a new conceptualization which, so far, dependency theory has failed to offer.

Is an empirical test possible?

It should have become clear by now that both modernization and dependency theories have made major contributions to our understanding of development and under-development, but that they are both greatly vulnerable to criticism. To go beyond such a general, even-handed (and therefore, trite) statement it would be necessary to subject both theories to the rigours of empirical testing in order to establish their relative validity and fruitfulness. As noted, however, the conclusive empirical testing of sociological theories is wrought with almost insurmountable difficulties, some of which are patently evident in this case.

For modernization theory

For the difficulties of testing modernization theory McClelland's thesis on the causal influence of the drive for achievement may serve as an apt example. McClelland claims to have found support for his thesis through empirical studies performed by him and his associates (see chapter 2). Most observers would make the more rigorous demand of having the theory tested through independent research. However, the type of cross-cultural quantitative research needed to test McClelland's thesis is cumbersome and expensive, and researchers with no *a priori* commitment to McClelland's point of view may well hesitate to invest the necessary time and resources. McClelland's conclusions must thus be accepted on faith (if at all), rather than on the strength of independent empirical evidence.

Indirectly, McClelland's theory, as well as modernization theory in general, would be empirically supported if it could be established that formal education has a causal influence on economic development. After all, modernization theory has stressed the quality of human resources, the pertinence of orientations and values for economic development, and the importance of education in influencing these (for example, Inkeles and Smith, 1974). If the causal influence of education on economic development could be established, the case for modernization theory would thus be greatly strengthened.

Various early comparative studies indeed established a positive relationship between the level of education in a given country and the level of its economic development (for example, Edding, 1966), giving rise to the belief that education does promote economic development. Subsequently, however, a greater degree of scepticism has set in. It has been pointed out, for instance, that some of the early studies merely established a correlation, rather than a causal connection, between education and economic development. Quite possibly, therefore, they merely pin-pointed the fact that wealthier countries tend to increase their expenditure on education. Some studies, to be sure, have pointed to a relationship between education at a certain point in time and *subsequent* economic development (for example, Peaslee, 1967). But even they have not clearly established that education has a causal effect on economic growth: To the extent that such studies have not held previous economic levels constant, it may well be that these countries' further economic growth is but the result of their previous economic development (which has affected their education as well), rather than the result of education *per se*.

In recent years, observers have also become more sensitive to various additional limitations inherent in this type of research. As Farrell (1975, p. 205), put it: 'We have different studies of different aspects of these general relationships, done at different times, in different societies, often using different methodologies, sometimes with apparently conflicting conclusions, with doubtful generalizability.' He therefore concluded that, on the whole, the evidence available on the impact of education on development is spotty.

Observers have also become more sensitive to the fact that education is far from being a homogeneous activity. Some types of education may be deliberately geared towards the inculcation of Western values — others may not; some types may be geared to equip children for industrialization, others may be focused on teaching them how better to cope with their rural environment; some types may be tuned to the requirements of the labour market, others may train people for jobs not available to them upon graduation. Hence, any attempt to reach conclusions on the basis of simple rates of enrolments at different levels of schooling seems to be grossly oversimplified and doomed to failure. Notwithstanding two decades of research on this topic, no definite conclusions have therefore emerged, and unassailable empirical support for modernization theory is thus still lacking.

For dependency theory

Attempts to subject dependency theory to empirical testing have not fared much better. One of the difficulties has been the problem of rival interpretations of unanimously accepted empirical data. To substantiate their claim that neo-colonialism has indeed perpetuated under-development in the third world, dependency theorists endeavour to demonstrate that after its emergence, despite alleged foreign aid and investments, the gap in economic growth between the West and the third world has constantly increased. Hoogvelt (1976) for one, cites some bourgeois economists as allegedly demonstrating that since the Second World War third world countries have been developing faster than developed ones. Hoogvelt agrees that their data on economic growth in the third world is most impressive — until calculations are made on a *per capita* basis. When this more stringent criterion is applied, the economic growth of developing countries does not measure up to that of their Western counterparts, because their population growth in recent years has been much greater.

Statistical data collected by the World Bank in 1970 substantiates this claim. This can be seen from Table 3.1 which compares average

Table 3.1 *Gross National Product (GNP)[a] per capita and average annual growth of GNP per capita in developing and industrialized countries, 1960–76*

	Total population (millions) 1976	GNP per capita United States dollars 1976	Average annual growth (per cent) 1960–76
Developing countries[b]			
Low-income countries	1,215·8	150	0·9
Middle-income countries	894·8	750	2·8
Oil Exporters	12·2	6,310	7·0
Industrialized countries	683·8	6,200	3·4
Centrally planned economies	1,207·7	2,280	3·5

Source: World Bank (1978), pp. 76–7.

[a]Gross National Product (GNP) is the money value of all goods and services produced in a country's economy during a given period (usually a year).
[b]The developing countries are divided on the basis of 1976 GNP per person into: low-income countries, with per capita income of $250 or below, and middle-income countries, with per capita income exceeding $250. The industrialized countries include the Western countries and Japan.

annual growth of Gross National Product *per capita* for developing and developed countries.

Except for the oil-exporting minority, developing countries clearly lag behind the industrialized (mainly Western) countries, in rate of economic growth.[9] It is here, however, that the problem of interpretation comes in. Modernization theory protagonists may well ask whether this is indeed a fair comparison. After all, it may be claimed, the industrialized states have long passed the stage of economic takeoff and achieved self-sustained economic growth. Would it not be more appropriate, therefore, to compare economic growth in today's developing countries with that of Western industrial countries in the nineteenth century, when they themselves were at the stage of takeoff and when their populations were also growing rapidly?

On this basis, today's developing countries would not seem to be faring quite so badly. This can be seen from Table 3.2, which presents average annual growth of GNP *per capita* in the major Western countries around the turn of the twentieth century.

Clearly, it might be claimed that neo-colonial penetration into the third world cannot have been so detrimental if it allows for economic growth that compares favourably with that of the neo-colonial powers

Table 3.2 *Average annual growth rates of GNP per capita in selected Western countries 1870–1913*

Country	Growth rate
France	1·4
Germany	1·8
Italy	0·7
United Kingdom	1·3
United States	2·2

Source: Cohn (1970), p. 7.

when they themselves were in the parallel stages of economic development.

To counter such claims, dependency theory would have to submit more detailed empirical proof showing that foreign aid and foreign investment in the third world have indeed resulted in economic retrogression in them. Such proof is not so easy to marshal, since the various empirical studies have not furnished unequivocal results. In an analysis of a number of Latin American countries, Kaufman and his associates (1975) did not find conclusive support for this contention. In a similar analysis on a sample of black African countries, McGowan (1976) found that the proposition that dependency is associated with poor economic performance is simply not corroborated by the empirical evidence.

On the face of it, such corroboration would be forthcoming from a review of a large number of comparative studies carried out by Bornschier *et al.* (1978). According to these authors, most of the studies show that while current inflows of foreign aid and investment have led to an increase in economic growth, the long-run, cumulative effect of such aid and investment has been to reduce the rate of economic growth. In this case, moreover, the direction of the causal influence could not have been the reverse of that indicated (i.e., that reduced economic growth engendered economic aid and investment). This is so, since in most of the studies reviewed, the dependent variable was defined as average yearly economic growth rates in years *subsequent* to the ones in which aid and investment were measured.

Even so, the possibility exists that the negative relationship between long-term investments and subsequent economic growth could have been spurious: the previous level of economic development was not allowed for in most of the studies reviewed. It is therefore conceivable that greater foreign aid was allocated to, and greater foreign investments reached, the more backward countries (because of their cheaper labour reserves), and that these more backward countries were also the ones in which the chances of further economic growth (irrespective of the level of aid and investment), were poorer.[10] Bornschier's review of studies therefore lends only very limited empirical support to the thesis that neo-colonialism has a detrimental effect on economic growth, and the results of empirical research on both modernization and dependency theories are still inconclusive.

Conclusion

Hence, all that can be said is that both theories brought to light some crucial factors in development and modernization, but neither paradigm is complete; and the variables which each has neglected are precisely the ones that have been best analysed by the other. Which is but another way of saying that the two theories are complementary and should be utilized in conjunction with each other for a better understanding of modernization and development.

Alexander (1979, p. 1) has indicated that:

The difference between these sets of approaches involves a significant conceptual shift and . . . that we are dealing with competing paradigms, using that concept as developed by T. Kuhn . . . . The choice of one or other paradigm alters the whole way the subject matter is defined and approached and the way that explanations are formulated. Proponents of each side tend to talk past one another in a fashion that indicates fundamental dissension rather than ongoing scientific debate.

But if this is indeed the case (as it undoubtedly is), then there is all the more reason for the proponents of the two schools to retune themselves towards each other. Such re-establishment of relations is called for not only so that a more fruitful scientific argument may ensue, but also so that a new paradigm may eventually unfold in which the most crucial variables of both theories may find their appropriate place.

However, new paradigms do not come into being merely because they are called for. In the meantime, the work of sociology must go on, and sociologists must make their own individual decisions as to the manner in which they wish to cut into social reality, and the social reality into which they wish to cut. This book, accordingly, works on the assumption, that Western and non-Western societies, although in constant contact with each other, and although greatly influenced by such contact, are still viable social units in their own right, and can be analysed as such. It is on this basis that the next part of the book deals with various aspects of modernization of Western societies, and of the changes which have occurred in these societies after modernization.

Selected readings

Baran, P. A., and Sweezy, P. M. (1966), *Monopoly Capital*, New York, Monthly Review Press.

Braverman, H. (1975), *Labor and Monopoly Capital*, New York, Monthly Review Press.

Chirot, D. (1977), *Social Change in the Twentieth Century*, New York, Harcourt Brace Jovanovich.

Frank, A. G. (1967), *Capitalism and Underdevelopment in Latin America*, New York, Monthly Review Press.

Hoogvelt, A. M. M. (1976), *The Sociology of Developing Societies*, London, Macmillan.

Marcuse, H. (1964), *One-Dimensional Man*, Boston, Beacon Press.

Part II

From a general discussion of modernization and development in both Western capitalist and non-Western countries we now turn to a more detailed discussion of modernization and subsequent changes in the West, divided into some major social spheres. The analysis of each sphere includes a presentation of the 'mainstream' and Marxist theories that are pertinent to that sphere. Some of these overlap the general theories presented above and others apply specifically to each sphere and therefore have not been mentioned before. There follows a presentation of the actual developments that have taken place in each area as far as these can be ascertained from historical and empirical data, and some tentative conclusions with regard to these theories and the actual developments are drawn. The first social area to be discussed in this manner is the economy.

Part II

4 · The advent and maturation of the modern economy

The development of the modern Western economy is exceedingly complex and only an economic analysis proper would be equipped to penetrate its complexity. The present discussion cannot hope to do more than to highlight some sociological aspects of this process. For this purpose, the following criteria for comparing the pre-modern and the modern economy and tracing the change from one to the other are suggested:[1]

(a) What is the nature of economic activity, including the sources of energy for production, the patterns of production and the role of knowledge, the structure of property and the role of profit, the organization of the economic enterprise and the composition of the workforce?

(b) What is the relationship between the economic sphere and other social spheres — specifically, what is the degree of differentiation or integration between them?

(c) What is the relationship between the economic enterprises themselves, and what is the resultant structure of the market — particularly the extent of free competition or the degree of monopolization in it?

(d) What is the level of economic performance, the degree of economic growth (or lack thereof) and the level of affluence of the population?

(e) What is the relationship between the participants in the economic endeavour: is there any conflict between them, and if so, what are its patterns?

Theoretical perspectives

Both the 'mainstream' and the Marxist theories have addressed themselves to these problems. Both conceptualize the advent of the modern Western economy as the rise of capitalism and industrialization; but since Marx and Weber have provided thorough analyses of this process, they focus their main theoretical effort on the changes that have occurred since then. According to the first school of thought, capitalism reached its full development in the nineteenth century and the changes that have occurred since have brought about a new and more viable economic order. According to the second school of thought the economic changes that have occurred since the nineteenth century merely spell the further development of capitalism, whose original problems have not been solved.

The 'mainstream' view

This school emphasizes first and foremost that since industrialization and the era of 'classical' capitalism in the nineteenth century an unprecedented economic growth has taken place. This growth has transformed the Western economy from an economy of scarcity to one of abundance, from an investment-oriented economy to a consumption-oriented one. This means that the populations of Western countries have reached previously unknown levels of affluence and that their standard of living is higher than it ever was before. It also means that the prime economic problem is no longer the inducement of saving but the inducement of consumption and that this is achieved through the recently proliferated and perfected media of advertising.

Another fundamental transformation from the nineteenth century onwards has to do with the relationship between economic structures and other institutional spheres. While the advent of capitalism up to that time entailed a process of differentiation between the former and the latter, the further development of the Western economy involved, on the contrary, some important mechanisms of reintegration, by which economic activity was brought back into line with wider sociopolitical needs (see chapter 2).

While the differentiation of the economy from other social spheres proceeded mainly up to the nineteenth century and was subsequently countered by reintegration, the differentiation within the economic sphere itself proceeded mainly from the nineteenth century onwards. At the time of classical capitalism, there was a rather large number of small enterprises in free competition with each other. Their internal division of labour was minimal, and their owners acted in the capacity of managers as well. Since then, capitalist enterprises have undergone a process of unprecedented growth. Many of them have become monopolies or oligopolies in their particular economic branches, many have become joint stock companies and there has been a process of differentiation between ownership and control.

In consequence, the character of the capitalist enterprise has radically changed, and entirely different forms of action are to be expected from it. Since the director rather than the owner is now in charge, the modern corporation is no longer geared primarily to profit and is no longer guided by greed. It is attempting to reach merely a satisfactory (rather than a maximal) level of profit, and it tends to assume a wide range of social responsibilities, including responsibilities towards workers, employers, customers, and the community at large. From a grasping operation, it has turned into a socially responsible institution.

The recent differentiation between ownership and control assumes an especially central place in the theory of Ralf Dahrendorf. As Dahrendorf (1959) explains, the major distinguishing feature of capitalism in the nineteenth century was the principle of private property, which implies the fusion of ownership and control, property and power. At that time the propertyless and the powerless (that is, the subjected class) also suffered severe material deprivation, and they had no way in which their grievances could legitimately be expressed. Hence they engaged in sporadic outbursts of unrestrained violence and capitalism was thus a rather unstable system.

Since then, however, ownership has come to be widely dispersed, while control is vested in a small group of managers; the economic situation of the propertyless has greatly improved and industrial conflict has been institutionalized through unionization, strikes and arbitration. For all these reasons the present-day economy is qualitatively different from the nineteenth-century capitalist one. As soon as the fusion between ownership and control broke down, the capitalist economy in effect ceased to exist. When industrial conflict became so greatly attenuated, a much more stable, post-capitalist society came into being.

The idea that capitalism has ceased to exist has similarly been expressed by Bell (1973) who also announced the coming of a post-industrial society. According to Bell, Western societies are approaching the post-industrial stage in that they are no longer centred on the capitalism of production and industry. Instead they are now centred on technocratic knowledge, which is aided by telecommunications and computers (see chapter 2).

Another concomitant change is the transition from a goods-oriented to a service-oriented economy. A most prominent indicator for both these transformations is a change in the occupational structure. In the industrial, goods-producing economy blue-collar workers formed the predominant occupational category. In the post industrial, knowledge-centred and service-oriented economy white-collar and service workers are fast becoming predominant. And within the latter category, the fastest growing occupational group is the academic-professional-technical group — that is, the group which is in one way or another concerned with knowledge.

In sum, then, the transition to the post-industrial society is one in which emphasis on goods production and industry with its large population of blue-collar workers has given way to emphasis on knowledge, services and white-collar work. Capitalism is no longer a relevant description of this economy since many of capitalism's original features have disappeared, and other (though not all) of its features are apparent in modern non-capitalist societies as well.[2]

The Marxist view
In contrast to this view, the Marxist writers claim that the changes from the nineteenth century and onwards do not mark the withering away of capitalism, but rather the further development through which its basic features have been enhanced. What the advanced capitalist economies still have in common, and what distinguishes them from all other economies, is their high degree of industrialization and the fact that the largest part of their activity is still under private ownership and control; in none of them does the state own more than a subsidiary part of the means of production.

Like 'mainstream' sociologists, Marxists maintain that the advent of classical capitalism produced a large number of enterprises competing on the market, that since then enterprises have undergone a process of unprecedented growth, and that giant corporations (many of them multi-national) now dominate the key sectors of the economy. Today, the typical economic unit in the capitalist world is no longer the small firm producing a negligible fraction of a certain output for an anonymous market, but a large-scale enterprise producing a significant share of the output of an industry, and able to control the volume of its production and its prices. Indeed, Marxists put even greater emphasis on the impairment of competition and the creation of monopolies (under which term they subsume oligopolies too).

But despite this development, they hold, or perhaps *because* of it, the basic features of capitalism are still there. For instance, it has been claimed that because managers rather than owners are now in control of the major corporations, these corporations are no longer greedy for profit. Nonsense, say the Marxists. Today's giant corporations are still as intent as ever on maximizing profit, except that now this aim is reached through even more systematic and rational means, such as technical expertise, operations research, market research, and management consulting. The object of these aids is to help the firm reduce costs; develop superior methods of production, marketing, and so forth; choose the most profitable alternative in policy formulation; and uncover new profit opportunities. Since the modern corporation is a steady enterprise, it has a longer time horizon. It may therefore defer smaller profits in the present for the sake of larger ones in the future, which may make it *seem* less profit-oriented. In fact, however, since the modern corporation is more rational, it is more, not less, geared to the logic of profit.

Moreover, while today's new, mega-corporation still resembles the previous small enterprise in its profit-seeking, it differs from it in the additional power it has gained — in its control over markets and in the influence it is able to exert over governments. Hence, it is not only each corporation which is committed to the maximization of its own profits, but the capitalist system as a whole which is increasingly influenced by such corporations, and is now built so as to maximize their overall profit. Capitalism, therefore, has become more, not less, powerful.

In monopoly capitalism the previous untamed competition is frequently eliminated, and whatever competition remains is often carried out through means other than the lowering of prices. This means that today's giant corporation is no longer a prices *taker* but a prices *maker*. And the prices it makes tend constantly to rise. Under monopoly capitalism the price system is one that works only one way: up. Now if today's giant corporations devise ever new methods of cutting costs while their products' prices rise constantly, and production increases, the surplus retained by capitalists must be rising as well.

Thus, although exceedingly powerful, capitalism is still beset by the crises of over-production and growing, unconsumed surplus. To counter them consumption is artificially stimulated, for instance through enormous investment in advertising. This phenomenon is thus not the outgrowth of abundance as 'mainstream' theorists have claimed, but rather the result of the internal contradictions of capitalism and without it, that system would speedily collapse. However, despite these and other measures (see chapter 3) the capitalist state is obviously incapable of coping with the basic problems of capitalism as is evident from recent developments (Baran and Sweezy, 1966; Miliband, 1973, ch. 2).

For although Western capitalism enjoyed a long wave of economic growth, especially since the end of the Second World War, this boom is now a thing of the past. It is being followed by a period of economic recession and crisis. Even in the years of economic growth, unemployment began to rear its ugly head. This is even more so today: its dimensions are clearly growing and no effective policies to counter it have been devised. As long as economic expansion was going on and unemployment was still relatively low, industrial conflict was indeed mitigated. But with the oncoming economic crisis and swelling unemployment, a new type of struggle is emerging, which may well be the start of massive anti-capitalist movements (Mandel, 1975).

Actual developments: capitalism and beyond?

How do the two theories stand up in the light of actual developments? As noted, the empirical testing of sociological theories is wrought with difficulties because of the abstract nature of their tenets and the divergent interpretations that may be imposed on the empirical data. Nevertheless, there are some developments that may be pinned down with relative objectivity.

Differentiation and reintegration
Historical analysis shows, for instance, that the development of capitalism was indeed accompanied by a certain differentiation of the economy from other social spheres and that subsequently a reintegration took place – as 'mainstream' sociologists have proposed. The process of differentiation was not only one of separating economic activities from kinship structures, but also one of separating it, to a certain degree, from political intervention.

This partial separation was not achieved all at once. During the transitional period between feudalism and capitalism, also known as the period of mercantilism (which lasted from approximately 1600 to about 1800), economic freedom was still seriously hampered by the state, and the traditional bonds and restrictions on labour and production had not as yet been abolished. State intervention (whose extent differed from country to country) was not deliberately aimed at impeding capitalism; some of it was explicitly designed to encourage its development, for instance through subsidies. However, such encouragement was frequently thought to defeat its own purpose and was not always welcomed by capitalists. Many of them therefore exerted pressure for, and eventually attained, a relatively large degree of autonomy for their economic activity.

The essence of the transition to this new period of relative autonomy is best brought out by an anecdote concerning Colbert, the finance minister to Louis XIV in France. 'How may we help you?' wrote Colbert to a prominent merchant. The reply was, *'Nous laissez-faire'*, which, translated into modern parlance would mean, 'Just let us do our own thing'. This expression subsequently became the slogan of the new nineteenth-century economic regime, which came to be known as the period of *laissez-faire* capitalism (Heilbroner, 1962, p. 71).

The desire to be left alone which, on the practical level, was expressed by the capitalists, was expressed on the theoretical level by Adam Smith and his fellow classical economists. These theoreticians taught that maximum freedom for the play of economic forces would, as though led by an 'invisible hand', eventually further the common interest of all. It would also lead to a perfect equality of opportunity: when there is perfectly free competition, everyone has an equal chance of success or failure. This extremely individualist theory thus furnished the theoretical basis, or perhaps the ideological legitimation, for the *laissez-faire* economic system.

This system, which culminated towards the middle of the nineteenth century, was indeed characterized by a relative freedom for the play of economic forces. This does not mean that government concern was absent. But many of the traditional restrictions of movement, choice of occupation and production, were abolished. Also there was a trend towards free trade, as duties were reduced, shipping restrictions were eliminated and other free-trade measures were introduced.

Some countries with strong feudal traditions, and especially Germany, did not leave economic activity to individual initiative to the same extent as did Britain and the United States, and retained a higher direction from above. But the thrust towards greater autonomy in the economic sphere was a widespread Western phenomenon (Knowles, 1932). Many of the laws and regulations which did exist were geared mainly to maintain law and to *prevent* the intervention of non-economic forces in the economic sphere. Consequently, the organization of labour was prohibited and the economic scene was composed of a large number of small, independent enterprises. These confronted each other on a relatively free market, which was regulated more than previously by competition and the forces of supply and demand.

Contrary to what Adam Smith and like-minded thinkers had claimed, however, this relatively free play of economic forces did not serve the interests of all. Not only did the system have a dehumanizing effect on the newly created industrial working class (of which more below), but it was also beset by the recurrent economic crises that had figured so prominently in Marx's theory, and which indeed posed an increasingly real threat to the persistence of the capitalist system. There were spells of general depression and slump between 1873 and 1879, 1882 and 1886, 1892 and 1896, 1900 and 1901, 1907 and 1908, 1912 and 1913. These crises reached their peak with the crash of 1929 and the subsequent depression in which, in the United States for instance, GNP declined from $104 billion in 1929 to $56 billion in 1933,[3] and nine million saving accounts were lost as the banks closed their doors.

As R. L. Heilbroner (1962) sees it, the causes for this depression are to be sought in the growing agricultural production, especially in the United States, coupled with inelastic demand and a consequent toppling of prices and intake; in the fact that farmers' buying power thus lagged behind, which reduced the market for industrial products; and in the general maldistribution of income, which distorted the purchasing power of the population. These causes can be interpreted in Marxist terms as the result of the internal contradictions of capitalism. But they may also be interpreted in 'mainstream' sociological terms as a result of excessive differentiation between the economy and the other sociopolitical spheres.

It has also been argued, however, that the situation was aggravated by a misplaced restrictive monetary policy by the United States government – entailing raised interest rates and diminished investments – which helped transform a normal recession into a major depression. According to this view, even the New Deal policy (introduced to counter the depression) was anything but helpful initially. Right through the mid-1930s the government policy aimed at a balanced budget. Only towards the later 1930s, when economic policy came to be based on J. M.Keynes's theory, were these errors corrected. Indeed, it is widely agreed that the depression only receded through the preparations for war which led to full employment.

In any event, the New Deal policy was the product of a new trend: from the end of the nineteenth century and onwards, the growing differentiation between the economy and the polity was patently reversed. Whether it was to alleviate the dreary conditions of the population (see below) to counter the threat posed to the system by these conditions, or to counter the recurrent economic crises culminating in the depression, the fact remains that the state began to intervene much more actively in the economic process. State intervention was inadequate to prevent the depression of the 1930s and according to some accounts even exacerbated it. But the New Deal policy marked a watershed;

thereafter, government guidance of the economy became more effective.

Such guidance came to be especially pronounced in France, with its five-year plans somewhat reminiscent of those in socialist countries. The New Deal notwithstanding, it is perhaps still least pronounced in the United States, where it has been countered by a traditionally strong ideological opposition. But state intervention has penetrated all Western economies, and is constantly growing. It has proceeded in several related matters, including the following:

Monetary intervention – governmental influence on the quantity of money, e.g. through the control of interest rates.

Fiscal intervention – intervention through the intake and the expenses of the government itself (as formally expressed in the government budget) including taxation, excises and levies; and on the other hand, subsidies, loans, welfare expenditure and the like.

Legal intervention – through economic legislation, for instance, with regard to tariffs, fair-trade practices, anti-trust laws (if any), and so forth.

Direct government participation – through government-owned (or partially owned) economic production, and through government purchasing – especially, but not exclusively, for defence purposes. Like other types of intervention, this type, too, has grown conspicuously. Thus in 1929 the American government purchased 8 per cent of the nation's GNP; by 1960, those purchases had swollen to 19·8 per cent of the GNP (Heilbroner, 1962, p. 174).

That these various forms of intervention did indeed constitute a reintegrative mechanism for the economy (as 'mainstream' sociologists have claimed) is evidenced by the fact that the recurring crises that were one of the most distinctive and destructive features of nineteenth-century capitalism were subsequently, if not eliminated, at least held in check. This is not to imply that economic recessions no longer occur. In fact, there has been one in the early and mid-1970s, and it is by no means certain whether it has yet been totally overcome. But it seems that since the Great Depression the disruptive effects of these recessions have not been as severe as before, although there is no certainty that this will continue to be so in the future.

Concentration and monopolization

There is one area in which 'mainstream' and Marxist theorists do not dispute each other. They both agree that the development of capitalism brought about relatively free competition and that another way (besides government intervention) in which this free play of market forces has subsequently been impaired is through the growth and concentration of economic enterprises. Although the Marxists put more emphasis on this development, both schools agree that this has led to ever more powerful corporations having monopolistic or oligopolistic control over the market. Perhaps this is because actual developments in this area are so clear-cut as to preclude controversy.

Observers usually agree that these developments are the outcome of industrialization (see below) and growing market demand, which together brought about standardized mass production. As a result, the larger enterprises have gained an advantage over the smaller ones since their economies of large scale and their more efficient production processes have enabled them to cut prices. This, in turn, has made it possible for them to eliminate, or take over, many of these small businesses, and thus to gain monopoly profits. At times, however (especially when equally powerful corporations confronted each other), standardized mass production has had the effect of intensifying competition and making it increasingly drastic and detrimental. Hence it has become more advantageous for the massive producers to limit such competition. In view of all this, it is usually agreed that concentration, the limitation of competition, and monopolization took place through a variety of interrelated processes:

(a) natural growth by means of larger investments and reinvestments;

(b) the buying out of smaller enterprises;

(c) mergers between companies;

(d) the creation of holding companies, where one company purchases sufficient shares in subsidiary companies to gain control over them and thereby co-ordinate their interests with its own;

(e) interlocking directorates, whereby the top directors of another company in which a certain company has some interests, are brought into the controlling company's board; and

(f) various explicit or tacit agreements to minimize competition between companies, such as trusts, cartels,[4] and price-setting.[5]

This last set of practices was first introduced on a massive scale at the end of the nineteenth century. In the United States the government reacted by introducing anti-trust legislation. The Sherman Anti-trust Act of 1890 declared illegal any contracts, combinations, and conspiracies in restraint of interstate trade. The Federal Trade Commission Act of 1914 prohibited unfair methods of competition in interstate commerce. Although at first these laws were not wholly effective, from the late 1930s onwards they became stricter and their enforcement more stringent.

In Europe the philosophy on trusts and cartels was entirely different and they did not encounter active government interference. Even in the United States there was a limit to what anti-trust laws could accomplish (or perhaps to what they were meant to accomplish). They might have prevented cartels, but they could not prevent tacit agreements of price-setting (for instance, where one corporation becomes a price leader and others follow), the standardization of products, and certainly not the advantage of larger companies over smaller ones.

As a result, monopolization has advanced practically unhampered. There are few cases where single enterprises control an entire market in a particular branch, but there are numerous cases where a number of large corporations reach tacit agreements that enable them to control the market in concert. Competition still takes place between different branches of industry (for example, between production of bottles and cans for the marketing of beer). But within the same branch much of the competition no longer revolves around prices, but has instead been relegated to the marginal areas of packaging and the creation and pro-jection of appropriate images. There are still many examples of new companies breaking into an industry, but this is no longer so in all or even most established branches.

Also, enterprises have continued to grow and vast economic empires have been created in all Western countries, and most conspicuously in the United States. At the beginning of the nineteenth century there was not even one enterprise in America that produced as much as 10 per cent of the products in any particular branch; in 1904 there were seventy-eight enterprises that produced over 50 per cent of the products in their respective branches. Today, the American market is divided into two: the one with which the man in the street is usually in contact is composed of a vast array of small businesses, together employing 40 per cent of the American workforce. This multitude of mini-businesses creates the illusion that the whole economy is decentralized. But, in fact, the combined power of all these businesses falls far below that of a small number of less visible giant corporations that form the core of the economic system (Heilbroner, 1962, ch. 5).

Today there are more than 200,000 industrial corporations in the United States, with total assets of $554 billion; but 100 corporations control 52 per cent of that sum. The financial world is equally con-centrated. Of America's 13,500 banks, the fifty largest control 48 per cent of all banking assets (Dye and Zeigler, 1975, pp. 109–10). The trend towards corporate growth has continued in recent years at an increasing rate. Indeed, it has somewhat humourously been suggested that if the present rate of centralization continues, the US economy will within 350 years turn into a super-giant corporation whose power will exceed that of the Roman empire.

Industrialization and the changing occupational structure

Another prominent change which accompanied the advent and further development of capitalism is industrialization. Basically, industrialization may be seen as the development of new scientific-technological knowledge, a consequent transformation in the sources of energy — from animal and human to mechanical — and a transformation in its forms and applications. Since this process was closely interwoven with the development of capitalism, the causes that brought about the latter are generally held to explain the former as well (see chapter 1).

Interestingly, the 4000 years prior to the beginnings of industrialization saw hardly any changes in this respect. In the fifteenth and sixteenth centuries, some initial changes came about with the invention of water- and wind-energy utilization. But it was only in the second half of the eighteenth century and at the beginning of the nineteenth century that the massive and rapid changes that came to be known as the industrial revolution occurred. Using its superior scientific advances, as well as the large amounts of capital gained through the capitalist organization of business and through foreign trade, Britain led the way to industrialization. Other Western countries — France, Belgium, Switzerland, the United States and eventually Germany, Netherlands and the Scandinavian countries — followed. In some of them (for example, France), industrialization was more gradual. But by the beginning of the twentieth century they were all substantially industrialized.

However, this does not mean that industrialization or even the industrial revolution was over at this point. In fact, many observers tend to divide the industrial revolution into various phases, the last of which has continued into the second half of the twentieth century. The initial phase, which began in mid-eighteenth-century Britain, was centred in the textile, iron, and coal industries, and the first genuine steam engine was probably its most important invention. The second phase began in the middle decades of the nineteenth century and was marked by the rapid growth of the railroad industry, the mass production of steel, the introduction of steamships, and the application of the new technology to agriculture. The third phase occurred around the turn of the twentieth century, and included the introduction of the automobile, electricity, the telephone and the petroleum industry.

The fourth phase came during and in the wake of the Second World War and was distinguished by a rapid development in aviation, electronics, nuclear power, computers, and automation (Lenski and Lenski, 1978, pp. 250–72).

The successive phases of the industrial revolution have brought about some basic changes in the occupational structures of Western societies. Before the first phase of the industrial revolution, the overwhelming majority of the labour force was engaged in agriculture. With the initiation of that phase, the proportion of the labour force engaged in agriculture began to shrink, and has been shrinking steadily ever since. Today only a minority in all Western countries is engaged in agriculture. At the same time, a growing proportion of the labour force came to be employed in industrial production, a trend that continued until the middle of the present century. From that point, that is, in the fourth phase of the industrial revolution, this trend has been reversed — at least in the United States. The percentage of the labour force engaged in industrial production has diminished, while a growing proportion is engaged in white-collar occupations. Also, up to that time, agricultural and industrial production workers made up more than half of the workforce. Subsequently, these combined categories have fallen below the 50 per cent mark. On the other hand, white-collar and service workers have overreached this mark, a trend which Bell has seen as indicative of the post-industrial society. This trend is illustrated in Table 4.1. Most other Western countries are apparently approaching the same situation, as can be seen from Table 4.2.

How much society benefits from that change is still an open question. For, 'No one knows for certain . . . whether more teachers, or more policemen or more accountants actually produce more of whatever it is that teachers or policemen or accountants produce' (Field and Higley, 1979, p. 154). But at any rate, in the United States the middle of the century has indeed marked a watershed between the industrial and post-industrial occupational structure, and a similar watershed has now been reached or is about to be reached by all other Western countries as well. Contrary to what Bell seems to imply, however, the emergence of a post-industrial occupational structure does not in itself provide a confirmation for the rest of Bell's thesis on the coming of the post-industrial society.

Economic growth and rising affluence
The development of scientific and technological knowledge and their application to production have also brought about a massive increase

Table 4.1 *Major occupational groups of the American civilian labour force 1900–77 (in percentages)*

	1900	1950	1977
White-collar workers	17·6	36·6	50·2
Service workers	9·0	10·5	13·7
Manual (blue-collar) workers	35·9	41·1	33·1
Farm workers	37·5	11·8	3·0
	100·0	100·0	100·0

Sources: Computed from: (1) US Bureau of the Census (1975), p. 139;
(2) US Bureau of the Census (1977), p. 406.

in such production and, consequently, unprecedented, long-term economic growth. Despite extensive population growth, all Western countries have witnessed a remarkable rise in Gross National Product (GNP) *per capita*, as can be seen from Table 4.3.

The table also shows that this remarkable economic growth, which had been going on for at least a century, was even further accelerated in the 1950s and 1960s. However, Table 4.4 indicates that while the growth continued in the early 1970s, the trend has slowed down from 1973 onwards. The recession induced by the rocketing oil prices is thus clearly visible. Although economic growth picked up again in 1976, it is still too early to know if it will continue, especially in view of the further upsurges in oil prices.

Overall, however, the economic cake has certainly grown and the population's share in this cake, as expressed by the average standard of living, has risen too, as 'mainstream' sociologists have correctly emphasized. Before modernization, the great majority of the Western population (like the great majority of the population all over the world) lived close to subsistence level. Since antiquity and up until the advent of capitalism and industrialization, there was no substantial increase in the standard of living, and the minor increase that did occur was spread over hundreds of years.

With the industrial revolution, and especially at the beginning of the nineteenth century, there was apparently even a deterioration in the living conditions of the bulk of the population. The nineteenth-century European economy was faced with massive population growth and with the requirement of feeding an unprecedented number of people. Whether this led to a decrease in real incomes, or whether the incomes of the bulging working population nevertheless rose slightly,

Table 4.2 *Major occupational groups in selected Western countries in the late 1970s*[a] *(in percentages)*

	Austria	Belgium	Canada	Denmark	Federal Republic of Germany	France	Italy	Netherlands	Sweden	United Kingdom
White-collar workers	32·0	38·7	46·2	36·3	38·4	33·4	27·2	41·3	44·8	41·7
Service workers	15·9	6·7	11·6	10·7	9·5	8·4	8·9	8·5	12·6	11·7
Manual (blue-collar) workers	39·6	45·2	28·3	38·9	36·1	34·6	42·0	35·3	35·8	40·0
Farm workers	11·6	4·5	5·4	10·5	7·6	15·3	16·5	6·2	6·0	3·0
Other	0·9	4·9	8·5	3·6	8·4	8·3	5·4	8·7	0·8	3·6
	100·0	100·0	100·0	100·0	100·0	100·0	100·0	100·0	100·0	100·0

Source: Compiled from: International Labour Office (1976), pp. 184–271; (1978), pp. 136–72.

[a] 1975–1978 – depending on the country.

Table 4.3 *Economic growth rates (GNP^a per capita) for selected Western countries (percentage per decade)*

Country	Growth per decade about 1860–1965	Growth per decade about 1950–65
Australia	10·2	23·9
Canada	18·7	21·1
Denmark	20·2	39·0
France	17·0	44·1
Germany (later Federal Republic of Germany)	18·3	63·3
Italy (from 1895)	22·9	60·4
Netherlands	12·6	38·9
Sweden	28·9	40·8
United Kingdom	13·4	27·8
United States	17·3	20·8

Source: Chirot (1977), p. 157.

[a]For a definition of GNP see Table 3.1.

is still a matter of debate. But it seems at any rate that the *quality* of life declined. The rapid flow of labourers and their families into the industrial cities created urban slums in which overcrowding, smoke, inadequate water supplies, lack of sanitation and consequent epidemics, made life unsupportable.[6] With wages still below subsistence level, women and children had to seek employment as well. The working day, for both adults and children, was generally from dawn to dusk.[7] Working conditions were dismal and job security or unemployment benefits were as yet unknown. Those who were incapacitated by old age or work accidents were not compensated but dismissed, and they, as well as the great masses of workers who were periodically hurled into unemployment or could not find work to begin with, had little to subsist on.

However, towards the middle and during the second half of the nineteenth century a substantial transformation began. For one thing, workers' real wages began to rise, and this process has been going on ever since. For instance, in Britain the increase in real wages between 1860 and 1891 was in the order of 60 per cent. Thereafter there was a slight decline until the First World War, but there was a further improve-

Table 4.4 *Index numbers of Gross Domestic Product (GDP)*[a] *per capita (excluding the services of government and private organizations) in Western countries 1960-76*

| | 1970 = 100[b] | |
	Non-communist Europe	North America[c]
1960	67	77
1963	76	83
1965	82	90
1969	96	101
1971	103	102
1972	107	107
1973	112	112
1974	113	110
1975	111	108
1976	116	114[d]

Source: United Nations (1978), Table 4, pp. 12–13.

[a] Gross Domestic Product (GDP) — is the money value of all the goods and services produced in a country's economy within a given period (usually a year), but excluding net income from abroad.
[b] Everything at 1970 prices.
[c] Canada and the United States.
[d] Growth rates are shown separately for each column, and are not comparable between columns.

ment of some 15 per cent between the later 1920s and 1938. In the United States too, real wages in manufacturing rose by about 50 per cent between 1860 and 1890 and by another 33 per cent between 1890 and 1913, and the trend continued in the 1920s (Bagwell and Mingay, 1970, pp. 219–20).

After the Second World War real wages continued to rise. In the United States the yearly median family income (expressed in 1974 dollars) rose from $6,691 in 1947 to $12,836 in 1974 (Broom and Selznick, 1977, pp. 163-4). In all, average *per capita* personal income increased from approximately $500 per annum in 1871 to approximately $5,500 in 1974,[8] an eleven-fold increase in little more than a hundred years (Lenski and Lenski, 1978, p. 281). Similar increases in real wages in recent years are evident in Europe too, as can be seen from Table 4.5. The table also shows that in recent years real wages have at least maintained their share of the growing economic cake and possibly increased it.

Table 4.5 *Average annual increase rates in real wages and salaries and average annual increase rates in Gross Domestic Product per capita (in percentages, at constant prices) in nine countries of the European Economic Community*

	Belgium		Denmark		Federal Republic of Germany		France		Ireland		Italy		Luxembourg		Netherlands		United Kingdom	
	1	2	1	2	1	2	1	2	1	2	1	2	1	2	1	2	1	2
1960/65	4·2	4·3	5·2	4·5	5·0	3·9	5·7	4·2	4·1	3·4	7·1	4·4	5·0	2·1	6·1	3·4	2·5	2·5
1965/70	4·9	4·4	3·9	3·7	5·4	3·8	4·3	5·0	6·0	4·2	6·2	5·3	3·4	2·9	6·2	4·5	3·2	1·9
1970/75	5·7	3·1	5·0	1·5	3·8	1·5	4·4	2·7	4·3	1·5	4·3	1·4	5·7	0·7	4·5	2·1	4·4	1·8

Source: European Economic Community Commission (1977), Table 5, pp. 206–7.

1 Average annual increase rates in wages and salaries – per cent.
2 Average annual increase rates in gross domestic product per capita – per cent.

In both Europe and America the long-term rise in real wages facilitated and was supplemented by improvements in the living environment, in housing, in health facilities, and in rising consumption. There was a marked proportional increase in expenditure on consumer durables stretching from stoves to iceboxes and sewing machines (Bagwell and Mingay, 1970, p. 220). This rising level of consumption was continued in recent years, as illustrated in Table 4.6.

This rise in consumption has apparently been the result not only of growing incomes, but also of the special efforts invested by producers to encourage consumption by means of advertising. As both 'mainstream' and Marxist sociologists emphasize (albeit from different angles), a high level of consumption has become a prerequisite for the growth and even the persistence of the present-day economy. Hence the importance of commercials which, according to most observers, are designed not only to win people over from one product to another, but also to induce more consumption of more products; not only to satisfy their existent requirements, but also to create new needs of which previously they may have been blissfully unaware. For this reason, commercial advertising which in previous centuries was very modest indeed, has now become an enormous industry in its own right. In the United States, for instance, close to 20 billion dollars were spent on advertising in 1970 (Hollander, 1973, p. 122). But even if partly induced through advertising, the rising level of consumption still indicates that Western societies had indeed become affluent, and their working populations have enjoyed a growing share of that affluence.

Improvement in working conditions and social welfare
Concomitantly, pressure from middle-class progressives, on the one hand, and from increasingly powerful labour movements, on the other hand, led to conspicuous improvements in working conditions and social welfare. While business interests opposed the measures, legislation was nevertheless introduced to gradually shorten working hours, limit child labour and increase welfare.

In Britain, the history of effective factory legislation began with the Factory Act of 1833, which appointed inspectors to enforce the law that children under the age of nine were not to be employed in textile mills, and that children under the age of thirteen were not to work more than nine hours a day. This does not seem much by present standards, but it was a step forward at the time. Acts of 1844 and 1847 extended the law to women as well. Even more important than the

Table 4.6 *Increase in two items of consumer durables – in nine countries of the European Economic Community*a *1960–75*

	Private cars per 1,000 inhabitants	Televisions per 1,000 inhabitants
1960	84	93
1975	274	265

Source: European Economic Community Commission (1977), Table 6, pp. 212–13.

aFor a list of these countries see previous table.

Factory Acts in restricting child employment were the provisions for compulsory education in the Education Acts from 1870 onwards. Eventually, laws reducing working hours were introduced all over Europe. In Germany, under Bismarck, new laws provided for sick leave and for compensation in the case of injuries sustained at work. In Britain Acts of 1880, 1896, and 1906, made similar provisions and equivalent laws were introduced in the other European countries at around the same time.

In the United States the introduction of effective factory legislation came much later, partly because the factory system itself was a more recent development there. By the beginning of the twentieth century, twenty-eight northern States had some child-labour laws, but these were neither adequate in scope nor fully enforceable. In the early twentieth century, new laws or amendments introduced such measures as compulsory education, a maximum working day of eight hours and prohibition of night work for children. By the time of the First World War, legislation in many States had extended to women; it also covered workmen's compensation and minimum wages. Some progress was thus made, but unemployment, industrial accidents, and unhealthy working conditions remained largely untouched. In 1925, twelve States still permitted children under sixteen to work up to sixty hours a week and child labour in agriculture was still largely unregulated. It was the depression in the 1930s and the New Deal that gave social reform a new impetus by way of federal intervention. The Fair Labor Standard Act of 1938 set minimum standards for all labour engaged in interstate commerce or in the production of goods for such commerce. It authorized the introduction of a maximum working week of forty hours and a minimum wage of forty cents an hour, and prohibited the employment of children.

During the same period, welfare legislation was introduced and government involvement in welfare was greatly extended. In Germany, old-age pensions and social security were provided by an act of 1889. In Britain, the foundations of the modern system of social security were laid in the first decades of this century through legislative measures and fiscal reforms. In 1908, old-age pensions were introduced for persons of limited means. In 1911 came the National Insurance Act. It was grafted on to the existing voluntary schemes of insurance provided by friendly societies and trade unions and provided protection against unemployment and sickness. At first these provisions applied to only part of the workforce but between 1916 and 1920 they were extended to cover almost all workers.

In the United States welfare legislation too came late and piecemeal. Legislation introduced in the 1930s, and especially the Social Security Act of 1935, represented a federal generalization of the limited measures previously introduced in some States to provide old-age pensions and unemployment insurance. In 1939, the measures in force still varied widely from State to State. Especially from the 1960s however, welfare legislation made headway in the United States as well and government involvement in such welfare was signally increased (Bagwell and Mingay, 1970, ch. 3). At the beginning of the twentieth century the social welfare expenditure of all Western countries comprised only a negligible proportion of their GDP. By the second half of the century, welfare expenditures have come to comprise a substantial and still growing percentage of these countries' GDP, as can be seen from Table 4.7. Together with successive welfare legislation, they have ushered in what is commonly known as the modern welfare state.

Unemployment
There is one important problem, however, that neither modern capitalism nor the modern state have been capable of solving: the problem of unemployment, which has evidently become more acute in recent years. Unemployment was, of course, extremely high during the depression in the 1930s. For instance, in 1932 the rate of unemployment reached 22.5 per cent in Britain, 23.6 per cent in the United States, 25.3 per cent in the Netherlands, 31.7 per cent in Denmark, 30.1 per cent in Germany, and 30.8 per cent in Norway,[9] and these rates did not substantially diminish until the approach of the war. In the post-war period unemployment was relatively low in most Western countries, but in recent years it has once more become a worrisome phenomenon (except in West Germany, where the

Table 4.7 *Changes in public welfare expenditure (excluding housing)*
in sixteen OECD member countries − in the early 1960s
and mid-1970s (per cent of GDP)

Country	Early 1960s	Mid-1970s
Australia	9·6	12·8
Austria	19·6	23·0
Belgium	18·6	23·2
Canada	11·4	18·9
Denmark	14·2	23·4
Finland	14·0	21·0
Federal Republic of Germany	16·5	20·6
France	17·0	20·9
Ireland	11·1	16·7
Italy	13·6	19·6
Netherlands	14·2	29·1
New Zealand	13·7	15·1
Norway	11·7	20·0
Sweden	13·6	21·9
United Kingdom	12·6	16·7
United States	10·3	15·7

Source: Australian Council of Social Service (1979), p. 16.

trend has been the reverse). This phenomenon is illustrated in Table 4.8.

Despite the problematic nature of unemployment statistics,[10] there can be no doubt that the rates of unemployment have grown substantially (although they have not approached those of the depression years). There are several theories to account for unemployment in general, and its growth in recent years in particular. It has been claimed, for instance, that when unemployment benefits are substantial, a large part of unemployment is voluntary; that unemployment results from rising wages, which decrease the demand for labour; that it results from insufficient market demand for commodities and services; and from displacement through automation. But whatever the explanation, the fact remains that unemployment is in some way the outgrowth of the system and that it is apparently not a transitory

Table 4.8 *Unemployment rates – five year averages, in selected Western countries, 1950–76 (in percentages)*

	France	Federal Republic of Germany	United Kingdom	United States
1950–4	2·4	5·8	2·3	4·0
1955–9	1·8	2·4	2·4	5·0
1960–4	1·5	0·5	2·7	5·7
1965–9	2·1	0·7	2·9	3·8
1970–4	2·8	1·1	3·5	5·4
1975–6	4·1	3·6	5·0	8·0

Source: Ashenfelter (1978), p. 136.

phenomenon. The question must therefore be asked whether these recently grown rates of unemployment pose a threat to the stability of that system. The advent of Nazism in Germany was preceded by a 30 per cent rate of unemployment. But the rate of unemployment in Norway at the time was even higher (30.8 per cent) and it was exceedingly high in many other Western countries too. Yet no similar occurrences took place. Pending more detailed research on the topic, therefore, no steadfast conclusions on the political effects of unemployment can be drawn. But the possibility of a destabilizing effect cannot be dismissed, and Western societies are increasingly faced with this possibility.

The regulation of industrial conflict

With the rise of capitalism and the industrial revolution, as the living and working conditions of workers in the newly established factories became intolerable, their potential grievances against their employers and against the system that had created these conditions evidently surged. Initially, however (as Dahrendorf has perceptively pointed out), there were no recognized ways in which the workers could express those grievances. Workers first attempted to organize for this purpose at the beginning of the nineteenth century, but were largely prevented from doing so. In Britain, laws enacted in 1799 and in 1800 prohibited the organization of workers, and any such attempts were severely punished. Although these laws were abolished in 1825, workers' organizations still did not gain full official recognition. Workers' organizations and unionization were not recognized in other European countries either, and in the United States these practices were still almost unknown.

Hence it is not surprising that the only way in which working-class people could effectively express their grievances was through out-bursts of violence. At the beginning of the nineteenth century such outbursts were frequently intermeshed with 'direct action' in the political arena, and violent rioting thus came to be a recurrent pheno-menon.

In Britain, such conflict is illustrated by Luddism and Chartism. Luddism was a violent movement of handworkers who felt themselves threatened by the new machinery and banded together to wreck it. It originated in 1811 and spread rapidly, especially among textile workers. Despite the severe penalties applied by the government, Luddite riots continued intermittently until 1818. A wave of rioting and machine-breaking also propagated itself among the starving farm labourers of Southern and Western England in 1830, and additional machine-breaking in the declining hand industries — threatened by the machine — took place in 1826, in the mid-1830s, and the mid-1840s. Chartism was a mass working-class movement for political reforms including universal male suffrage and paid parliamentarians.[11] It instigated violent outbursts in Birmingham and Newport in 1839, in which twenty-four participants were killed. Subsequent Chartist out-bursts in 1848 reflected general unrest throughout Europe, but there-after the movement died a natural death.

In the United States Dore's rebellion (in Rhode Island in 1842) was the first of many violent civil disturbances instigated by the workers. Like the Chartist agitation in Britain that it followed by three years, this rebellion too was centred on political demands, but it apparently resulted from worsening economic conditions.

Gradually workers began to organize as official opposition to such organization diminished. In Britain, attempts to link all labourers together in general trade unions began in 1818. After 1825, trade unions extended their activities and began bargaining on working conditions. But their scope was still rather limited, and they still had no firmly structured organizations with stable leadership and co-ordination. In France, the penal code which made concerted industrial action a crime, was repealed in 1864. Trade unions, which since 1791 had laboured under the stigma of illegality, were now tolerated and thereby strengthened. However, here, as in most other European countries, trade unions did not gain full legal recognition until somewhat closer to the end of the century.[12] Only then could they grow rapidly, gain mass membership and become powerful enough to exact improved economic conditions for their members. Efforts were also made to create more nationally unified labour organizations and to link them up internationally. This led, in 1913, to the establishment of the International Federation of Trade Labour Unions (IFTU), which represented the bulk of organized labour in nearly every European country.

In the United States worker organization lagged behind. Massive organization came about only after the introduction of the New Deal. At that time, enterprises first signed contracts with unions, thereby recognizing them as official representatives of the workers. By the late 1930s, four million workers were unionized, although opposition was still rather fierce. In the 1940s, opposition declined and membership rose to eight million. A peak was reached in the 1950s, when membership rose to eighteen million. To this day, however, only less than a quarter of all American workers are unionized, and the growth in real wages has thus been attained with only limited union impact.

In the West, in general, the growth and proliferation of labour unions was accompanied by an increase in strikes, which became the predominant mode of industrial conflict. This was particularly marked at the end of the First World War, when there was a multitude of huge strikes in both Europe and the United States, although these abated to some extent in the 1920s. After the Second World War, the Western societies were once more subject to large waves of strikes and since then many working days have continued to be lost through such action.

Like any other mode of conflict, strikes entail a power struggle. As such they have a potentially destabilizing effect on the system. However, with the spread of strikes, industrial struggles that had previously spilled over into wider socio-political spheres have gradually come to be contained within the industrial sphere alone, and certain 'rules of the game' have come to be institutionalized: strikes have come to be recognized as a legitimate economic weapon; employers have come to refrain from introducing strike-breakers; and workers have undertaken to refrain from violence. Thus, and once more in line with Dahrendorf's conception, the revolutionary potential of industrial conflict has been drastically reduced.

Conclusion

The two theories juxtaposed in this chapter have been at odds with each other on the depth of the change that has taken place in Western societies since capitalism unfolded in the nineteenth century, and on whether a new social order has emerged since. However, the latter seems to be a non-issue since present-day Western society is obviously new in some ways and old in others. It is post-industrial (or on the verge of becoming so), in that the bulk of its workforce is no longer engaged in industrial production. But, at the same time, it is still capitalist in that the principle of private property, despite some modifications, still dominates its economy. But this in itself is not very instructive. The question is rather whether the basic problems of nineteenth century capitalism (the recurrent, aggravating economic crises, the grim living and working conditions of the labouring classes and the uncontrolled, violent industrial conflicts) have been solved or alleviated and whether the system has therefore attained a viability which it apparently lacked at that time.

The foregoing analysis shows that the recurrent crises of capitalism have been brought under a certain degree of control, even though they have not been eliminated. It also shows that the general level of social security, prosperity and consumption of the Western populations (including the working classes) has risen quite dramatically.[13] The latter rise has been due, in part, to the change of the economy to an expenditure-dependent economy and to the economic establishment's consequent tendency to encourage 'consumerism'. But it has, nevertheless, been a significant achievement. If industrial conflict has thus become less intense and violent, this is to be attributed not only to the institutionalization of such conflict, but also to increased prosperity, that has taken the edge off the workers' grievances.

But while the diagnosis of the past thus tallies, at least in part, with the 'mainstream' theoretical point of view, recent developments indicate that the prospects for the future are far less clear-cut. For one thing, until recently, whatever economic crises did take place had their source in some defects of the Western economies as such, and could therefore be controlled at least to some extent through government intervention. Recently, however, economic problems have also been caused by external factors, especially the OPEC-initiated oil price rises, and in view of the predicted depletion of existent oil resources, further price rises may reasonably be expected. The development of alternative energy sources may mitigate such tendencies, but (at least within the next quarter of a century or so) it probably will not be able to avert them. It must therefore be asked whether the capitalist system, which has been rather successful in coping with internally induced crises, will be equally successful in coping with externally induced ones — over which it may have only marginal control, and which may well impend on it in the future.

Also, and partly in connection with this, there has been a growth in unemployment, a problem whose solution does not seem in hand or even in sight. The political implications of unemployment are not at all clear. Among other things, it is quite possible that whatever adverse political effect unemployment may have has recently been countered by more generous unemployment benefits. Nevertheless, the recently grown rates of unemployment signify that a certain (albeit still small) percentage of the population has not shared in the affluence of capitalist society. Hence, if Western stability is, at least in part, the result of such affluence, there is no certitude that unemployment may not eventually pose a threat to this stability as some Marxists have predicted.

Selected readings

Baran, P. A. and Sweezy, P. M. (1966), *Monopoly Capital*, New York, Monthly Review Press.

Bell, D. (1973), *The Coming of the Post-Industrial Society*, New York, Basic Books.

Dahrendorf, R. (1959), *Class and Class Conflict in Industrial Society*, Stanford University Press.

Heilbroner, R. L. (1962), *The Making of Economic Society*, Englewood Cliffs, N. J., Prentice-Hall.

Mandel, E. (1975), *Late Capitalism* (trans. J. De Bres), London, New Left Books.

5 · The advent and maturation of the modern class structure

In the foregoing chapter it could be seen that Western societies have undoubtedly enjoyed a rising prosperity. But the recently growing rates of unemployment served as a preliminary indication that not all have shared equally in this prosperity. This chapter analyses in greater detail the inequality in the distribution of prosperity's benefits; how it differs from inequality in pre-modern society and whether it has diminished or increased in recent years. The assumption guiding the discussion is that the *relative* prosperity (or conversely the relative deprivation) of various groups of the population is no less important than their absolute level of prosperity or deprivation. For, as H. P. Miller (1969, p. 134) has aptly remarked, 'Our needs stem not so much from what we lack as from what our neighbors have.' Specifically, the discussion will relate to the following criteria:

(a) What is the basis or what are the bases of inequality; what factor or factors determine who gets what?

(b) Does inequality find expression in the division of society into distinct classes, or are the boundaries between various levels on the hierarchy blurred so that only a continuum is discernible?

(c) To the extent that distinct classes exist, what is the upper class or the dominant class in the system and on what is its dominance based?

(d) How great is the gap in material rewards between the upper and the lower classes, or those who are high and those who are low on the hierarchy?

(e) What are the chances for people of lower positions to advance into the upper ones? In other words, how open is the system and what are the chances of social mobility?

(f) What is the prevalent ideology that defines the desired class system? Does it accept inequality as legitimate and desirable, or does it call for equality of opportunity, or even for complete equality?

(g) Finally, to the extent that distinct classes exist, what is the relationship between them: do the lower classes accept their lot, or is a potential or actual class struggle evident, and if so what is its pattern?

114

In combination, some of these criteria yield a qualitative index of the degree of inequality in a given society. The clearer the boundaries, the more distinct the classes, the larger the gap in material rewards between them, the smaller the chances of social mobility,[1] the less egalitarian the society.

Theoretical perspectives

The changes that have taken place in these respects with the advent and maturation of modern society have once more been conceptualized by the two (by now familiar) schools of thought: the 'mainstream' approach claims that by each of these criteria there has been a decrease of inequality; and the Marxist theory maintains that inequality is as rampant as ever and the classes as divided as before.

The 'mainstream' view
As noted, scholars of this school of thought are of mixed theoretical ancestry, and in the area of class analysis they do not always present a united front. Some are close adherents of Weber, while others attempt a combination of Weber and Marx; some couch their analysis mainly in structural-functional terms, others tend to lean more towards the power and conflict school. Nevertheless, they have a common core: they tend to emphasize that structured inequality is as old as society itself.[2] There never has been a society where complete equality prevailed: even in societies where formally all are equal, in fact some are more equal than others; some tell others what to do, while others can do whatever they want, as long as they do what they are told. Indeed, it is doubtful whether a totally egalitarian society is at all possible.

Most of these theorists conceptualize inequality in terms of stratification, defined by some as inequality in the distribution of rewards. They claim that such inequality is inevitable because it is functional or even essential for the very existence of society. Greater rewards must be attached to the most important positions and to those for which major efforts and lengthy training are required, in order to induce the most qualified persons to fill these positions and to perform the associated duties to the best of their ability (Davis and Moore, 1945). After all, who would invest the time and effort for the training needed to become a doctor (or even a sociologist) if they did not expect greater rewards at the end of that strenuous road?

Other theorists of this school see inequality as imposed on the weak by the strong, but nevertheless regard such inequality (at least of power and authority) as inevitable, because they see it as a requirement of social organization itself (Dahrendorf, 1959). But while all societies are beset by some inequality, societies differ a great deal with regard to the structure and degree of their inequality. Modern Western societies, are clearly beset by less inequality than the societies that preceded them, as the gap in material rewards between the various strata has decreased: 'A process of relative homogenization takes place, reducing the gap or range separating the top and the bottom of the scale' (Inkeles, 1960, p. 341; see also Barber, 1973).

In the wake of Weber, most sociologists of this school of thought have adopted a multi-dimensional view with regard to the bases of inequality. Like Weber they hold that in principle there are three main bases of such inequality: economic resources, power, and prestige (or status). However, these three dimensions are concomitantly regarded as rewards, and societies are seen as differing with regard to the basis or bases on which these rewards are allocated. In medieval society the one central basis for the allocation of all three types of rewards was land tenure. The landholding nobility was thus the upper class. In early modernity property-holding in general and ownership of enterprises in particular came to fulfil this role; large property-holders or capitalists joined and later superseded the nobility as the upper class; the property-less formed the working class and those with small property – the middle class. In more recent years the situation has become more variegated with occupation, education and ethnic affiliation gradually added to property as the main bases for allocating economic rewards (income), power and prestige. Since there are now multiple bases of social stratification, there exists a sizeable minority of people who are high on one count but low on another. Their position in the social structure of stratification is thus uncrystallized and they are not easily classifiable into one social class or another (Lenski, 1954).

The decrystallization of social positions has had a most significant effect on the nature of the upper or dominant classes. In early modernity, and up to the peak of capitalism in the nineteenth century, these classes were made up of aristocrats and capitalists whose position was based on combined ownership and control of land or economic enterprises and who therefore held both wealth and power. However, because of recent differentiation in economic enterprises between ownership and control (see previous chapter), power (but not necessarily wealth), is now vested in a newly emergent managerial class. According to James Burnham (1944), a managerial revolution has occurred whereby this class has gained not only economic power, but political power as well, and has come to control not only economic enterprises, but society as a whole.

More recently, 'mainstream' sociologists have taken exception to some aspects of Burnham's view, but many, nevertheless, concur that the separation of ownership and control has indeed produced two sets of roles whose incumbents differ greatly from each other. Their modes of recruitment are different: capitalists reach their position through the accumulation and/or inheritance of capital, while managers ascend through the educational and/or the bureaucratic ladders. Their social origins, modes of thought, values and interests, also diverge: while capitalists are concerned chiefly with profits, managers are concerned first and foremost with the success and growth of the companies they head, and with the power that accrues to them therefrom. And, while the ownership of enterprises has been increasingly dispersed among large numbers of shareholders, control has become ever more concentrated.

Hence the managers who exercise such control have become increasingly powerful both in relation to owners and in relation to employees. While they may not have become political overlords, as Burnham has suggested, they have still accumulated great economic power, and thus have become a most prominent part, if not the most prominent part, of the dominant class of contemporary Western societies. These societies are thus seen as qualitatively different from nineteenth-century capitalist societies not only because a new socio-economic system has come into being (see previous chapter), but because a new class has gained ascendancy in them (Dahrendorf, 1959, ch. 7).

This view is pushed somewhat further by Bell (1973), who maintains that it is a newly constituted 'knowledge class' (rather than a managerial class) which has gained ascendancy in modern society. In industrial society, in which capital was the central resource, the capitalist class was dominant. In post-industrial society, in which knowledge forms the central resource, those who possess such knowledge (including scientists, professionals, academics, engineers, and other experts) approach dominance.

Thus, the nature of property has changed. No longer does it consist solely of tangible entities; nowadays it also consists of grants and contracts. Expertise in these areas, that is, legal knowledge, has thus become a *sine qua non* for property-holders. Moreover, as the economic production process and the political decision-making process become more complex, they too must be based on expert knowledge. Ultimately, it is not the technocrats who make the decisions, but the capitalists and the politicians; these last thus continue to enjoy considerable advantages. But neither capitalists nor politicians can get along without the expertise provided by the 'knowledge class'; hence its power has increased, and with it, its share in the rewards of income and prestige. So while the 'knowledge class' has not become the sole dominant class, it has a greater leverage on others than ever before.

According to the 'mainstream' view, the bottom of the class structure is still made up of the working or lower class, and there is still a middle class in between.[3] However, the boundaries of these classes are constantly bombarded not only by people who are in one class by certain criteria and in another class by other criteria, but also by a growing barrage of people moving from one class to the other. Since knowledge is now so important as a basis of social position, those who have the potential to marshal such knowledge — the talented, the intelligent, the ambitious — tend to rise to the higher classes at the expense of those whose talent is unequal to their birth. Hence contemporary Western societies have very high rates of social mobility, while ascriptive criteria of birth and descent have decreased in importance. Those who had the prenatal intelligence to select the right kind of parents still have a definite head start in the race for success. But the very fact that a race now takes place is in itself a definite stride forward.

Bell once more pushes the argument even further, claiming that post-industrial society is approaching a state of meritocracy, that is, a state of complete equality of opportunity, where birth privileges no longer count and where people advance solely by merit. The term 'meritocracy' was coined by Michael Young in his sociological fable *The Rise of Meritocracy, 1870–2033* (1958), in which he argues that in modern society progress depends on the extent to which power is matched by intelligence. Hence it is to be expected that a social transformation would occur in which intelligence would become the chief qualification for entry into the elite. According to Young's fable, such a transformation in fact occurs in British society at the turn of the twenty-first century: by 1990 or thereabouts, all adults with an IQ above 125 belong to the elite, or meritocracy.

On the face of it, this practice seems to usher in the perfect society, craved by utopians and reformists throughout the ages. And yet there is an unexpected and puzzling upsurge of dissatisfaction: since complete equality of opportunity now prevails intelligence and hence success now depends exclusively on heredity. Thus, paradoxically, the very society that was set to abolish the effects of heredity in fact assigned more weight to it than any previous society has done before. Previously, moreover, all social classes had had their fair share of intelligent people: those who could not rise in the hierarchy could still salve their self-esteem by telling themselves that they had not been given a fair chance. But now the inferior classes are, by definition, inferior in intelligence as well, they therefore no longer have a buttress for their self-regard; they bear the stigma of inferiority and lose all self-respect. Furthermore, when talent was dispersed, all classes had their natural leaders; hence there was a potential for conflict and change. Now that all potential leaders are part of the elite, the lower classes are left totally passive and helpless. Nevertheless, a populist revolt eventuates; the leadership is recruited from the elite, especially from elite women who sympathize with the plight of the lower classes in their demand for equality rather than equality of opportunity. The revolt is crowned with success, and meritocracy comes to an end.

According to Bell, the evolving post-industrial society is not one of complete meritocracy, but has a tendency to approach that state. Its logic, if not its reality, is one of meritocracy, for without intelligence one cannot belong to the newly ascendant 'knowledge class'. And indeed, although society is merely approaching meritocracy and has by no means attained it, the populist revolt or something very much like it is evident even now, at least in the United States. It finds expression in increasing pressure for 'fair admission' and 'fair employment' of blacks, women, and members of other disadvantaged groups. In practice, this means pressure for increasing admission of such people to student bodies, to university faculties and other desirable places of employment.

This principle was basically accepted by the US government in the 'affirmative action' program first proclaimed by President Johnson in an executive order of 1965. Henceforth, all federal projects and places of employment using federal funds would be required to prove that they had sought out qualified applicants from disadvantaged groups, and had hired such applicants whenever their qualifications were roughly equivalent to those of others. The test of whether a certain employer fulfilled the federal requirements eventually became whether persons of disadvantaged groups were hired in proportion to their percentage in the relevant population. For instance, if 30 per cent of all PhDs were women, 30 per cent of all faculty members were to be women as well. In theory, this policy was designed to eliminate discrimination; in practice, it replaced it by a quota system.

Evidently, this system raises severe problems of its own: lowering of standards through employment of the less-than-best-qualified, and injustice to the more talented whose only crime is that they do not belong to the right minority group. The struggle against discrimination was originally aimed at its denial of a justly earned position because of group affiliation, but it has been replaced by a system that also allocates positions on the basis of group affiliation. It may well be asked whether this is not merely another form of discrimination.

The moral of Bell's fascinating analysis seems to be that while society today is more egalitarian than it was before, the ideal of total equality of opportunity, or of total equality, simply cannot be attained. Whenever attempts are made to reach either of these states, they boomerang, resulting in self-defeating measures, and in social paradoxes and contradictions that necessarily lead to the reintroduction of inequality in a different guise.

But while Western society has not reached (and cannot reach) complete equality, or complete equality of opportunity, opportunities have nevertheless widened. The resultant increase of mobility (see above) has led to an increase in the proportion of people belonging to the middle class (Barber, 1973) and in the number of people acting as if they did. Because of the growing prosperity and the diminishing gaps in material rewards, the boundaries separating the classes have become blurred and the working class has been undergoing a process of embourgeoisement. As Morris Ginsberg (1930, p. 536) has observed, 'it is extremely difficult to say what exactly one is conscious of when one is class conscious'. Nevertheless, sociologists of this school are widely agreed that working-class people have failed to develop a collective class consciousness of their own and that, instead, their craving for social status has led them to adopt middle-class standards of living, lifestyles and outlooks. The contemporary West has thus been regarded as having become an overwhelmingly middle-class society (Goldthorpe *et al.*, 1969, ch. 1).

Concomitantly, there has been a marked diminution of class conflict. As Dahrendorf, Bell and other 'mainstream' sociologists see it, capitalist society was at one time (especially in the nineteenth century) beset by an all-pervasive potentially explosive class struggle, which overshadowed practically all other social cleavages. However, with growing prosperity, decreasing inequality, increasing mobility, the blurring of class boundaries, the decline of class consciousness, and the embourgeoisement of the working class, class conflict has become less salient. It has shrivelled into industrial conflict, which has in turn become regulated and therefore less intense and violent (see previous chapter). But while class consciousness has diminished, ethnic identification has intensified. Hence racial-ethnic divisions have recently generated more pervasive, disruptive, and explosive conflicts than have class divisions, which no longer hold a central place in contemporary Western society.

The Marxist view

Class conflict, which figures only marginally in 'mainstream' sociology holds a central place in Marxist theory. In contrast to 'mainstream' theory, Marx and his present-day followers have not focused on stratification (that is, on hierarchical gradations in society), but rather on classes that confront each other as potential conflict groups. Such classes have as their central basis the relationship to the means of production. Every society is divided into those who own and control these means of production, and consequently wield great economic power — the ruling class(es); and those who do not — the subjected or exploited class(es). In contrast to 'mainstream' sociology, Marx and his followers do not recognize multiple bases of class formation. Class consciousness is important in turning a 'class in itself' into a 'class for itself', that is, in turning what is merely a category of people into a militant entity. But it is the relationship to the means of production which is the basis of class formation, and on which class consciousness, too, is based.

In feudal society, which featured an agrarian economy, the most important means of production was the land. Hence those who held and controlled the land — the feudal nobility — formed the ruling class. With the advent of capitalism, this basic principle persists: ownership and control of the means of production still constitute the central basis of the class division, even though the means of production themselves have changed. And just as the nobility controlled the means of production (land) in feudal society, so the capitalists — the bourgeoisie — control the means of production (financial resources and machinery) in capitalist society.

In feudal society the subjected class was made up of serfs who were tied to the land; in capitalist society it is made up of the proletariat which is 'free' to sell its labour on the market. But the basic principle is the same: in both societies, the subjected class is the one without control over the means of production. In capitalist society there is another class between the ruling class and the subjected class: the petty bourgeoisie, composed of people who own minor means of production and are self-employed. Below the subjected class, the proletariat, there is yet another class: the *Lumpenproletariat*, a label which has been termed more an insult than a concept; it covers various types of marginal and parasitic elements for whom Marx had little sympathy. According to Marx, as capitalist society advances, the majority of the small bourgeoisie is absorbed into the proletariat, while a minority manages to work its way up into the bourgeoisie. In this manner, society is gradually polarized into two mutually opposing classes. The class consciousness of the proletariat is heightened until it is ready for the final showdown, the revolutionary class struggle, which will bring about the demise of capitalist society.

Many present-day Marxists have reservations with regard to Marx's polarization thesis and believe that the middle class, at any rate, is still very much in evidence. But they have even stronger reservations with regard to transformations which 'mainstream' sociologists deem to have occurred in Western class structures. They believe that the bourgeoisie is still the dominant class in capitalist society and that indeed the dominance of this class – characterized by the ownership of the means of production – is still one of the main features that distinguishes capitalist society from all other societies, past or present.

The idea that a supposedly new 'managerial class' has become the dominant class is thus dismissed as misguided. For one thing, many companies are still controlled by individuals or families who combine ownership and control. In other companies, managers are not only from a similar social background to that of owners, but frequently own stock in their own right and, in any event, draw salaries that are nothing but profits in disguise. Consequently, their values and interests are not basically different from those of property-owners. Their motives (like those of owners) may be complex, and include prestige, power, and self-realization. But the constraints of the system are such that they are pushed into a capitalist mode of action. Thus managers are not separate but the most active element, the forefront, of the capitalist class proper.

Bell's view that a supposedly new 'knowledge class' is becoming dominant is similarly considered as being off the mark. Anthony Giddens (although not a Marxist) concurs with the Marxists in this respect. He writes (1973) that the old saying 'knowledge spells power' is oversimplified. The expert does not always have power himself; like the scribe of antiquity he may well serve to increase others' power rather than his own. Following G. Sartori (1971), he holds that there is a fundamental difference between the situation in which the powerful hold knowledge and the situation in which the knowledgeable hold power. When power-holders have knowledge it adds to their power, but knowledge itself does not confer power.

The theoretical-technological expert, proceeds Giddens, is certainly more essential to the modern decision-making process than any expert ever was before. But if functional indispensability were to spell power, then in a slave economy the slaves would be supreme. The modern expert merely presents the decision-makers with clearer options; he does not take decisions himself. Indeed, the structure of modern organizations testifies to the incorrectness of Bell's view: there is usually a division between staff (the experts) and line (the regular gradation of authority). The experts are outside the general line of authority and enjoy a certain degree of autonomy. But, on the other hand, they do not enjoy much authority over others.

The 'mainstream' sociologists' claim that a new dominant class has come into being is thus flatly rejected, as is the claim that inequality between the classes is decreasing. While this might have been so to a marginal extent at an earlier point in time, it is certainly no longer the case today. This, in itself, would not be so bad if existent inequalities were not already so large; and, moreover, they may even be increasing.

The openness of mature capitalist society is also not as great as it is claimed to be, and social mobility is not more, but, if anything, less, widespread than previously. There is a great deal of movement of individuals between social positions, but more of it covers fairly short distances of social space; it is movement within rather than between classes. Movement from manual to non-manual occupations — on which many mainstream sociologists build their case — is not seen as indicative of class mobility, since lower-rank white-collar workers are classified by many Marxists as belonging to the working class. The advance from the working class to the middle class is still wrought with great difficulties and recruitment to the upper class in particular still has a distinct hereditary character to it. Thus the advantages of the well-born are still great; indeed, the careful selection of one's parents has become more, not less, important than it was before. Those who fear the advent of meritocracy, in which everyone would start equally and be judged on merit alone, need not be alarmed: the race is still effectively rigged against working-class competitors.

Marxists further disagree with their adversaries' embourgeoisement thesis. They admit that the workers' standard of living has risen but hold that class position is not merely a matter of consumerism. The workers do not and cannot resemble the bourgeoisie because they are still in a subordinate position in the production process. Some of the Marxists concur that a certain blurring of class boundaries has occurred and that such boundaries can no longer be drawn with the precision of lines on a map. This, however, they do not consider very crucial, for what should be of concern to sociologists, according to their view, is not the placing of people neatly into pigeon holes, but rather the basic class structure. And despite the blurring of boundaries, this structure has not significantly altered.

The same holds for the class struggle too. Many Marxists recognize (as do 'mainstream' sociologists) that the revolutionary class consciousness which Marx had expected the proletariat to develop did not materialize. Some also admit that class conflict was recently institutionalized and reduced to economism – the bargaining for scarce rewards. This they attribute, among other things, to the growing alienation and resulting apathy of the working class and to the perfection of hegemony, that is, the cultural domination of the working class by its capitalist exploiters (see chapter 3).

However, several Marxists believe that the potential for the class struggle is still there. The fact that class conflict has recently been regulated demonstrates not that it has become less salient, as some sociologists have claimed, but rather that the opposing interests have remained as contradictory as ever, and that the struggle between them is still as potentially disruptive. Indeed, the very fact that it had to be regulated proves that its basis still exists; and that, if left alone, it could have posed a major threat to the capitalist system. Moreover, in recent years, as economic recessions have set in and unemployment has increased, the potential for class conflict has been greatly augmented and the advent of a massive revolutionary movement can no longer be regarded as a remote possibility.

To the claim that ethnic and racial conflict has largely supplanted class conflict as the most explosive struggle in modern society, Marxists retort that such ethnic-racial conflict is nothing but class conflict in disguise. In the United States, for instance, racial and ethnic minorities such as blacks, Puerto Ricans, and Chicanos are nothing but an exploited class, disadvantaged by exclusion from control of the means of production no less than by hereditary social barriers. In mature capitalist society, therefore, classes and class conflict are not scheduled for disappearance (Baran and Sweezy, 1966; Mann, 1973; Miliband, 1973; Mandel, 1975; Connell, 1977).

Actual developments: the medieval class structure

Here, as in other spheres, the evaluation of the two opposing approaches

through an examination of empirical developments is beset with difficulties as some of the empirical evidence is lacking and some of it is
open to conflicting interpretations. Nevertheless, an attempt can be
made to discern certain patterns of development through the bits and
pieces of evidence that are available.

Both schools of thought concur that in medieval times the major
basis of the class structure was land tenure. The latter was not only the
basis of economic power but the basis of political power as well. The
feudal lord, who was the landholder, derived not only economic advantages therefrom but political advantages too: he exercised full administrative and judicial authority over his dependents. On their part, these
dependents, the serfs, were not only economically disadvantaged by
being obliged to hand in part of their crops or working powers to the
lord, but were deprived of their political freedom as well, as they were
not entitled to leave the land at will. Landholding was also the main
basis of prestige: the landholders formed the nobility (and eventually
the hereditary nobility) to which all others deferred.

Thus there was but one basis for the class structure: those who held
the means of production and economic power were the holders of
political power and prestige as well. The church was outside this main
structure, but it too was a feudal hierarchy based on land rights, which
were closely tied in with position in the church, political power, and
prestige rankings.

The system as a whole was in the form of a hierarchy of classes
(towards the end of the era these came to be more crystallized and
known as estates), each of which was itself hierarchical. In this hierarchy of hierarchies the gap in power and prestige between the top and
the bottom of the scale was, not surprisingly, large; and in most countries
it was further bolstered by legal provisions. Even so, at the beginning
of the Middle Ages the gap in material rewards was apparently not as
great as is commonly thought, and only later on did it gradually increase. Until the end of the eleventh century, even the nobility had to
make do with relatively simple food, clothing, and dwellings. Only from
then on did the wealth and living standard of the nobility gradually
rise, while that of the peasants remained stationary.[4]

However, even at a certain point in time the gap between the classes
was not uniform since the nobility had several gradations in it. The
highest echelon was comprised of those overlords who had obtained
their grants of land (fiefs) directly from the ruler (king or prince) in
return for military or administrative services rendered. They in turn
granted land rights for part of their lands to vassals, who did the same

to their own subvassals, and so forth. In this manner economic power and well-being, as well as political power and prestige, diminished gradually as one descended the pyramid (parallel gradations prevailed in the church).

The lower class was similarly graded. In some areas the top echelon was composed of freeholders, that is to say, of farmers who cultivated their own (variously sized) plots of land, many of whom were relatively privileged in economic terms. The second echelon was composed of serfs. Their land officially belonged to their feudal lords, who exacted part of their crops or various services (or both) in return for the right to cultivate it. At the bottom of the scale were the slaves, the remnants of antiquity, most of whom became serfs as the medieval period progressed.

Peripheral to the main class structure was yet another social grouping, the burghers, first evident in the towns that emerged around the twelfth century. This entity was similarly graded: it was headed by merchants and artisans who, in turn, could be graded internally by the size of their enterprises and workshops and the magnitude of their property. Somewhat lower were the apprentices in training to become merchants or artisans. At the bottom were the labourers whose lowly positions were permanent.

From the medieval period to the industrial revolution this entity of town dwellers comprised but a small proportion of the population, apparently no more than 10 per cent. Its chief significance lay not in its numbers but in the fact that it was the prototype of the modern class system, the upper echelons being the pioneers of the modern bourgeoisie. Modernization of the class structure thus set in rather early in towns, whereas in rural areas, which comprised the great majority of the population, some elements of feudalism survived well into the eighteenth century and beyond.

In all parts of the medieval class structure the prevailing ideology was avowedly non-egalitarian. The privileges of the aristocracy and the wealthy merchants were generally accepted as legitimate. Even those who were disadvantaged by them did not generally question their legitimacy. No significant counter-ideology developed, and a person who strove for change was not intent on transforming the system as such. In B. Barber's (1957, p. 486) words, 'He did not believe in equality for all, at least not here on earth, though he might, if he was a firmly believing Christian, look forward to it in heaven.' Rather he was set on improving his own position in the system.

This, however, was not easy since feudalism gradually evolved into a hereditary system. At its heart was the personal contract between the suzerain (overlord) and his vassal, which specified the rights and duties of each party. Initially, this was a lifetime bond that had to be renewed for each generation. But as the Middle Ages progressed, and especially from the tenth to the twelfth century, it gradually became hereditary with renewal a mere formality.

Despite this, the widespread idea that the strata of medieval society were hermetically closed does not bear scrutiny and some – albeit narrow – avenues of social mobility remained open. In France, England and other major feudal countries, they included the following:

(a) *The achievement of knighthood through prowess on the battlefield.* As Stanislav Andreski (1965, p. 157) put it: 'Strong and daring men, by joining various war bands, often succeeded in entering the ranks of the nobility. There was, for instance, a whole category of knights raised from serfs, whom medieval documents call "ministeriales".' This path was not open to all since it generally required initial means such as military equipment (armour) and training. It apparently narrowed even further during the twelfth century when private wars within the knightly class became less common, but it did not close completely.

(b) *Advancement in the rulers' administrations.* This path widened from the twelfth century onwards as states became somewhat more centralized and their administrations began to expand. But it remained relatively limited until well after modernization, for only then did the state bureaucracies reach sizeable dimensions (see next chapter).

(c) *Advancement in the church hierarchy.* Members of the higher echelons of the church were generally recruited from the nobility. But since the church was not a hereditary, self-recruiting class like the nobility itself, the possibility for talented and ambitious lower-class people to advance through its hierarchy was not completely absent.

(d) *Escape of serfs to the cities.* As the medieval rulers were chronically short of funds, they were interested in the growth of cities, from which taxes could be obtained in hard cash. Hence many encouraged serfs to escape to the cities, where by hard work they could accumulate wealth and property. Many rulers decreed that anybody residing in a city for a certain period was automatically freed from the bonds of serfdom.

(e) *The purchase of land and titles by rich burghers.* Rulers were inclined to encourage this route of advancement as yet another source of cash income, but were obliged to restrict it so as to prevent the inflation of titles, and hence the devaluation of this cash source.

Although these various routes of mobility, even combined, were rather narrow, they were of great importance since they served as what has been termed 'safety-valve institutions'; they opened an alternative for the most ambitious, for those whose lot in the lower classes was unbearable to them. Thus they diminished the chances of potentially subversive action, and strengthened the system more than they weakened it (Barber, 1973).

Actual developments: the advent of the modern class structure

Even so, the system eventually disintegrated and gave way to the modern capitalist class structure. This transformation was gradual and therefore cannot be timed with any precision. It apparently reached its peak towards the end of the eighteenth and the first half of the nineteenth century, but it began centuries before that, and continued thereafter as well. The causes of this transformation are to be sought in the development of the capitalist economy, in technological advancement, in the industrial revolution in which this advancement culminated, and in the large-scale urbanization these developments brought in their wake. Hence the factors that account for these economic and technological developments – including the value constellations (discussed in chapter 1) – may be held to be indirectly responsible for the transformation of the class structure as well. The French Revolution undoubtedly had some relevance for this transformation, but the Revolution was probably the product of earlier changes in the French class structure no less than it itself was the catalyst for further change. As it alerted the aristocracies all over Europe to the fate of their French counterpart, it probably had some ramifications in increasing their flexibility. But the main roots of the transformation are clearly to be sought in the development of capitalism, its antecedents and consequences.

This should be evident from the nature of the transformation itself. It entailed, first, a change in the basis of the class division: land tenure rights gradually gave way to property (including financial assets and industrial machinery) as the foremost basis of membership of the dominant class, and the newly expanding bourgeoisie came to fill the role of such a class. The landholding aristocracy continued to have great wealth, power and prestige well into the nineteenth century. But eventually it either merged with the bourgeoisie or faded into the background.

Since the bourgeoisie was basically an entrepreneurial class, its ascent marked the ascent of a new, entrepreneurial type of stratificational ideology: that of equality of opportunity. According to this newly prevalent ideology, men differ from each other in many ways, for instance in intelligence and ambition; hence not all can be entirely equal. But there is one sphere in which all are entitled to equality: in their rights and opportunities. This will ensure that differences in social position no longer reflect the privileges of birth and inheritance, but only those of ability and effort. Concomitantly, another ideology developed: that of fully-fledged equality, which took root in the various socialist and communist movements that proliferated in the Western world after the end of the eighteenth century.

Perhaps it is in connection with these ideological developments that the legal differences between the classes or estates (wherever they had existed) were gradually abolished and replaced by equality of all before the law. This, to be sure, was merely a formal gesture that did not lead (and was not meant to lead) to actual equality. The gap in material rewards between the classes not only prevailed but, at least up to the second half of the nineteenth century, it apparently increased: from the fifteenth century onwards, the aristocracy and the merchants began to reap the benefits of the increased trade with the Orient and the discovery of the New World, but these benefits apparently did not trickle through to the peasants. Moreover, as increasingly large numbers of peasants were forced to leave the land and flock to the cities to swell the ranks of the working class, their quality of life evidently declined, and the discrepancy between theirs and that of their employers was clearly unprecedented.[5] Two greatly divided and mutually hostile classes thus confronted each other, the newly enriched bourgeoisie and the growing and impoverished proletariat. In the nineteenth century, the aristocracy was still powerful and a middle class of small producers, shopkeepers and white-collar workers existed as well, but these did not wholly avert the confrontation. Not surprisingly, intermittent class conflict (expressed in violent industrial and political struggles) broke out (see chapters 4 and 7).

However, at the same time, new avenues of social mobility were opened, avenues which in the medieval period had either been non-existent or exceedingly narrow. The first of these was entrepreneurship and the accumulation of capital. Even in the Middle Ages, and especially since the fifteenth century, business ventures, and later industrial ventures, were frequently initiated by 'new men', by pioneers who brought as their sole investment their energy, intelligence, and cunning (Pirenne, 1939, p. 516). But by the beginning of the nineteenth century this path had apparently widened considerably, through its relationship with technological development and industrial innovation. As Andreski (1965, pp. 242–3) put it:

> In the West new forms of economic activity were being created by 'new men', men who gained wealth and rose in status in virtue of their pioneering efforts . . . . Although . . . great vertical mobility is not sufficient for technical progress, certain forms of it seem to be a necessary accompaniment. Technical progress involves not only the invention but also the organization of new units of production able to apply new methods. The motives of inventors are complex: it is quite probable that disinterested curiosity is more important than any thought of material reward. But in the case of businessmen, it is fairly obvious that they are motivated by the quest for wealth and power. The attainment of these involves climbing the social ladder. New methods of production will therefore be introduced only if innovating activity is rewarded by a rise in status.

Another widening path of social mobility was that of occupational advancement, especially into white-collar occupations. This, too, was the result of the advancing technology and economy which led to a continual repatterning of the occupational structure (see chapter 4). But while an increase in mobility did take place, it was (at least up to the second half of the nineteenth century) the inadvertent by-product of economic and occupational change rather than the result of a deliberate societal response to a changed ideology, or the outcome of deliberate government action. And although the channels of mobility had widened to some extent, they were still accessible to only a small minority; most of the growing working class had neither the training nor the opportunity to avail themselves of these channels.

The changes in the class structure that occurred with modernization and up to the middle of the nineteenth century thus point in two divergent directions. The discrepancy between the classes in material welfare apparently increased; but so did the opportunities for social mobility, although even then they were not widely accessible.

Actual developments: the maturation of the modern class structure

Of even greater interest, however, are the later developments. For while the two schools of thought — the 'mainstream' and the Marxist — would probably not dispute most of the changes outlined so far, they are diametrically opposed on what occurred thereafter: it has been reasonably well established and generally agreed upon that an upper (or dominant), a lower (or working) class and an intermediary (or middle class still persist. But the two schools of thought disagree fundamentally on the recent changes in the material gaps between these classes and in the possibility of advancing from one to the other. It is here that the crux of the controversy is located.

Trends in inequality
Has the gap in material rewards between the classes decreased substantially from the second half of the nineteenth century, as the 'mainstream' sociologists have suggested, or has it decreased but marginally, only to increase again later on as the Marxists have claimed? The empirical evidence indicates that in fact there has been a movement towards lesser inequality in earnings in many Western societies over the years for which figures are available, that is, roughly since the beginning of the twentieth century, and especially since the interwar years.[6] Thus, according to Heilbroner (1962), between 1936 and 1958 the income of the lowest fifth of the American population grew to a much greater extent than did the income of the highest fifth, although the intermediate groups made even higher advances, as can be seen from Table 5.1.

Table 5.1 *Per cent increase in average income (1950 dollars) for the American population − 1936-58*

Highest fifth	57
Second fifth	91
Third fifth	107
Fourth fifth	116
Lowest fifth	101

Source: Heilbroner (1962), p. 172.

This analysis is corroborated by Lydall (1968, ch. 6) who cites a great variety of statistical evidence, all of which indicates that there was a fairly rapid decline of dispersion in income in the United States between 1939 and 1949. The analysis is further supported and updated by Chirot (1977), who traces changes in the American income distribution between 1929 and 1970. These data are shown in Table 5.2.

Similarly, Broom and Jones (1976, p. 52), report that in Australia in

Table 5.2 *Percentage of national income received by families in the United States, 1929–70*

	1929	1950	1970
Top five per cent	30·0	17·3	15·6
Top fifth	54·4	42·7	40·9
Second fifth	19·3	23·6	23·8
Third fifth	13·8	17·4	17·6
Fourth fifth	9·0	11·9	12·2
Lowest fifth	3·5	4.5	5.4

Source: Chirot (1977), p. 189.

1915 the top 1 per cent of male income-earners received 14·6 per cent of the total net income reported by adult males, a figure that declined to 7·9 per cent in 1969. Over the same period the Gini coefficient[7] of income inequality fell from an estimated 0·42 in 1915 to 0·34 in 1969. They conclude that in the half-century from 1915 to 1969 income inequality among adult men decreased by close to one-fifth.

Parallel developments are reported by Lydall (1968, ch. 6), for the United Kingdom, Canada, and Belgium. Analysing various types of surveys, he concludes that there was a certain decline in the overall dispersion of income in these countries during the first half of the twentieth century. On the other hand, reports Lydall, the evidence does not suggest that there has been any substantial change in the dispersion of income in Sweden, Norway, Germany (later West Germany), Austria and France. Partially contradicting this, a United Nations report on income distribution (United Nations, 1967) states that there was a general though not a very strong decline in income inequality in Germany, Sweden, Denmark, and the Netherlands.

However, the evidence also indicates that the decline in income inequality occurred mainly up to the end of the Second World War. Since the early 1950s, such inequality appears to have declined only marginally, if at all. This is clearly evident for the United States, where the income of the top fifth of the population was reduced by approximately 12 per cent from 1929 to 1950, but by only 2 per cent between 1950 and 1970 (see Table 5.2). The same holds for Australia: Broom and Jones (1976, p. 52) report that from 1950 onwards the gap between the highest and lowest quarter of taxpayers narrowed, but the gap

between the two middle quarters widened so that the overall discrepancy remained more or less as it was.

Moreover, Lydall reports that in the United Kingdom and Canada
income dispersion even widened slightly in the 1950s; and the aforementioned United Nations Report on income distribution states that
from the 1950s to the 1960s income distribution has slightly decreased
only in one European country — Norway. In all others it has slightly
widened or remained constant. Finally Berthoud (1976) reports that
the Gini coefficient of inequality for net income in Britain remained
stable in the 1960s (it was 0·24 in 1961 and 0·25 in 1971) and Shanon
(1975) reports on the basis of a detailed analysis that in the 1960s there
was not much change in income dispersion in the other European
countries either.

According to Heilbroner (1962, p. 171) the decrease in income dispersion in many Western countries in the first half of the twentieth
century was brought about by the intervention of trade unions, by the
introduction of minimum wages, and through the passsage of welfare
legislation. The changes were thus due, to a much greater extent than in
the nineteenth century, to deliberate public policy. If this analysis is
correct, then it follows that the apparent stabilization of the income
gaps from the 1950s onwards is due at least in part to a slackening of
the push towards greater equality in the public policy of Western
countries, even though inequalities of income, and even more so of
wealth, are still very large.

For instance, for the United States, Table 5.2 shows that in 1970 the
top fifth of the population enjoyed an income that was almost eight
times as great as that obtained by the bottom fifth, and that the top
fifth of the population enjoyed around 40 per cent of all income. Table
5.3 shows that income inequalities in other Western countries equal or
exceed that of the United States.

Income in turn, was found to be closely related to wealth, although
the latter was found to be even more concentrated at the top. In the
United States, for instance, the top 2·5 per cent of the population own
39 per cent of the country's wealth, while the bottom 50 per cent of
the population own no more than 4 per cent of that wealth; and in
Britain 5 per cent of the population own 54 per cent of the country's
wealth.[8] Even in Sweden, where the distribution of wealth is much
more egalitarian, the differences are still very great: the top 2 per cent
of the population own as much as 20 per cent, while the bottom 50 per
cent own only 25 per cent of the country's wealth (Lenski and Lenski,
1978, p. 337).[9] In America and in other Western countries a small

Table 5.3 *Income inequality in Western countries (pre-tax income)*

	Percentage of income received by		
	Lowest 40% of the population	Middle 40% of the population	Top 20% of the population
Australia (1968)	20·0	41·2	38·8
Canada (1965)	20·0	39·8	40·2
Denmark (1968)	13·6	38·8	47·6
Federal Republic of Germany (1964)	15·4	31·7	52·9
Finland (1962)	11·1	39·6	49·3
France (1962)	9·5	36·8	53·7
Netherlands (1967)	13·6	37·9	48·5
New Zealand (1969)	15·5	42·5	42·0
Sweden (1963)	14·0	42·0	44·0
United Kingdom (1968)	18·8	42·2	39·0
United States (1970)	19·7	41·5	38·8

Source: Ahluwalia (1974), p. 8.

minority thus owns a considerable portion of all wealth, hence it wields a decisive share of economic power and there are no signs that this concentration of wealth and power is diminishing.

And just as the top of the pyramid has not displayed any clear levelling tendencies in recent years, neither has the bottom. Thus, Myrdal (1969) has argued convincingly that while many Americans are benefiting from a rise in their living standards, at the base of the hierarchy there is increasing inequality, manifested in the emergence of an 'underclass' of the unemployed and the unemployable. Unemployment, in turn, is related to poverty and the poor make up sizeable parts of Western populations. Thus it has been estimated that in 1959 some 39·5 million people, or 24 per cent of the American population, lived in poverty. And although the proportion has substantially decreased, a sizeable cluster of the population, some 12 per cent, still do so today (Broom and Selznick, 1977, p. 164).[10]

Nor is the existence of such a cluster confined to the United States. For instance, Abel-Smith and Townsend (1965), using data from the

British Ministry of Labour's National Survey of income and expenditure in 1960 estimated that 7½ million persons, or some 14 per cent of the British population, were living below generally accepted subsistence standards.[11] Also, various studies conducted in Australia have shown that pockets of poverty have been very much in evidence in that country. The National Commission's Enquiry into Poverty conducted in 1975 reported that over 10 per cent of all households in Australia were below an austere poverty line, and an additional 8 per cent were less than 20 per cent above it (Henderson, 1975).[12] Similar situations are to be found in several other Western countries as well, and with the recently growing rates of unemployment (to which poverty is related), Myrdal's concept of an underclass seems increasingly appropriate.

Moreover, unemployment and poverty are in turn related to racial and ethnic affiliation. For instance, in the United States in recent years, while the overall poverty rate among whites has been about 9 per cent, the rate for blacks has been around 31 per cent, and that for persons of Spanish origin around 23 per cent. Closely related to this is the fact that over the past twenty years non-whites' unemployment has been double that of unemployment among whites, and has tended to extend for longer periods of time and thus to be more harmful (Broom and Selznick, 1977, pp. 164, 474). Although there seems to have been some occupational upgrading of blacks in the United States as more of them have recently been engaged in white-collar occupations, it nevertheless remains true that there are many blacks who are either poor or unemployed, or both, and who therefore fit in with Myrdal's characterization of an underclass. Whatever tendencies for the diminution of inequalities have thus existed for the bulk of Western societies, these have apparently bypassed the groups at the top and bottom of the class spectrum.

Trends in social mobility
The second major controversy between the 'mainstream' and the Marxist schools of thought concerns the degree of openness (or closure) of Western class structures. Has mobility increased substantially since the second half of the nineteenth century and is it uniformly high today — as 'mainstream' sociologists have claimed, or is it still largely innocuous, as the Marxists have proposed?

In many Western societies and especially in the United States, people are certainly led to believe that mobility is very high indeed. According to Merton (1957b), the legend promoted by the establishment is that the lofty goal of success is open to all; that the American dream of advancement from rags to riches is a realistic possibility; that however lowly the starting point, ambition and talent will lead to the very top. But what is the situation in actual fact?

Empirical analysis has shown that although this belief is obviously a myth, the sources of mobility have recently changed and the rates of certain types of mobility have thereby increased, at least in the United States. Economic concentration and the growth of corporations and administrations (see chapters 4 and 6) imply that the opportunities for 'new men' to start enterprises of their own and thereby climb the ladder of wealth have clearly decreased, while the opportunities for mobiity through advancement on bureaucratic ladders have clearly increased.

Also, until recently, differential rates of fertility constituted an important factor of social mobility. For all industrial countries for which data are available fertility has tended to vary inversely with income and class position (Lipset and Bendix, 1964). Since upper-level occupations have been expanding, this implies that even if all higher-class fathers had bequeathed their sons their own or equivalent positions, there would still be room at the top into which lower class people could rise. There is a popular saying: the rich get richer and the poor get children. Actually,however, the fact that the poor get children has (until recently) signified that some of these children at least have become richer as well. But the class differential in fertility has recently narrowed and the failure of the upper classes to replace themselves demographically is no longer an important factor in social mobility (Jones, 1974, p. 44).

The most important source for recent trends in social mobility, is to be found rather in the upgrading of the occupational structure of Western societies (see Tables 4.1 and 4.2), and especially in the growth of the white-collar occupations, which enjoy a relatively high prestige and many of which enjoy a relatively high income.[13] Although interpretation of such shifts in terms of precise rates of social mobility is far from simple, they indisputably imply the opening of mobility channels for significant proportions of the population. This process of occupational upgrading has been accelerated in recent years at least in the United States. As Table 4.1 indicates, the proportion of people engaged in white-collar occupations grew by 19 per cent in the fifty years between 1900 and 1950, and by roughly 13 per cent in the twenty-five years between 1950 and 1975. Also, while the number of manual workers continued to grow between 1900 and 1950, it has clearly shrunk from 1950 onwards. This would seem to signify that social mobility should have been increased in recent years. Has this in fact been the case?

A large number of empirical studies have addressed themselves to this topic. And although they are not in agreement on the optimal method of measuring social mobility, they did arrive at the common conclusion that, at least in the United States, certain types of upward mobility have in fact been increasing. Thus Thernstrom (1966), in a study comparing mobility rates in a small but representative American city in the middle of the nineteenth century with parallel rates for several large American cities and for national samples around the middle of the twentieth century, found that the chances of mobility had clearly increased. Only one labourer in twenty from the earlier sample rose into a non-manual occupation, as against one in ten from the later large-cities sample. Only one labourer's son in ten from the earlier sample achieved a non-manual position as against one in five from the later national sample.

In another study (Thernstrom, 1973), the author traced mobility rates in a large, representative American city — Boston — from 1880 to 1970. He found that in general the rates of mobility have remained constant (and rather high). Throughout the whole period, roughly a quarter of all the sample members who pursued a blue-collar occupation moved over to a white-collar job before the end of their working life. But although the occupational structure as a whole became neither notably more, nor notably less, fluid, the mobility chances of unskilled workers increased during this period: only 32 per cent moved out of their occupation in 1880–90, but 53 per cent did so in 1958–68.

Similarly, Duncan (1965), in a re-analysis of several nationwide surveys concludes that there was more upward mobility and less downward mobility of American men[14] in 1962 than there was in 1932, and that there has been a specially large increase of mobility into professional and technical occupations. Also, Blau and Duncan, in a 1960s nationwide survey of some twenty thousand American men, came up with the result that the younger men enjoyed greater opportunities for advancement than did their predecessors in earlier decades[15] (Duncan, 1965; Blau and Duncan, 1967, pp. 90–111). Hauser and Featherman (1973) concluded, on the basis of another study, that there was no further increase in mobility in the 1960s, but that the general trend of high mobility in previous decades continued.

It has been argued that a distinction ought to be drawn between structural mobility (that is, mobility resulting from the *upgrading* of the occupational structure) and circulatory, or exchange mobility (that

is, the mobility resulting from the *openness* of the occupational structure).[16] Having made this distinction, observers conclude that circulatory
mobility in the United States has remained more or less constant in
recent years; the recent increase is only in structural mobility. Thus
Hauser and his colleagues (1975a, 1975b) conclude on the basis of their
studies that when changes in the American occupational structure are
controlled there is a striking lack of trend in the rates of mobility. It
is only when those changes in the occupational structure are not
neutralized, but rather incorporated into the analysis, that the increased
rates of upward mobility become evident. At the same time, a comparison of a national sample of men in England and Wales with a similar
study carried out in 1949 shows that no changes in circulatory mobility
have taken place, and that consequently English society is no more
open today than it was thirty years ago (Hope, n.d.). However, this
comparison does not report on structural mobility, which may well
have increased during this time-span as it did in the United States.

Singling out circulatory mobility for exclusive analysis is justified
for some purposes but not for others. As F. Jones (1974, p. 51) aptly
points out, for the members of a society the distinction between structural and circulatory mobility is largely irrelevant: what counts is
whether they do or do not have a chance of getting ahead. Hence the
fact that in the United States mobility has increased in recent decades
(even if only because of changes in the occupational structure) is still
highly significant.

It is also significant that the rates of mobility in many Western
countries seem to have been rather high, at least where the transition
from manual to non-manual occupations is concerned. For instance,
S. M. Miller (1969), who compared manual to non-manual intergenerational mobility in twelve Western nations in the 1940s and 1950s,
reports that nine of them had mobility rates of 20 per cent and over.
Similarly, Lipset and Bendix (1964), who surveyed the same type of
mobility in eight Western nations over approximately the same time-
span, reported that all but one (Italy) had mobility rates of 20 per
cent or more. The results of the two comparative analyses do not tally
precisely. For instance, while Miller reports a mobility rate of 30 per
cent for France and 25·5 per cent for Sweden, Lipset and Bendix
report rates of 39 and 31 per cent respectively for these two
countries.[17] Nevertheless, the similarities between the analyses are
sufficient to warrant the conclusion that movement from manual to
non-manual occupations, though differing widely in different Western
countries, has been substantial in most of them. This conclusion is

further corroborated by Broom's and Jones's (1969) comparative study of Australia, Italy and the United States in the 1960s. On the basis of national surveys in all three countries, the authors conclude that intergenerational mobility from manual to non-manual occupations has been 20 per cent or more in all three (20 per cent in Italy, 31 per cent in Australia, and 36 per cent in the United States).

It will be recalled that Marxists do not accord much weight to findings of this nature, as they claim that taking on a non-manual occupation does not necessarily elevate the incumbent out of the working class. According to this view, the truly significant mobility is not into non-manual occupations *per se* but into the dominant class. Accordingly, it is of interest to mention S. M. Miller's (1969) comparison of mobility in nine Western countries, if not into the dominant class proper, at least into what he calls the elite (that is, the occupational groups with the highest standing — comprising between 3 and 16 per cent of the population in different countries).[18] According to Miller's study, only between 0 (Belgium) and 7·8 (USA) per cent of all persons whose fathers were manual labourers had been fortunate enough to advance into the elite, with the percentages in most of the nine countries somewhere in between. As Miliband (1973, p. 37) points out on the basis of this study, in post-war Europe only some 5 per cent of manual workers' sons made the leap into business and the professions.

It must be remembered, however, that the elite and/or dominant class comprise but a small percentage of the population. So even if complete equality of opportunity prevailed, only a small proportion of the working class could make its way into these groups. Not surprisingly, therefore, a somewhat different picture emerges when the proportion of the elite or dominant class originating in the working class (rather than the percentage of the working class admitted into this class) is examined. Lipset and Bendix (1964), for instance, report on a number of studies concerning the social origins of the business elites in Britain, the Netherlands, Sweden, and the United States. Despite some methodological problems, these studies have indisputably established that, in all the said countries, between 10 and 15 per cent of the members of the business elites are of working-class or lower white-collar origins, and an additional 15 per cent are descended from the lower middle class. So between a quarter and a third of these business elites, which in effect can be identified with a certain part of the dominant (capitalist) class, have their origins in lower social classes. Descendants of these lower classes are still greatly under-represented in the capitalist class, but they are not totally barred from it.

The growth of the middle class and the embourgeoisement controversy
Mobility into the capitalist class, or rather the lack thereof, has been especially emphasized by Marxists. 'Mainstream' sociologists, on the other hand, have put special emphasis on mobility into the middle class, which, recently, has indeed led to a growth of that class. In addition to the traditional or 'old' middle class (small businessmen, shopkeepers, small-scale producers and the like), which continues to persist, there has been an expansion in the number of non-manual salaried employees, who fall into the intermediate brackets of the income scale and who have come to be known as the 'new' middle class. The strengthening of the middle class may also be conceived as the development of a growing buffer between the upper and lower class. It is perhaps one of the main reasons why the revolutionary class struggle envisaged by Marx has not (as yet?) eventuated.

Has the middle class also been strengthened through the embourgeoisement of the working class, as 'mainstream' sociologists have claimed? Since the general affluence of the Western working classes has increased, and since consumption products have become more standardized, some working-class consumption patterns have indeed come to resemble those of the middle class to a greater extent than previously. Consumer surveys in Britain have shown that the possession of various kinds of consumer durables — television sets, vacuum cleaners, washing machines, and so forth, was apparently becoming fairly general not only among the middle class but among the working class as well. Increasingly, too, manual workers were invading the hitherto almost exclusively middle-class preserves of car and home ownership (Goldthorpe *et al.*, 1969). Clothing, too, has become more standardized, and nowadays seems to be differentiated by age to a greater extent than by class. Seen on a superficial level, the life-styles of the various classes thus seem to converge.

However, less standardized and more expensive items of consumption, such as antique or crafted furniture, Oriental carpets, original paintings, or other art exhibits displayed in the home, as well as the education required to appreciate those items, are still confined to those in the middle class and above. These items are more subtle in their effect, as well as more secluded, than, say, cars. Much 'conspicuous consumption' has thus become less conspicuous because it has been withdrawn into the interior of homes where it is open to perusal only by those of similar social position in the framework of informal social relations. Although it therefore figures less in the awareness of the public (and of sociologists), the ability to engage in it and to appreciate it still differentiates the various classes from each other, and serves as a status symbol for the higher ones.

Also, a study of the most affluent part of the working class in an English town shows that even the 'workers' aristocracy' does not tend to resemble the middle class in its patterns of sociability, aspirations, ambitions and political attitudes. For instance, most of the workers who formed part of the study retained their union membership and their electoral support for the Labour Party, although they tended to do so for the sake of individual advantages to be gained rather than for reasons of class solidarity. The researchers conclude that the idea that even affluent workers turn middle-class is a questionable one, and what holds for the most advantaged of workers must certainly hold for the multitude of less affluent workers as well (Goldthorpe *et al.*, 1969).

Conclusion

An unbiased evaluation of the recent changes in the class structure of Western societies leads to the conclusion that the situation is neither as encouraging as it has been depicted by 'mainstream' sociologists, nor as bleak as the Marxists have made it out to be. Income inequalities have indeed decreased and mobility has increased (at least in the United States), and relatively high rates of mobility from manual to non-manual occupations have been achieved, with some variations, in all Western countries. It seems that within the white-collar category itself there have also been high rates of social mobility, as expressed in ascent on the various bureaucratic hierarchies with which modern societies are so generously endowed. And while mobility into the capitalist class proper has been much more limited, it has apparently not been quite as restricted as Marxist observers seem to believe.

On the other hand, the process of decreasing inequality was arrested some thirty years ago. This process in any case bypassed the very top and the very bottom of the class spectrum, so while a certain narrowing of gaps has occurred for the bulk of the population, the small wealth-holding (capitalist) class at the top and the 'underclass' at the bottom have not shared in this trend.

Also, to the extent that mobility has increased, it has done so because of changes in the occupational structure (structural mobility), rather than increasing openness of the system (circulatory mobility). It was pointed out above that it makes little difference to people whether the advancement they enjoy is due to structural or to circulatory causes.

But this is true only for any given point in time. Not so when the dynamics of the system and especially its prospects for the future are considered. For occupational structures cannot be upgraded indefinitely, and mobility resulting from it may be expected to come to a halt as soon as that process of upgrading has exhausted itself. As Hauser and Featherman (1973) caution, this trend is strictly limited by the impending depletion of occupational groups, such as farm-workers and un-skilled labourers, which hitherto served as sources of recruitment into higher-status occupations. It is further limited by the fact that the category of industrial labourers in general is not likely to continue shrinking substantially beyond a certain limit. Barring the opening up of the occupational structure to increased circulatory mobility, which so far shows no signs of taking place, the increases in mobility that have occurred may well be approaching their end, and in the future mobility may even be shrinking.

Decreasing inequality and increasing mobility thus seem to have halted or to be on the verge of halting. Moreover, this seems to have occurred at a point at which considerable inequalities still remain. This fact is not generally evident because people are encouraged to believe in the possibility of success for all and because inequality is so much less visible today than it was previously. The latter is so in turn because of the general rise in affluence which makes it possible even for those lowest on the scale to afford a certain standardized minimum. Inequality is also less obvious than it used to be because it is more subtly expressed, and many present-day class symbols (such as art and craft objects) are of a nature that precludes perusal by outsiders as well as quantitative analysis.

While 'mainstream' sociologists, basing their case largely on the spread of standardized consumer goods, have concluded that a process of embourgeoisement of the working class is taking place, the present analysis indicates that another conclusion is warranted. A certain type of (perhaps inadvertent) manipulation has been occurring, whereby the semblance of equality and equality of opportunity has increased to a much greater extent than equality and equality of opportunity itself. Consequently, the *feelings* of relative deprivation amongst the working class are smaller than might have been expected on the basis of actual relative deprivation. At the beginning of this chapter Miller's succinct observation was reported to the effect that our needs stem not so much from what we lack but rather from what our neighbours have. But this cannot hold true when we are unaware of what our neighbours do have, as frequently seems to be the case in Western societies.

As 'mainstream' sociologists have recognized, the decrease in inequality (which has been substantial) has been an important factor in
the erosion of class consciousness and in the mitigation of class conflict.
It seems, however, that the even greater decrease in the *semblance* of
inequality has been no less important (although less clearly recognized)
in this respect. A British conservative leader, Stanley Baldwin, is reported
to have said, 'If you want people to be conservative, then give them
something to conserve.' It seems that Western societies have succeeded
in doing just that by raising the general level of affluence, by decreasing
inequality, and even more so the semblance of inequality, and by giving
working-class people the sense that they are not much worse off than
anybody else. Hence they, too, feel that they have a stake in the
system, and that by overthrowing it they have much more to lose than
merely their chains. This is not to say, however, that this may not
change in the future, if class disparities continue to persist, if channels
of social mobility close up, and if the small but growing 'underclass'
continues to be excluded from the benefits of the system.

Selected readings

Davis, K., and Moore, W. E. (1945), 'Some principles of stratification',
   American Sociological Review, 10, pp. 242–9.
Etzioni, A., and Etzioni-Halevy, E. (eds) (1973), *Social Change* (2nd
   edn), New York, Basic Books, chs 21, 36.
Giddens, A. (1973), *The Class Structure of Advanced Societies*,
   London, Hutchinson.
Goldthorpe, J. H. *et al.* (1969), *The Affluent Worker in the Class
   Structure*, Cambridge University Press.
Lenski, G. (1954), 'Status crystallization', *American Sociological
   Review*, 19, pp. 405–13.
Miliband, R. (1973), *The State in Capitalist Society*, London, Quartet.

6 · The advent and maturation of the modern polity (A): the power of governments and ruling elites

The maturation of the Western class structure has brought about a significant (though imperfect) decrease in inequality between classes and a certain mitigation of class conflict. Can an equivalent statement be made about the maturation of the Western polity? The major change in that polity with modernization and after, we are told, is the transition from feudalism to absolutism and subsequently from absolutism to democracy. This statement in and of itself, however, does not tell us very much. What we would wish to know is − what changes have actually occurred (especially with the transition to democracy) in the character of governments and ruling elites and in the power inequality (or power gap) between them and the public.[1] For as S. P. Huntington (1968, p. 1) has forcefully reminded us − the most significant difference between various regimes is not the *type* of government but the *degree* of government.

More systematically, the following criteria are hereby suggested to guide us in the comparison of Western democracies, with their historic predecessors, and in analysing the transformation from one regime to another:

(a) What is the degree of power the governments, and through them, the ruling elites, exercise over the public?

(b) What is the extent of the public's participation in the political arena and what is its impact on public policy?

(c) Who rules: from what social classes are the ruling elites recruited?

(d) In whose interest is their political power exercised?

(e) And finally − what is the manner in which the elites attain and preserve political power and the manner in which the conflict over the attainment and preservation of such power is waged?

Theoretical perspectives

Once again the 'mainstream' and the Marxist schools of thought have

144

differed in the manner in which they have addressed themselves to these questions. However, in this particular field of study the 'mainstream' is customarily subdivided into the pluralist model and the elitist model. This chapter presents a brief overview of each of the three models and then juxtaposes them with actual historical developments with regard to the power and interests of governments and elites. Developments in public participation and political conflict are analysed in the following chapter.

The pluralist view[2]

The pluralist model has been prevalent for many years, especially in the United States, although recently it has become somewhat less popular. It holds that after modernization in the West, and especially in the twentieth century, political power has come to be increasingly fragmented and diffused. Absolutism marked the growth of centralized state power (without which modernization would have been impossible). The subsequent advent of democracy, however, marked the reversal of this process.

Accordingly, the contemporary Western, and especially the American, political system is seen as an intricate balance of power amongst overlapping economic, religious, ethnic and other groups. Each group is held to exercise a certain influence on the policy-making process, but none of them is seen as possessing a monopoly or decisive share of power, since the different groups all check and counterbalance each other. Thus no distinct power elite is discernible and the idea of such an elite is held to be more fiction than reality. The government, to be sure, is vested with a degree of power; but it is increasingly subject to pressures from the various interest groups. In order to keep itself in office, it must display maximal responsiveness to these pressures, so as to keep everybody reasonably happy. The independent power held by the government is therefore minimal.

Moreover, since it is the government's task to balance out the various pressures, it cannot act in a partisan fashion to support the interests of any one group. Indeed, the government helps countervail the power of some (for example, business) interests by acceding to the demands of opposing (for example, labour) interests. In this manner, competition between different groups is endorsed by the government itself, ensuring that everybody's interests are taken into account, at least to some extent.

This view has had its proponents in all the major social sciences.

In sociology, for example, it has been concisely expressed by David Riesman (1961), who wrote:

> There has been in the last fifty years a change in the configuration of power in America, in which a single hierarchy with a ruling class at its head has been replaced by a number of 'veto groups' among which power is dispersed (p. 206).
>
> In the amorphous power structures created by the veto groups it is hard to distinguish rulers from the ruled (p. 214).
>
> Even those intellectuals . . . who are frightened of those who they think have the power, prefer to be scared by the power structures they conjure up than to face the possibility that the power structure they believe exists has largely evaporated (p. 223).

In political science, this view has been expressed for instance, by Robert Dahl (1956, p. 137), who asserts, 'all the active and legitimate groups in the population can make themselves heard at some crucial stage in the process of decision'. And in economics this view has been propounded among others by J. K. Galbraith in his early writings (1952, p. 141): 'Without the phenomenon itself being fully recognized, the provision of state assistance to the development of countervailing power has become a major function of government; perhaps *the* major domestic function of government.'[3]

Closely akin to the pluralist view of political power is what may be referred to as the democratic view of political participation. This position holds that prior to modernization there were practically no institutionalized avenues of political participation for the rank-and-file public, which was therefore effectively excluded from the political decision-making process. Modernization and recent developments in the political sphere (particularly, but not exclusively in the West) have resulted in an unprecedented increase in the public's political participation. As a larger range of groups and wider strata of the population have increasingly been drawn into political participation there has been a dramatic increase in the influence they have brought to bear on the political arena. As Eisenstadt (1966, pp. 15–16) put it:

> The broader strata of society tend more and more to impinge on its central institutions, not only in making various demands on it, but also in the sense of developing the aspirations to participate in the very crystallization of the center . . . . The growing participation of broader strata in the center of society and in the civil order can be seen as two basic attributes of modern nation-building, of the establishment of new, broader political and social entities.

Or, as V. O. Key Jr (1958, p. 9) saw it, in modern Western democracy, and especially in the United States, 'the people may not really govern themselves, but they can stir up a deafening commotion if they dislike the way they are governed.'[4]

The elitist view

An alternative perspective on political modernization and more recent political changes has been offered by the elitist model. This model was originally developed by Vilfredo Pareto, Gaetano Mosca, and Roberto Michels and was further elaborated by C. Wright Mills.[5] Recently it has found new proponents such as T. R. Dye, L. H. Zeigler, G. L. Field and J. Higley. The basic contention of this school of thought is that all societies are divided into the few who rule and the many who are ruled. The first group (the elite) effectively monopolizes power and is able to enjoy its advantages. It almost invariably gets its way whenever important public decisions are made, while the second group (the masses) acquiesces in this arrangement and is mostly passive. Even if the ruling elite is periodically overthrown or otherwise deposed, its removal merely sets the stage for the emergence of another elite, so that nothing changes as far as the masses are concerned.

The evolution of modern democracy is not viewed as a departure or even as a mitigating factor in this inevitable pattern of domination and subjugation. Even in democracies elites continue to rule as exclusively as they ever did before. Indeed, some theorists, like Suzanne Keller (1963, pp. 88–106), have proclaimed elite rule as a requisite that must be met if society (including democratic society) is to survive.[6]

Democracy has been claimed to be 'government by the people'. In fact, however, say Dye and Zeigler (1975), the survival of democracy rests broadly on the shoulders of elites rather than on the shoulders of the people. They term this the 'irony of democracy': it is the elites, not the masses, who are most committed to democratic values. If democracy were not safeguarded by the elites it would have disappeared long ago, or perhaps never even have come into being in the first place. Democracy has come about and survived because elites, not masses, govern.

Similarly, Field and Higley (1980) stress the elite-determined character of democracy. They argue that there is a necessity for a unified, well-off and secure elite before any stable pattern of government involving substantial personal freedom and meaningful electoral choice can be established, and that these conditions can come about only through the stratagems of the elite itself. Elites require the support of non-elites and are checked by them. But the basic character of the polity is determined by the elite structure.

According to Joseph Schumpeter (1962) (who has been classified as a 'democratic elitist'), democracy gives people the ability to choose between competing elite groups but not necessarily the ability to influence their policies once they come to power. Aron (who may be classified in a similar manner) sees elite power in democracies as formidable, but as dispersed to a greater extent than it is in other regimes (see chapter 2; see also Sartori, 1962). But elitists proper regard the impact of the public and the dispersion of power, even in a democracy, as very limited indeed.

For Mills, for instance, the dominance of the elite in such a society is eminently secure. Not only has this dominance not been eroded by the advent of democracy, but in recent years it has, in fact, been growing while the masses have become increasingly powerless, politically impotent, and therefore alienated and apathetic. 'In many countries', argues Mills (1959b, p. 324), 'they lose their will for rationally considered decision and action; they lose their sense of political belonging because they do not belong; they lose their political will, because they see no way to realize it.' Accordingly, there has been an increasing polarization of political power: the elite has been amassing more and more of it while the masses have been receiving less and less. More recent elite theorists such as Dye and Zeigler (1975), concur that most communication between the elite and the masses flows downwards rather than upwards, and even elections confer no real political power on the public; they are important mainly for their symbolic value.

Recent elite theorists accept the pluralist thesis on the proliferation of interest groups, but the leaders of the most powerful of these groups are seen as part of the ruling elite. Interest groups are therefore not regarded as a counterbalance to elite power either, but rather as a platform for that power.

What is the composition of the ruling elite and in whose interests does it act? Mills (1959b; 1973), who has addressed himself to this problem in great detail, holds that in America the ruling elite (or the power elite — as he terms it) is composed of three interlocking groups: high political office-holders, the leaders of capitalism, and the top military command. These groups exist in an uneasy alliance with each other. Drawn together by common, disproportionately high, socio-economic and educational background, by social interaction, by the common mentality of success, and by the interchangeability of their positions, they nevertheless vie with each other for dominance. As a result, the relative power of each of the three groups changes over time and none of them is permanently in a controlling position. Since the

Second World War, capitalists and the high military command have held hegemony, but the political elite has not necessarily been subdued on a permanent basis. At all times, the power elite represents and promotes the interlocking self-interests of the three groups of which it is composed. This is so, not because the elite is made up of selfish crooks who are out to take advantage of the public. Rather, it comes about because the elite members' mentality leads them to equate the good of society with their own interests.[7]

It is intriguing that such diametrically opposed conceptions have been applied to characterize the same developments in the same societies and that they co-exist so peacefully in modern social science. It is even more intriguing that a third point of view, the Marxist view — which to a certain extent disagrees with both — should have been able to assert, or to re-assert, itself and that it too should have found a legitimate place in contemporary social science, gaining in popularity and stature in recent years.

The Marxist view

The point of departure for this school of thought is Marx's idea — as expressed most forcefully in the *Communist Manifesto* (1973, p. 33) — that 'The executive of the modern state is but a committee for managing the common affairs of the whole bourgeoisie.' As Ralf Miliband (1973) points out, although Marx in some of his other writings refined and qualified this view, he never abandoned it.

To this, contemporary Marxists add the distinction between governing and ruling. Governing, they say, concerns the execution of the day-to-day routine work of administration and decision-making that makes the political process run smoothly. Ruling, on the other hand, implies the holding of decisive power which constrains the political process and determines how it will be run and in whose interests. It makes little difference who *governs* in modern capitalist society; in any event it is the bourgeoisie, the capitalist class, that *rules*; the governing group (frequently referred to as the state apparatus) merely serves the interests of the ruling capitalist class. Indeed, adds Nicos Poulantzas, the state best serves the interests of the ruling class when the latter is not a governing class and does not participate in the routine, day-to-day running of the political system.

Before the advent and maturation of capitalism, Miliband points out, government was in the hands of the aristocracy. Today, in most Western capitalist countries, the capitalist class still has a significant share in manning the state apparatus, although it does not monopolize it to the same extent that the aristocracy did in an earlier age. But even though the capitalist class does not govern exclusively, it still rules exclusively, and thus the basic situation is as it was: the political system still works overwhelmingly to promote the ruling class's interests.

The state apparatus has a relative autonomy *vis-à-vis* the ruling class, but this itself works in the interests of that same ruling class. This is so since the state can only serve the common interests of the ruling class as a whole in so far as it is not exclusively committed to any of the diverse and frequently warring factions of that class. It is precisely this relative objectivity of the state which enables it to organize the hegemony of this class as a whole (Miliband, 1973, Poulantzas, 1975).

Some Marxists agree with the elitists that the power of governments has been growing in recent years, but add that this, too, has benefited none other than the capitalist ruling class. Some Marxists further agree with some of the elitists' view that – to put it bluntly – democracy is little better than a sham, designed to lend the public a sense of power without actual power. The electoral system (as Miliband, 1973, pp. 63–4, sees it) gives people the illusion that insurmountable cleavages between parties exist and that momentous issues are at stake:

> The assertion of such profound differences is a matter of great importance for the functioning and legitimation of the political system, since it suggests that electors, by voting for one or other of the main competing parties, are making a choice between fundamental and incompatible alternatives, and that they are therefore, as voters, deciding nothing less than the future of their country.

In actual fact, however, there is a basic consensus among all political parties: they all work within the general confines of the capitalist system.

> What is really striking about *these* political leaders and political office-holders, is not their many differences but the extent of their agreement on truly fundamental issues . . . the political office-holders of advanced capitalism have, with very few exceptions, been agreed over . . . the existing economic and social system of private ownership.

This being the case, it really makes very little difference who people vote for and which party is elected. In any case the victor will perpetuate the capitalist system no less than his defeated opponent.[8]

Actual developments: the growth of government power

The difficulties which beset the testing of theories in other areas, permeate the political area as well. But like politics in practice, the testing of political theories is the art of the possible and it is with the realization of what is possible that the following pages are concerned.

Perhaps the least equivocal data concern the development of government power. Political power has been defined as the ability to control or influence the allocation of resources — which affect people's life chances — through the political process. It will be seen that Western governments have increased their ability to do so through centralization and rationalization of the governmental process, by branching out into a wider range of activities and by gaining more control over more effective means of (military) coercion.

The centralization of government power

Scholars of all three schools of thought would undoubtedly agree that the transition from medieval feudalism to the absolutism of early modernity, marked a clear centralization of power in the hands of West-European governments. Despite large differences between various countries, it may be said in very general terms that in medieval times, Western Europe was characterized by a decentralized system of political rule. This was necessitated by the poor systems of communication, furthered by the relative self-sufficiency of the local agricultural economy, and buttressed by the feudal system of stratification. Because of the poor communications, the stability of society depended largely on the ability of the feudal lords to maintain order. But this ability also made it possible for them to resist the encroachments of the crown into their domains of power (Crossman, 1939, pp. 13-19). The feudal lords thus maintained quasi-autonomous socio-political units of which they were not only the economic masters, but the political masters as well. The Catholic church was centralized to a much greater extent, but within the various political domains, it served to countervail the power of the secular rulers; it therefore had a decentralizing rather than a centralizing effect on each domain's internal power structure.

Thus the feudal system was based on an uneasy balance of power and on intermittent power struggles among three centres of power: the crown, the great feudal lords and the church. In this power struggle the crown did not necessarily emerge as the victor on all or even most occasions. It was only with the beginning of modernization that the balance gradually shifted in favour of the crown: as the king's power successively increased, that of the church gradually decreased, while that of the feudal nobility was increasingly bent to the king's purpose. This is not to say that the power of the aristocracy was eliminated, but rather that it was increasingly incorporated into the structure of the state and became one of its major bases.

In this way, a two-sided process of the centralization of power occurred: a process of territorial centralization whereby quasi-independent feudal domains became incorporated into the state[9] and a process of functional centralization, whereby military, administrative, judicial and other functions previously carried out independently by these domains' feudal lords, successively came to be monopolized by the states' central governments. In these, the descendants of those same feudal lords now filled the top-ranking, most powerful positions. This change, summarized here in a few words only, was actually an exceedingly complex and protracted process that lasted for several centuries and culminated in the emergence of the European territorial nation-state with its centralized government and absolute ruler. By the end of the sixteenth century, Western Europe included a number of such states and absolutism was firmly entrenched, developing further in the seventeenth and eighteenth centuries.

While popular representative institutions had been gradually developing by that time, the key turning point for most absolutist regimes came towards the end of the eighteenth century, following the French Revolution, its repercussions and aftermath throughout the Western world. It is from this time on and throughout the nineteenth century that democratic institutions seriously encroached on the power of absolutist rulers (see chapter 7). Does this mean, however, that the process of centralization of government power was now reversed?

The evolution of the modern state administration
It is at this point that the modern state bureaucracy comes in. For while absolutism brought about the gradual development of a large, modern bureaucratic state administration — to replace the limited, small-scale administration of the medieval ruler — the subsequent decline of absolutism did not effect a reversal of that trend. Indeed, the bureaucratic administration continued to grow and develop as absolutism declined. It not only did so with the evolution of democracy in the nineteenth century, but has continued to do so well into the twentieth century, and it is apparently still in a process of growth. For instance, in the United States, the number of civilian employees of the federal government has gone steadily up for the last century and a half:

Year	Number of employees
1821	7,000
1861	37,000
1901	239,000
1941	1,438,000
1974	2,866,000

Source: Lenski and Lenski (1978), p. 311.

Moreover, this growth is far outdistancing the growth of the population as a whole. While the latter has increased twenty-fold, the former shot up four-hundred-fold. Also, while in 1929 the civilian employees of the American government[10] comprised 6·8 per cent of the total American labour force, they comprised 17·8 per cent of that force in 1973 (Chirot, 1977, p. 195). Similar trends are reported in other countries. In France, for example, civil servants increased from 3·7 per cent of the labour force in 1866 to 16·7 per cent in 1962 (Lenski and Lenski, 1978, p. 474).

The bureaucratic administration has become a most powerful tool of the modern, Western, democratic state (just as it has become a powerful tool of the modern communist state). So much so, in fact, that some observers believe that modern bureaucracy has turned from an instrument of power to a master in its own right — frequently deferred to rather than utilized by modern governments.

But whether politicians rule bureaucrats, or top bureaucrats rule politicians or whether (as seems most plausible) they both wield interlocking power — is not crucial for the present discussion. In any event, it is clear that the modern bureaucracy can accomplish more of whatever it is meant to accomplish than any state administration ever could before and that this has greately augmented government control over the allocation of resources, i.e., government power.

The rationalization of government power
This is so, among other things, because the expansion of the modern government bureaucracy no less than the centralization of government activities, marks a trend of rationalization, that is, of growing efficiency and effectiveness of the government functions. Thus, centralization brought about greater uniformity. Diverse practices based on local customs were gradually replaced by standardized procedures based on state-wide laws and regulations, which simplified the government's tasks and thereby rendered their execution more effective.

This process was interrelated with and enhanced by the development of the modern state bureaucracy. For not only did this bureaucracy grow, but it also became more rational and effective, approaching, to a much greater extent than before, Weber's ideal-type model of bureaucracy with its clear hierarchy, formal, impersonal and standard regulations, and a clear-cut division of functions among its personnel. Although Weber has been criticized for overemphasizing the rational aspects of modern bureaucracy, and although bureaucracy itself has been criticized for its alleged rigidity, it can hardly be doubted that modern bureaucracy is more rational and effective than whatever haphazard administrations existed in earlier periods. This is not to say, however, that the further proliferation of bureaucracy, especially in the twentieth century, inevitably adds any further to this effectiveness, as the optimum of bureaucratic effectiveness may well have been passed by this time. The recent growth of bureaucracy, however, is related to another aspect of growing government power: its increased pervasiveness.

The growing pervasiveness of government activity

The volume of activities undertaken by modern governments is greater than that undertaken by any previous government, and the range of such activities is broader than it ever was before. Modern governments tend to penetrate spheres that in pre-modern societies would have been considered completely outside the scope of their jurisdiction. This expansion becomes evident from the persistent rise in government expenditure. For instance, in the United States public (all levels of government) expenditure rose from 7 per cent of GNP in 1890 to 21·3 per cent in 1932 and to 33 per cent in 1974. In the United Kingdom such expenditure rose from 8.9 per cent of GNP in 1890 to 38 per cent in the 1960s (see Musgrave, 1969, p. 92; and Chirot, 1977, p. 194).

The general trend of proliferating government activity is most clearly evident in its growing intervention in the economic sphere. Some government intervention in the economy was prevalent in Europe in the eighteenth century, during the period of mercantilism, but was reduced to some extent during the period of nineteenth-century *laissez-faire* (see chapter 4). It was revived once more, and to a much greater extent, towards the end of the nineteenth century, and even more so during the twentieth. For instance, Galbraith (1967) reports that in the United States, federal, state and local government activity accounted for 8 per cent of economic activity in 1929, and for about 25 per cent of that activity in 1967. The government's share in economic activity has grown to a similar extent in other Western countries.

Government activity has branched out into other spheres as well. For instance, during the Middle Ages education (or what little of it there was) was carried out exclusively by the Catholic church. Only in modern society has education been taken over by the state. Although in many Western countries parallel religious and/or private educational systems continue to exist, the modern state now carries the main responsibility for funding, planning and carrying out the education of the bulk of the young population (see chapter 8). Other activities taken over by the modern government include welfare, sanitation, and lately, in many Western countries (though not in all) health services as well.

It has been claimed that this expansion of the government's activities has caused an 'overload' and detracted from its ability to govern: government activity has therefore become not more, but less, rational and effective. The contrary claim would be, however, that with the growth in the government's responsibilities in many areas came what is merely the other side of the coin – the growth of government control over what is provided in each of these areas. Overloaded or not, the government thus has control over more resources and hence over the growing numbers of people whose life chances are dependent on these resources. As more and more people obtain more and more services provided by the government, their lives are also increasingly affected – some would say interfered with – by the government agencies that furnish those services. As greater numbers of people are employed by the government; as an increasing percentage of people have their economic activities, education, welfare and health monitored by the government, they also become more dependent on it for their livelihood, and in some cases (i.e., health services) for their very lives.

The growth of military power
Yet another aspect of the augmentation of government is the growth of its military potential. This is evident not only in the monopolization of the means of violence, which were previously dispersed among feudal lords, and in the growing effectiveness of these means of violence, due to technological development, but also in the absolute and relative growth of the military, as a government organization parallel to, and no less important than the civilian administration.

Throughout the medieval period, most people lived for most of their lives completely outside the confines of the military and the rulers were quite limited in the type of armed forces they could summon up. From the eleventh and twelfth centuries onwards, when the most embryonic form of the modern state began to develop, the king or prince depended mainly on the military forces mobilized by his vassals. Those, however, were quite restricted in the time-span of their obligatory service. The ruler's own army was usually small and temporary as well. If he wished for a permanent, standing army, he had to resort to mercenaries. Those, however, had to be paid and the ruler was usually limited in the funds at his disposal. In the days of absolutism there still was no compulsory conscription and even Napoleon was restrained in the numbers of men he could induct into the army (Jouvenel, 1952).

This is in marked contrast to the situation in recent times, when compulsory conscription has been introduced whenever deemed necessary by the government, usually (except for the most recent years) without effective protest from the public. Even where there is at present no compulsory conscription, governments continue to maintain sizeable, well-equipped, standing armies. For instance, in the United States the federal military forces comprised 142,000 men in 1909, reached a high of 3,408,000 in 1968 — during the Vietnam War — and then settled to the respectable number of 2,202,000 men in 1973 (Chirot 1977, p. 195).

Ostensibly, the military power amassed by the modern government in both weaponry and personnel is aimed at foreign enemies. But actually it can be used to fulfil domestic functions as well. Internal military coercion is probably used more sparingly in Western democracies as compared with most alternative regimes. But the potential of military intervention to quell possible insurrections is certainly there and cannot fail to buttress government power. Indeed, it is not very far-fetched to assume — as Key (1958) does — that non-violent methods for the settlement of political conflict often work because of the implicit threat of government coercion in the background.

The growth of government power — an explanation

How can this growth of government power be explained? It seems that several interrelated, economic and non-economic factors may be held accountable for this development.

Economic factors
The general process of economic development which marked the advent

of capitalism and the attendant improvement in the systems of communication both required and facilitated the growth of state power. Most important, however, was the development of taxation, which itself was closely related to the general trend of economic development. As Jouvenel (1952) points out, neither the centralization of government functions nor the expansion of government intervention, nor the unprecedented growth in the state's administration and the military, could have come about without the increase in the government's economic potential through the development of taxation.

In medieval times the ruler usually could not marshall the funds for extensive government operations. He was limited mainly to the revenue that accrued from his own land. When under major pressure, for instance because of war, he could turn to the church and, if the latter concurred with the objectives of his campaign, it would hand over to him a certain percentage of its own revenues for a limited period of time. Another source of revenue were the cities, where the rudiments of taxation were pioneered. But all these sources were usually insufficient and the medieval ruler was habitually under much financial pressure, and therefore very limited in what he could accomplish.

In the thirteenth and fourteenth centuries the kings increased the pressure on various segments of the population for the extraction of payments at progressively shorter intervals. However, such payments had to be consented to by the people. Hence the kings were obliged to visit the major population centres periodically in order to convince the people to make their monetary contributions. As parliaments developed, the rulers succeeded in mobilizing them for the extraction of taxes from the public. But in return they had to make various concessions to their demands in the matter of policy and justice.

Eventually, taxes turned into a permanent feature of political life, but even at the peak of absolutism, the public's resistance to the payment of taxes was strong, and a continuous struggle on this issue was taking place between that public and the monarchy. Indeed, dues and taxes of all kinds which were imposed on the peasantry were one of the prime causes of the French Revolution. It is only with the advent of democracy that the public reluctantly acquiesced in the paying of taxes. Hence, in the twentieth century, taxation soared (as is illustrated by Table 6.1). Only in recent years have some taxpayers' revolts been evident especially in the United States. But there are no signs as yet that they have led to a reversal of the trend of growing taxation.

While growing taxation was of overriding importance in increasing the *ability* of the modern government to expand its activity, the

Table 6.1 *Taxation increase in two Western countries (expressed as a percentage of the GNP)*

	US internal revenue collections	Australian Commonwealth taxation collection
1880–1	1·3	
1900–1	1·7	
1902–3		4·2
1930–1	3·3	
1932–3		8·6
1957–8	18·2	
1960–1		17·1
1970–1		19·3

Source: Compiled and computed from: US Bureau of the Census (1960, F. 1, p. 21; Y. 264, p. 279); Australian Commonwealth Bureau of Census and Statistics (1971, pp. 1042, 1044).

differentiation and increasing complexity of the economy and the growing specialization in the occupational structure were important in increasing the *demand* for such activity. As various theorists have pointed out (see chapter 2), developments such as these necessitate mechanisms of reintegration; the government emerged as the most suitable body for this task of overall co-ordination.

Ideological factors: the development of the nation-state

Although this may not seem evident at first glance, another explanation for the augmentation of government power may be found in the development of the modern nation-state. In medieval Europe there existed the rather weak supernational empire on the one hand and the sub-national or non-national minute political unit on the other hand. Towards the end of the medieval period, as the empire disintegrated and the smaller units were increasingly integrated into the larger political entity, their many languages were incorporated into, or replaced by, a single national langue. This language then became the carrier of the new national culture and both together became the identifying marks of the nation. The nation in turn became the focus of intense identification (Berger, 1971, p. 27). In this manner the first European nation-states emerged in France, Spain and England. By the sixteenth century, several European political entities had emerged as nation-states; others were added throughout the following centuries through the unification of smaller ones (for instance, in Italy towards the end of the nineteenth century) and through the dismantling of the Austro-Hungarian Empire following the First World War. Today practically all Western states are variations on the nation-state.

The importance of this development for the increase of state power lies in the ability of the nation-state to mobilize a much higher level of commitment of its citizens than any prior political unit was capable of doing. It is this type of national-political identification (or patriotism if you will) that apparently makes citizens willing (or at least less unwilling) to serve the state, for example, through increased taxation or military conscription, while it also makes people more willing to accept the government's decrees in matters of resource allocation and to adopt its leaders as figures of authority.

It has sometimes been claimed that, in recent years, nationalism has lost in importance in the Western world. In fact, however, the evidence does not support this conclusion. Wherever different national minorities have been incorporated into one state this has been a source of conflict or at least pressure to change, as the case of the United Kingdom eloquently illustrates. While in the United States (and possibly in other Western democracies as well) young people have become wary of compulsory conscription, in general the allegiance of citizens to their states is apparently still stronger than it was before those states could draw on nationalism for their legitimation.

Ideological factors: the advent of democracy

Paradoxically, another explanation for the increase of government power especially with the advent of democracy has been given in terms of that democracy itself. Musgrave (1969, p. 86), for instance, claims that the transition to democratic government changed the public's perspective as to what it was entitled to and hence strengthened the public's effective demand for government services such as for job training, unemployment assistance, recreational facilities, geriatric care and the like. The provision of an increasing number of such services by the government, carries with it, as we have seen, as an inevitable correlate, the augmentation of its control over how these services are allocated, hence the augmentation of its power.

It has also been claimed (Jouvenel, 1952) that as long as the people felt that they were ruled by the alien forces of absolutism they would not entrust the state with excessive power and they opposed, to the best of their ability, any moves on part of the ruler which might conceivably result in the augmentation of such power. But with the advent of democracy, people came to feel that they themselves were now the masters of their rulers. Consequently, they no longer feared the increment of government power and even welcomed it. Hence it is under the cloak of democracy that governments have been able to amass more power than any government could have hoped to have acquired before.

Government power and interest groups

Whether or not this explanation is accepted, it would seem in any event that the growth of government power with the transition to democracy and especially in recent years, runs counter to the pluralist perspective. What, however, about the various countervailing interest groups, pressure groups or 'veto groups' on which the pluralist thesis largely builds its case?

It is clear, on the one hand, that interaction between governments and various representatives of organized interests have taken place all through history. Estates, guilds, professional organizations and local communities were some of the more recent forerunners of modern interest groups. It is also clear, on the other hand, that the increasing heterogeneity and complexity in modern society implies the multiplication of specialized interests and is therefore reflected in the unprecedented proliferation of groups representing such interests (Key, 1958, ch. 6).

In America, for instance, Key (1958, pp. 142-3) proceeds, interest groups have existed since the founding of the Republic; yet the great proliferation of such groups came in the twentieth century:

Specialization has as its corollary interdependence; interdependence has as its consequence friction. New cleavages produced new frictions and put to government new problems in the mediation of conflicts born of the new relations among interests within society . . . . Increased specialization almost inevitably means increased governmental intervention to control the relations among groups. In turn, governmental intervention or its threat, stimulates the formation of organized groups by those who begin to sense a shared interest . . . . Organization begets counter organization . . . . The upshot of these processes has been the erection of an impressive system of agencies . . . for the representation of group interests before Congress and other governmental agencies. Perhaps around

500 organizations [now] have a continuing interest in national policy and legislation.

In other words, some of the very factors that brought about increased government intervention and therefore increased governmental power are also the factors that brought about the proliferation of interest groups. These now include such diverse groups as business and industrial organizations, for example, in the United States, the Chamber of Commerce of the United States, the National Association of Manufacturers, farmers' organizations (for example, the National Farmers' Union), labour organizations (for example, the AFL-CIO), religious and/or ethnic organizations, veterans' organizations and many others.

But the increase in the number of interest groups does not necessarily spell an increase in their power. Indeed, to the extent that interest groups multiply, some of them may well countervail each others' pressures thereby granting the government greater leeway in exercising its power than would otherwise have been the case.

Moreover, interest groups clearly have a bias built into them. Although in some manner they channel influence from 'below', they do not necessarily do so in a representative fashion. For not all interests are organized and represented; at the extreme, some elements of the population may be entirely excluded from representing their interests in matters that deeply concern them, or else may be at a relative disadvantage in doing so, while others – especially the more prosperous, the more articulate, the better organized, the ones that have a leverage over crucial resources – are at a distinct advantage. Like the ruling elites themselves, interest groups are thus skewed in favour of the most powerful sections of the community (McConnell, 1967, p. 7).

Consequently, one may safely assume power differentials, or even a power hierarchy of interest groups. The most powerful groups, those at the top of the pyramid, those whose power is truly compelling and relates to the country's most central policy issues and is not cancelled out by opposing pressures – these probably are as few today as they were in the past. Furthermore, there is no evidence to support the thesis that they have become more powerful than they had been and that they have thereby eroded the government's power to a greater extent than they did in earlier periods.

Assuming, then, that some of the lesser pressure groups may well cancel each other out, that the power of some select pressure groups is great but has not necessarily been increasing, and that the power of governments, on the other hand, has very clearly been growing, we must conclude that the elitist and the Marxist schools have a stronger case than the pluralist school, and that the power of governments has indeed been increasing as over that of countervailing groups.

The changing composition of the ruling elites

Who, however, are those who man those governments and control their policies, that is, the ruling elites — and from what classes are they recruited? Both the elitists and the Marxists concur that in all Western, capitalist countries the ruling elites (or the state apparatuses) have been recruited overwhelmingly from the privileged classes, and that in recent years this tendency has been mitigated to some extent, but has not been abolished. Historical and contemporary empirical analysis supports this view, while at the same time pointing to some differences between countries.

Up until the French Revolution, political elites in Western countries were recruited mainly from the aristocracy. The bourgeoisie (not to mention the working class) was effectively excluded. Indeed, it has been claimed that the capitalist class's inability to gain a foothold in the political elite was one of the main factors which triggered the Revolution. Since the bourgeoisie was a major power in the Revolution, it gained substantial benefits from it: in France, its representation in the ruling elite was patently increased, but the working class was still excluded for a long time to come.

In Britain during the nineteenth century representation in the political elite was still largely monopolized by the aristocracy, although the capitalist class was gradually beginning to make some inroads. For instance, in 1840 over 72 per cent of the members of the House of Commons were landholders and some 8 per cent were manufacturers (Putnam, 1976, ch. 7). The composition of cabinet at that time is illustrated by the following table:

Table 6.2 *The social structure of cabinet membership, 1830–68*

Large territorial lords and their sons	56
Country gentlemen (lesser landowners)	12
Mercantile and administrative upper class (mainly rentiers)	21
'New men' (mostly lawyers)	14
Total	103

Source: Guttsman (1963), p. 38.

Clearly, at that time there was no effective working-class representation in Britain either, and this holds for both the parliament and the cabinet. Only towards the end of the century did the first Labour candidates win admission to the House; even then, and for some years to come, their numbers were negligible. The Labour Party itself was not established until 1900 and the first Labour government was not formed until the 1920s.

Even when Labour came to power, its representatives were not necessarily working-class people themselves. Nevertheless, class representation in the political elite shifted to some extent. For instance, while in 1840 the dominant classes accounted for over 85 per cent of the House of Commons (over 72 per cent landholders and some 8 per cent capitalists) and workers were not represented at all, this was no longer so at the beginning of the twentieth century. By 1911 the propertied classes accounted for about 63 per cent of parliament (some 25 per cent landholders and some 38 per cent capitalists) and by the 1920s workers had roughly a 22 per cent share of the House (Putnam, 1976, pp. 174-5). While the working class had not been represented in cabinet throughout the years 1868-86, it accounted for 21 per cent of all cabinet members throughout the years 1935-55, and for 14 per cent throughout the years 1955-70 (Guttsman, 1963, p. 242; Putnam, 1976, p. 177). Also, in all Labour cabinets from 1927 until 1950, over half of the members have been of working-class background, and in 1951 and 1970, 37 and 26 per cent respectively of Labour members of parliament were actually manual workers (Butler and Pinto-Duschinsky, 1971, p. 303).

In nineteenth-century America, as in Britain, the ruling elite was composed mainly of the socio-economically advantaged. But unlike their British counterparts, American political leaders have not been exclusively the representatives of the dominant classes proper – either landowners or capitalists – and have been recruited to a much larger extent from the professions. Admittedly, professionals who became members of the ruling elites were disproportionally successful and affluent; but they were still professionals rather than capitalists. This can be seen from Table 6.3, as compared to Table 6.2.

A similar situation still prevails. Top leaders in government are still recruited predominantly from the legal profession (56.1 per cent), from government itself (16·7 per cent), and from education (10·6 per cent) (Dye and Zeigler, 1975, ch. 4). At the same time, the American system still favours people with ample means. For instance, 28 per cent of United States senators have a net worth of one million US dollars or more, compared to 0·3 per cent of such millionaires in the general population (Lenski and Lenski, 1978, p. 339). Here, too, working-class people have recently gained a foothold: 18 per cent of the American legislative elite has recently been composed of people from working-class backgrounds. But even today the majority of that elite is still composed of people from middle- and upper-class families.

Table 6.3 *United States presidents, vice-presidents and cabinet members' initial occupations (in percentages)*

	1789-1824	1825-76	1877-1934
Professionals	77	89	81
Proprietors and managers	13	8	13
Large landowners	8	2	0
Other farmers	2	0	2
Clerical and manual workers	0	1	3
Total	100	100	99

Source: Putnam (1976), p. 187.

Similar tendencies are apparent in other Western countries: in Italy and West Germany persons of working-class background have recently made up 36 and 30 per cent respectively of these countries' legislative elites. But penetration into top government positions has been more modest: In France and West Germany, from the late 1940s up until 1960, only 7 and 11 per cent respectively of all cabinet members were of working-class background (Putnam, 1976, pp. 23, 177).

It must be concluded, then, that working-class people have made some inroads into the system, but ruling elites are still drawn disproportionately from the privileged classes and the higher the rank, the smaller the representation of the working class.

Contrary to what is sometimes claimed, however, elites' class backgrounds tell us little about the interests which these elites represent. Some Marxist empirical studies (for example, Connell, 1977), have endeavoured to show that the ruling elites or state apparatuses do, in fact, promote the capitalist class's interests, thereby turning it into a ruling class. Other studies, however (for example, Etzioni-Halevy, 1979), have endeavoured to show that ruling elites serve basically their own interests, and that in some cases they even exploit the capitalist classes so as to promote those interests. The issue thus still awaits conclusive empirical evidence. In the meantime it can only be said that the increase in government power (dealt with above) may have benefited the capitalist classes. But there is no reason to believe that it has not given an added leverage to the ruling elites as well.

Selected readings

Dahl, R. (1956), *A Preface to Democratic Theory*, University of Chicago Press.
Domhoff, G. W. (1967), *Who Rules America?*, Englewood Cliffs, N.J., Prentice-Hall.
Dye, T. R., and Zeigler, L. H. (1975), *The Irony of Democracy* (3rd edn), North Scituate, Mass., Duxbury Press.
Etzioni, A., and Etzioni-Halevy, E. (eds) (1973), *Social Change* (2nd edn), New York, Basic Books, chs 4, 14, 22.
Mills, C. W. (1959), *The Power Elite*, New York, Oxford University Press.
Poulantzas, N. (1975), *Political Power and Social Classes* (trans. T. O'Hagen), London, New Left Books.

7 · The advent and maturation of the modern polity (B): public participation and political manipulation

It was argued above that the increasing power of Western governments and elites has not been countervailed by pressure groups to a greater extent than previously. But has it perhaps been countervailed by growing political participation of the rank-and-file public? The basic principle of democracy is that the power of the rulers is legitimate so long as it is exercised with the consent of the ruled, as expressed through free elections and other mechanisms of political participation and representation. Have Western democracies in fact realized this principle to a greater extent than previous regimes? And have they done so to a greater extent as they matured? The pluralist-democratic model claims that this has in fact been the case, while the elitist and Marxist models oppose this claim. Which of these views is supported by actual developments?

Consent and participation

One of the most important developments that took place with the advent of democracy is the evolution of the principle of consent itself. Previously, the possession of power carried with it only a limited obligation to render account for the manner in which it was exercised, and often no obligation at all.

In medieval Europe the prevailing concept was of power and authority as deriving from the law, and from a contract between the ruler and the ruled. This implied the notion that if the ruler did not uphold the law, his rule was illegitimate and if he did not fulfil his obligation towards those he ruled, they need not fulfil theirs towards him. Also, because of poor communications, the medieval ruler depended on local feudal lords for administration and the raising of soldiers. Those whose help was vital to the ruler were in turn able to insist that laws or taxes not be imposed without their consent. The principle of consent was thus implied in theory and necessitated in practice. But this was a very rudimentary version of the principle.

Later, during the period of absolutism, even this principle was superseded by the doctrine of the divine right of kings, and the rulers' demands for the absolute obedience of their subjects to that divinity. This new conception of sovereignty developed in France towards the end of the sixteenth century and was introduced to England by James I. 'Kings', he wrote, 'are breathing images of God.'[1] And just as God does not owe His rule to the consent of the ruled, it now became unnecessary for monarchs to do so. The doctrine of the divine right of kings thus furnished the legitimation for the centralization of power and for the monarch's absolute rule.

Only the breakup of this regime led to the actual development of the doctrine of consent as expressed, for instance, in the American Declaration of Independence and in the French Declaration of the Rights of Man.[2] The American Second Continental Congress (held on 14 July 1776), for instance, made the following declaration:

We hold these truths to be self-evident that all men are created equal, that they are endowed by their Creator with certain inalienable Rights, that among these are Life, Liberty, and the pursuit of Happiness. That to secure these rights, Governments are instituted among men, deriving their just powers from the consent of the governed.

Thus the principle of consent was now explicitly formulated and formally adopted, and it became the central basis for the legitimation of the power of democratic governments. Moreover, a variety of bodies, procedures and mechanisms came into being whose rationale was to translate this principle into practice through the facilitation of public participation in politics. Foremost among these were the development of freedom of information and organization and the development of representative institutions and elections.

Information and organization

Two basic prerequisites for effective political participation of the public and hence for translating the principle of consent into practice are the possibility of gaining information on what is going on in the political centre and the possibility to organize for political action to either support or oppose those occurrences. Like the adoption of the principle of consent itself — the substantial realization of both of these possibilities is a rather recent phenomenon.

The mass media and freedom of information

At present most of our daily information on the occurrences in the
political arena derives from the mass media of communication or from
informal communication which — in turn — relays and interprets the
messages of the media for us. In the absence of such media in pre-
modern society, the rank-and-file public was thus only sparsely informed
on politics. This situation changed first through certain technological
developments such as printing and improvements in transportation
which made the appearance and circulation of newspapers possible.
Later on it changed even more drastically with the more modern
techniques for collecting news, printing and distribution of papers, and
the appearance of a much larger literate public (see next chapter)
which ensured a dramatic growth in circulation,[3] and finally with the
invention of radio and television which vastly accelerated and further
increased the circulation of news.

What was important, however, were not only the technological
breakthroughs which facilitated the development of the media. No less
significant was the increasing freedom from government interference
which the media came to enjoy in Western democracies. Freedom of
speech and of the press was considered as a basic democratic right and
was widely supported in the first half of the nineteenth century; it was
often embodied in the new written constitutions of Europe.[4] But the
actual realization of this right did not come at once. For instance in
France, although the Declaration of the Rights of Man, adopted
immediately before the Revolution, called for freedom of the press, the
press was still heavily censored and controlled until roughly the middle
of the nineteenth century. Only in the second half of that century were
the press controls gradually relaxed and only in 1881 were special laws
enacted to safeguard the press from government interference. In
Britain, too, laws limiting freedom of speech and of the press were only
gradually reformed. The Reform Bill of 1832 attenuated some of the
restrictions on the freedom of the press, but limitations against the
publication of libel, obscenity, treason, etc., continued. Only a later
succession of laws clarified the legal meaning of these phenomena,
thereby reducing the incidence of legal repression.

It was only with this reduction of legal repression, mostly during
the second half of the nineteenth century, that the press began to
publicize the inside machinations, intrigues, corruption and other
disreputable facts about the ruling elites. It was then that public indig-

nation first rose to such a high pitch as to force resignations, dismissals and even trials of leading politicians. At this time, then, the political significance of what today is commonly referred to as 'public opinion' made itself felt on the political scene of all Western countries, to a greater extent than before (Thompson, 1967, pp. 369-75).

Some recent sociological research has come to the conclusion that there are certain limitations to the impact of the media on public opinion. Other research has shown that despite wide exposure to the media, large proportions of the public are still ignorant of the more complex political issues. Also, doubts have arisen as to the extent to which the absence of legal restraints, that is, the formal freedom of the media, has brought about actual freedom of the media as well (see below). However, even cynical observers can hardly doubt that since the end of the nineteenth century, both media and public opinion have had a greater impact on the political scene than they did earlier.

The freedom of organization and direct action

The freedom of speech and of the press could not have carried much weight, had it not been accompanied by the development of the freedom of association and organization. This was also regarded as an inherent right of democracy; but it, too, was only gradually realized, mostly towards the end of the nineteenth century. In Britain, the right to freedom of association came to be legally accepted only in 1871; in France, freedom of association was granted only in 1884 and it was only shortly before the end of the nineteenth century that freedom of association was securely recognized in all Scandinavian and Western states (Thomson, 1967, p. 369).

It has been claimed that in several Western democracies certain limitations on the freedom of organization, formally or informally, continued to prevail even afterwards. As an example, limitations on communist organization in the United States, especially during the McCarthy era, are frequently cited. But in a wider perspective these may be seen as aberrations of the general principle of freedom of association, which still prevails in Western democracies to a greater extent than in previous or other contemporary regimes.

Closely related to the freedom of organization is the development of actual, anti-establishment political organization. This led to the introduction of protest, demonstrations, or what is usually referred to as 'direct action' as a common manner of waging political conflict.

Instances of rebellions and riots can be cited from various chapters of history. But only in modern Western societies has direct action become a more or less integral part of the political scene.

The role of direct action in Western society is illustrated in Britain by the Wilkes movement in the second half of the eighteenth century, which agitated for freedom of the press and parliamentary reforms. This movement utilized a wide range of methods which have since become common forms of protest, and it marked an evolution from sporadic rioting towards organized conflict. Other well-known protest movements in Britain include Luddism and Chartism. In America, the efforts of impoverished farmers, industrial workers and immigrant groups to establish basic social and economic rights have similarly involved many instances of civil disobedience and riots (see chapter 4). Also significant was the suffragette movement which pressed for the enfranchisement of women in various Western countries, especially at the beginning of the twentieth century. Recently, the best-known instances of direct action are the civil rights movement and anti-Vietnam protest in America, and student protest in American and in various Western countries in the 1960s, as well as the women's and homosexuals' liberation movements.

Some observers regard direct action of this kind (especially when non-violent) as legitimate and even desirable within a democratic framework, while others perceive it (even when non-violent) as threatening the basic institutions of democracy. But whether one approves of them in principle, or not, it is clear that many of the protest actions and movements — while themselves facilitated by more permissive attitudes of political establishments towards anti-establishment organizations — have played significant roles in furthering the freedom of such organizations, as well as other civil liberties, parliamentary-electoral reforms and the improvement of social conditions. Recent protest movements have apparently played no less significant roles, for example, in the termination of the Vietnam War, in promoting civil rights legislation for blacks and in (at least partial) school desegregation in the United States. Legitimate or not, then, it is a clear instance of an avenue of public political participation that has opened up and has increasingly been utilized in modern Western societies.

The development of representative institutions

In contrast to direct action whose democratic legitimacy has sometimes been questioned, the development of representative institutions — parliamentary assemblies and political parties — has been widely acclaimed as one of the foremost achievements of Western democracies.

Parliamentary assemblies

In principle, it would seem, parliaments can exist as representative institutions only when their members are elected by those they are supposed to represent. Historically, however, parliaments antedated modern elections. The first parliamentary assemblies developed in Western Europe in the late medieval period. (In England, for instance, the parliament dates from the second half of the thirteenth century.) But at that time they fulfilled mainly judicial functions, served as advisory councils or as consultative links between rulers and their subjects and took part in various bargaining processes on behalf of their communities and other interests.

Although in this sense assemblies had representative roles, at first this did not involve electoral representation. The power of such assemblies was rather meagre and membership of them was therefore considered a burden rather than a privilege. Hence there was no question of competing candidates standing for office. Only during the fourteenth and fifteenth centuries, when parliaments gained more political importance and membership of them became worth campaigning for, did competitive elections for parliamentary candidates develop. But, later on, parliamentary assemblies were overcome by absolutism. At the beginning of the seventeenth century, all continental West European countries had assemblies of estates, but by the end of that century most had been eliminated or reduced in power. In France the last Estates General until the Revolution met in 1615. In the Kingdom of Naples parliamentary proceedings ended in 1642. Towards the end of the seventeenth century absolute rule was re-established in Sweden. Only in England were the attempts of the monarchy, at the beginning of the seventeenth century, to curtail parliament's power unsuccessful.

In continental Western Europe the process of parliamentary decline was eventually reversed: the power of parliaments grew, in the wake of the French Revolution, and the monarchy was eventually supplanted by parliamentary government. In England the power of parliament asserted itself even further after the revolution of 1688. Until that time there had been a dual system in which parliament and the king had shared the responsibility of government. The revolution abolished this dualism; parliament became the dominant institution (Huntington, 1968). In the Australian colonies (to cite another example) legislative assemblies originally were appointed by the colonial governors and had very limited powers; but towards the middle of the nineteenth century their powers gradually increased to resemble those of their British counterpart. In the United States — according to Huntington — there was no place for either absolutism or parliamentary supremacy. But as authority was divided between Congress and the executive, the latter came to be an important part of the governmental structure as soon as this structure was set up — at the end of the eighteenth century.

Parliamentary power thus greatly gained in importance when the franchise was still restricted (see below). Hence the exercise of that power was still vested in the representatives of only a minority of the population. Only the extension of the franchise, especially towards the end of the nineteenth century and the beginning of the twentieth, towards universal suffrage brought about the final convergence between parliamentary government and popular representation.

Some observers claim that the power of parliaments had reached its peak in the latter half of the nineteenth century, when in many Western countries they gained the right to dismiss cabinets through no-confidence votes, and that their power shrank again precisely with the final extension of the franchise in the twentieth century. It is claimed that in many countries parliaments now mainly ratify government-initiated legislation and governmental decisions; thus serving as a 'rubber stamp' for the executive, and that their representative functions have thus shrunk, precisely at a time when their representative basis has widened.

However, the decline in parliamentary power and in its representative functions ought not to be exaggerated. The American Congress can certainly be seen to be a formidable countervailing power to that of the president; in other Western democracies government initiatives may also at times be defeated or amended by parliament; the need to maintain a supportive majority in parliament is still a major constraint under which Western governments operate; and no-confidence votes, although not routine, do occur occasionally.[5]

Moreover, that parliamentary power has indeed declined to some extent is due, in large measure, to the development of party discipline which now makes a government's majority in parliament safer than would previously have been the case.[6] Whatever diminution has occurred in parliamentary power may thus be traced back (at least in part) to the evolution of another type of representative institutions: political parties.

Political parties

Democratic political parties (defined here as durable organizations with distinct political programs, that compete for power peacefully through popular elections) are a very modern phenomenon. In contrast to parliamentary assemblies, parties of this kind, with a potential of forming an organized opposition against the government, are the product of the nineteenth and twentieth centuries. In 1800 they existed only in the United States; today they exist throughout the Western world.

Political opposition, and competition, are of course universal. But stable organizations for the institutionalization of opposition and the peaceful conduct of such competition have been rather rare in history. Temporary coalitions and alliances of one kind or another existed in ancient Athens and in Rome as well as in various medieval (for example Italian), political domains. But these groups were not very stable and frequently their competition was anything but peaceful. At the beginning of modernity there was hardly a place for competing and opposition parties, as long as monarchs claimed to rule by divine right and the only contribution they expected from their subjects was their unfailing obedience.

Political parties had scope for development only when rulers and ruling elites accepted the principle of having to legitimize their rule by popular consent, and the principle of the legitimacy of opposition to that rule. Not surprisingly, this change of attitude was not easily achieved, and came about only after a protracted struggle.

Once the ruling elites had accepted the development of political parties as legitimate (or perhaps as inevitable) they gradually came to utilize them as an instrument of mobilizing support for themselves, just as potential alternative elites did not fail to utilize them to mobilize opposition. But parties also became a most important instrument of public representation – since they structured alternatives which popular elections could resolve. They thus became, in S. M. Lipset's (1967, p. 48) words, 'by far the most important representative structure in complex democratic society'.

The first groups of this kind emerged in the eighteenth century. At that time rival parliamentary groups (to which the names Whigs and Tories were applied) came into being in Britain, and similar groups were formed in the Swedish parliament and later on in other Western parliaments as well. But these were still parliamentary factions rather than parties; they were based mainly on personalities, family ties or regional economic interests, and only to a minor extent (or not at all) on common political programs.Their full potential was not realized at the time and only retrospectively could they be recognized as embryonic forms of a party system that developed much later (James, 1974, ch. 2). The first groups that may accurately be referred to as parties, identified with political programs (or at least with political labels such as Democrats, Republicans, Conservatives, Liberals), emerged at the end of the eighteenth century in the United States and at the beginning of the nineteenth century in several other Western countries. But, mostly, these parties were still confined to parliamentary activity and their memberships were still greatly restricted.

It was after the middle of the nineteenth century, with the extension of the franchise, that parties, as concerted bodies, first vied with each other for support in elections. This entailed the formation of permanent organizations to collect funds, present programs and solicit votes. While the parties' leadership remained in the legislative assemblies, organized support now came from a wider number of participants. But party organizations were still weak, political programs less than binding, and lower class people — though solicited to vote — were deliberately left out. Only at the turn of the century did parties become identified with more binding political programs; party leadership became partly divorced from parliamentary status; members and activists were widely solicited and mass support was actively mobilized. According to most observers, it is at this point that parties — in their present format — emerged (Macridis, 1967).

The development of elections

Neither parliaments nor political parties could have acquired whatever significance they now have were it not for the development of elections, the central process of political participation and political conflict in a democracy. Elections are of such central importance because (when open, free and competitive) they are the only channel of political participation in which all citizens have an equal say, as opposed for instance to direct action, where an active, militant minority may outweigh a moderate, silent majority. Moreover, although the importance of elections is frequently belittled (see chapter 6), they still serve as the basic mechanism for waging conflicts over political power by certain, generally accepted rules. As such, they also serve as the basic mechanism for selecting the ruling elite and for holding it accountable for its performance through the constant, potential threat of replacement.

Perhaps it is for this very reason that the development of free, competitive elections in the Western world was in many ways an unprecedented phenomenon. Some elections had taken place in ancient times, for instance in Greek and Roman assemblies. But electorates did not include women and slaves, a sizeable part of the population. In medieval Europe some kinds of elections apparently survived at local levels and at regional assemblies. But the medieval, hierarchical feudal structures did not accommodate elections very well; in practice, most official positions came to be inherited. Moreover, in most countries absolutism put an end even to those feeble medieval electoral practices.

It was only from the seventeenth century onwards that modern-type elections developed. Several features characterized these elections: they came to be interlinked with representative institutions, including political parties competing for office (see above); they came to focus on the individual as the unit to be counted; they became increasingly free from harassment and intimidation and they developed towards universal suffrage and a large-scale participation.

Individual representation and deferential voting

The concept of individual representation through elections seems self-evident to us today, but was alien to pre-modern society. When parliamentary power was mainly a matter of bargaining with the crown, members of the assembly were regarded as the representatives of communities, local interests and estates rather than of individuals. From the seventeenth century onwards, parliament gradually reduced its representation of localities and took on a function as the collective representative of the nation on the one hand, and as the representative of individual rights on the other. In the United States senators and congressmen continued to owe their primary loyalties to their constituencies, but at the same time they came to represent their individual constituents as well (Huntington, 1968).

It was only when this conception of individual representation through parliament developed that elections by independent individuals seemed to make sense. Yet for some time to come it was still customary in many European countries, for people — even those few who had the franchise — to vote as directed by their powerful patrons, such as large-scale landowners and major employers. This practice, known as deferential voting, ensured that candidates for parliament still directly represented large-scale interests, rather than individual voters. Throughout the centuries this practice gradually diminished, but in Britain, for instance, it could still be found throughout most of the nineteenth century, and only towards the end of that century was it effectively abolished. It was only when this occurred that the principle of individual representation could effectively assert itself in practice. Another practice which aided the development of individual representation was the development of the secret ballot.

The secret ballot
Initially, elections were by an open voting system; this encouraged harassment and intimidation by actual or threatened violence, and thus the subjugation of individual voters to powerful interests. To eliminate this pressure the secret ballot was advocated. But for quite a number of years this proposal met stern resistance. For instance, in Britain the secret ballot was advocated as early as 1780, but the principle was invariably rejected by the House of Lords. The proposition met similar opposition of vested interests in Australia, for instance, ostensibly on the ground that it was unconstitutional and un-British for people to be secretive about their political leanings.

Despite this opposition, the ballot was pioneered in Victoria, Australia, in 1856.[7] The other Australian colonies rapidly followed and almost all had adopted it by the late 1850s. What came to be known as the Australian secret ballot[8] was introduced in Britain in 1872; towards the end of the nineteenth century it was adopted by most Western European countries; and by 1900 most American States had adopted the ballot as well.[9]

As shall be seen below, the secret ballot could not eliminate certain electoral malpractices. But in most cases it had a formidable success in eliminating intimidation and violence. Thus − observers agree − free elections could not have eventuated without the secret ballot, and were it not for the introduction of that ballot elections could not have acquired whatever significance they now hold.

The extension of the franchise
Another development without which elections could not have acquired their present significance − is the extension of the franchise. The democratic doctrine of government by consent of the governed clearly calls for universal suffrage. But this seemed a threatening proposition to the upper classes and the ruling elites, who feared that extending the franchise to the propertyless and the young − those who did not have a stake in the existing order − would jeopardize that order and with it their own privileges.

Accordingly, up to the eighteenth century participation in elections was limited to a minority of the population, mainly property-holders. With the French Revolution, all citizens were declared equal, but in practice the franchise remained restricted to the few, and property and income qualifications were still attached to it. In most Western countries it was only after severe struggles that financial qualifications were made less stringent and eventually abolished, and the right to vote was gradually extended from the more privileged to the middle classes, to the peasantry, and finally to the working class. But by the beginning of the twentieth century most Western countries had universal suffrage for men; women attained the vote in most countries in the first decades of the twentieth century, especially after the First World War.[10]

Table 7.1 illustrates the gradual extension of the franchise in Britain by showing the proportion of adults with the vote at different times:

Table 7.1

Before 1832	5%
1832	7%
1867	16%
1884	28%
1918 (almost all men enfranchised; women enfranchised at the age of 30)	74%
1928 (universal male and female suffrage)	96·9%
1948	96.7%

Source: Leonard (1968), pp. 10–11.

In America there were variations by States but, all in all, property qualifications gave way rather early to tax requirements, which were also abolished for the most part before the Civil War. By 1870 all but four States had universal male suffrage and women attained the vote in 1920. In the various Australian colonies manhood suffrage was attained throughout the second half of the nineteenth century and women got the vote after the establishment of the Commonwealth in 1902.

Even after universal suffrage was ostensibly attained, some groups continued to be over-represented in the electoral system while others continued to be disadvantaged. In some countries plural voting (i.e., voting on the basis of more than one qualification) for the well-to-do and the educated persisted. For instance, in Britain plural voting was not abolished until 1948. In some countries racial minorities were still effectively barred from voting. In the United States, for instance, blacks were formally enfranchised in 1867 and the 15th Amendment to the Constitution (introduced in 1870) forbade the States to deny the vote to anyone on account of race and colour. In practice, however, blacks in the South were frequently discouraged, or even prevented, from voting. This practice became more rather than less frequent, and by the turn of the century the Southern States had, in practice, disenfranchised the blacks. This was accomplished through State laws that were ostensibly non-discriminatory, but actually discriminated against blacks. Literacy requirements were introduced at a time when most blacks were still illiterate. A requirement was introduced to interpret the Constitution — which made it possible for election officials to discriminate by asking simple questions of white voters and difficult ones of black voters. To ensure their effectiveness, these discriminatory practices were supplemented by pressure and even violence.

Another means of disenfranchising blacks became prominent at the beginning of the twentieth century: this was the white Democratic primary. Blacks were prevented from voting in these primaries on the ground that the Democratic Party was a voluntary organization and hence was not subject to the anti-discriminatory laws which ruled general elections. Since the Democratic nominees were invariably elected to almost any public office in the solid South, blacks were effectively prevented from participating in their election.

But this process was reversed towards the middle of the twentieth century. In 1944 the Supreme Court outlawed the white primary; the situation was further improved by civil rights legislation in the 1950s and 1960s. It was only then that the proportion of Southern blacks who registered to vote came to resemble that of a population with a comparable level of education under 'normal' circumstances. The United States was thus among the first Western countries to achieve white manhood suffrage, but among the last to achieve effective universal suffrage.[11]

In this manner universal suffrage was painstakingly won and today it has been attained in all Western countries. But the legal right to vote does not guarantee that this right will be exercised. Participation in elections depends not only on the franchise but on several social factors as well. The extension of voting participation thus followed, but did not stand in a one-to-one relationship with, the extension of the franchise.

The extension of voting participation
Voting participation may be measured as a percentage of the population (or the adult population) or as a percentage of those entitled to vote

(voting turnout). These two measures have not always followed the same trends and have differed from one country to another — as can be seen from Tables 7.2 and 7.3.

Table 7.2 *Voting participation in the United Kingdom 1885–1979*[a]

Year	Votes as percentage of population	Votes as percentage of electorate (turnout)	Year	Votes as percentage of population	Votes as percentage of electorate (turnout)
1885	12·9	81·2	1931	47·0	76·4
1886	8·1	74·2	1935	47·0	71·1
1892	12·1	77·4	1945	51·0	72·8
1895	9·5	78·4	1950	56·8	83·9
1900	8·6	75·1	1951	56·9	82·6
1906	13·0	83·2	1955	52·5	76·8
1910 (Jan.)	14·8	86·8	1959	53·6	78·7
1910 (Dec.)	11·7	81·6	1964	51·3	77·1
1918	25·0	57·0	1966	50·0	75·8
1922	32·5	73·0	1970	51·1	72·0
1923	32·6	71·1	1974 (Feb.)	55·9	78·8
1924	37·0	77·0	1974 (Oct.)	52·2	72·8
1929	49·6	76·3	1979	53·6	76·0

Source: Etzioni-Halevy (1979), p. 30.

[a]
 No data for the period prior to 1885 have been presented because, according to the authorities on this subject, it was not possible to calculate the percentage of voting turnout with any degree of accuracy for that period.

In both Britain and America voting participation as a percentage of the population has increased rather steadily with only small setbacks while voting participation as a percentage of the electorate has slumped perceptibly in both countries after the First World War. This is usually explained by the enfranchisement of new groups. Some newly en-franchised groups, it is suggested, temporarily have relatively low political involvement; they require some time to catch up with the involvement of previously enfranchised groups. Those enfranchised during the course of the nineteenth century, it is pointed out, were of relatively higher socio-economic strata that already had a high level of

Table 7.3 *Voting participation in the United States (presidential elections) 1824-1976*

Year	Votes as percentage of population	Votes as percentage of electorate (turnout)	Year	Votes as percentage of population	Votes as percentage of electorate (turnout)
1824	3·8	26·9	1900	18·4	73·2
1828	11·3	57·6	1904	16·5	65·2
1832	10·4	55·4	1908	16·8	65·4
1836	11·6	57·8	1912	15·8	58·8
1840	16·5	80·2	1916	18·2	61·6
1844	15·8	78·9	1920	25·1	49·2
1848	15·8	72·7	1924	25·4	48·9
1852	14·5	69·6	1928	30·6	56·9
1856	16·7	78·9	1932	31·9	56·9
1860	17·0	81·2	1936	35·6	61·0
1864	—[a]	73·8	1940	37·8	62·5
1868	—[a]	78·1	1944	34·7	55·9
1872	15·4	71·3	1948	33·3	53·0
1876	18·3	81·8	1952	39·2	63·3
1880	18·3	79·4	1956	36·9	60·6
1884	19·0	77·5	1960	38·1	64·0
1888	18·8	79·3	1964	36·8	61·7
1892	18·5	74·7	1968	36·5	60·6
1896	19·5	79·3	1972	37·2	55·7
			1976	37·9	59·2

Source: Etzioni-Halevy (1979), p. 31.

[a]No popular vote was counted for the Southern States in 1864 and 1868.

political involvement; those enfranchised towards the end of the nineteenth century belonged to the lower strata, which usually have low political involvement. In the United States the newly enfranchised at the turn of this century, it is further pointed out, included large numbers of new immigrants whose political alienation was based not only on their low socio-economic status but also on their cultural estrangement. In fact, however, the greatest slump in voting turnout occurred when women were newly enfranchised and it is women (and not so much lower-class people) who took some time to catch up with previously enfranchised groups.

It can also be seen from the tables that until the First World War the United States was ahead of Britain in voting participation by both measures. But gradually Britain edged forward and today it is clearly ahead of the United States. Indeed, in recent years, voting turnout in the United States has lagged behind that of practically all other Western democracies as well.[12] This has been explained, in part, as a result of different recording procedures, different registration requirements and different geographical mobility; more people in the United States have recently moved and thus do not meet residency requirements. However, it ought to be conceded that these factors alone cannot explain such large differences and that contrary to what is popularly thought to be the case, the American public displays a lower level of political involvement than that of other Western democracies.

Despite such differences, Britain and the United States — together with other Western democracies — display a common trend: a rather steady increase of voting participation as a percentage of the population. This is apparently due to a combination of factors, including not only the extension of the franchise, but also rising levels of education, greater exposure to the media and (in some countries), the introduction of compulsory voting. But, in R. E. Lane's (1959, p. 18) words: 'Whatever the reason, it is significant that generally speaking, decade by decade . . . a constantly increasing proportion of the population has registered its preference in national elections.'

It must be concluded, then, that recent changes have been towards variously expressed, broader participation of the public in the political arena. This conclusion would seem to support the pluralist-democratic view of political participation. Or does it? On the face of it, it looks as if the elitist and the Marxist views have little to go on, except for one phenomenon (which so far has not figured in the present discussion): political manipulation.

Political manipulation[13]

Both the elitist and the Marxist schools of thought put major emphasis on the recent pervasiveness of political manipulation[14] of the public engaged in by political elites or ruling classes in order to entrench themselves in power. As Mills (1959a, p. 310) put it: 'the public . . . has become the objective of intensive efforts to control, manage, manipulate'.

The doctrine of democracy demands, as noted, that the people exercise sovereignty by extending their consent to the government, which thereby becomes authorized to act in their name. According to the pluralist-democratic theorists, growing political participation of the public (especially in elections) implies that governments do indeed increasingly depend on the consent of the people. However, the claim made by elitists, Marxists and some other observers is that it is actually the ruling elite (or class) which moulds the people's consent to itself, thereby ensuring its own rule. According to this view, consent thus descends from the top, rather than ascending from the bottom. To quote Mills again (1951, p. 110):

> In modern society . . . those who hold power have often come
> to exercise it in hidden ways: they have moved and they are
> moving from authority to manipulation . . . . No longer can
> the problem of power be set forth as the simple one of changing
> the processes of coercion into those of consent. The engineering
> of consent to authority has moved into the realm of manipul-
> ation.

The growing political participation by the public (these scholars argue) has thus been offset by growing and more effective manipulation of the public by the ruling elites (or classes) and therefore is not really meaningful. Instead of enabling the public to exert more influence on the political scene, this increasing participation has merely been utilized by the ruling groups to put and keep themselves in power. The avenues of increasing democratic participation, instead of being instruments in the service of the public, have been turned into manipulative devices in the service of the elites. The extension of democratic rights merely implies that the political elites have had to modify their struggle for power to include, to a greater extent than before, the manipulation of the public.

This raises the question whether political manipulation of the public has indeed increased over time during the modern period. It is clear that certain types of political manipulation could have come into being only with the evolvement of democratic institutions themselves. For instance, it is only with the development of elections that electoral manipulation (see below) became feasible. The question, however, is whether political manipulation has developed even further in recent years, after the evolution of the basic democratic institutions has been completed.

To explore this, a distinction must be made between two types of manipulation: symbolic and non-symbolic manipulation. The former is manipulation through the use of words, visual images and other symbols. The latter is manipulation which resorts to other devices and is not centrally focused on symbols. Let us review some examples of the latter first.

Non-symbolic manipulation: co-optation

It has been shown above that participation in the ruling elites has been extended to wider social strata, specifically to labour parties, presumably the representatives of the working class. This, however, claims Michels (1949), is only an apparent increase in the political power of the working class. This is so because those who have come to power are not labourers, but labour leaders; not the working class, but an elite from among the working class.

As soon as labour-class persons become labour leaders, an increasing gap widens between themselves and the labour class that they supposedly represent. While the interests of the latter are to bring about such changes of the system as will improve their lot, the interests of the former are to maintain themselves in power. Moreover, not only do their interests diverge, but their mentalities become different as well. Having attained the success of power, the labour leaders' outlook upon the world now comes to resemble that of the ruling elites and ruling classes more than that of the working classes. Give a man (it has been said) a large salary, a carpeted office, a car and a secretary, and the vital problems he set out to confront will lose much of their urgency (unless, of course, they concern that very salary, car and secretary).

In other words, a subtle type of manipulation is taking place here which — most likely — has not been intentionally designed by anyone, and yet is very effective; in modern sociology it has been termed co-optation. The principle of co-optation is that when a power structure is threatened by a certain group, the leaders of that group are incorporated into power positions within that very structure. Since they now share in the responsibility over the system and in the rewards of power which accrue from it, they also share in the interest of maintaining that system, and the cutting edge of their threat is, if not eliminated, at least considerably dulled. This, some elitist observers claim, is precisely what happened to labour leaders when they came to share political power in Western societies.

The Marxist view is very much in line with this conception. In fact, Miliband (1973) substantiates and complements the same argument even though he does not apply the same terminology. He attempts to show that whenever labour parties have come to power, they have become much more moderate than their followers have meant them to be. Once in power, labour leaders have not shown any marked tendencies to transform the system, at least not drastically or immediately. They have assured representatives of prevailing interests that they were 'acutely aware . . . that Rome was not built in a day, and that its building must in any case be approached with the utmost circumspection' (p. 91). They have practically looked for excuses not to embark on those reforms which they had previously promised their electors.

Miliband cites two major examples to prove his point. First, the Popular Front which came to power in France in 1936. This party did introduce some reforms such as a shorter working week, higher wages, enlarged trade union rights and the like. But it did not, and was not designed to, replace the system, or even to effect a genuine redistribution of economic power.

Second, the Labour Party government in Britain in 1945 which — according to Miliband — was renowned for the modesty of its ambition for reform. It did have a substantial nationalization program (including nationalization of the Bank of England; coal, gas and electricity works, railways and the steel industry). But when this program of nationalization was carried out, representatives from the private sector were drawn to the boards of the newly nationalized enterprises. This, and the fact that the goal in the first place was a mixed rather than a nationalized economy, made it easy for the Conservatives to reverse some of the processes as soon as they came back to power. Thus, while it is true that in the twentieth century labour leaders, for the first time in history, have obtained a share of power, they have exercised or have been manipulated to exercise that power predominantly in the interests of the ruling class.

Non-symbolic electoral manipulation

Another type of non-symbolic manipulation concerns a certain manipulation of elections, of which several sub-types may be distinguished. There is, first, electoral fraud which has been rather common in most democratic countries, at one time or another. For instance, in many electorates all over the Western world, persons who had moved away or had passed away continued to vote, by courtesy of the electoral officers who were also party supporters. Or else fraudulent procedures were introduced by 'stuffing' ballot boxes with fictitious votes, or by introducing errors into counting procedures. It has been told about Frank Hague, one-time Democratic boss of New Jersey, for instance, that his vote counters practically determined the outcomes of elections and in one electorate only his generosity enabled his opponent to poll 120 out of 4600 votes cast. As one observer consequently remarked, 'It ain't how the ballots go into the box that counts. It's how they come out' (Steinberg, 1972, p. 40). Eventually, various systems (such as non-partisan polling officers combined with rival party scrutineers, and voting machines) have been devised to curb this practice and today — observers agree — it has markedly declined or even disappeared in all Western countries.

Another, and more subtle, type of electoral manipulation was not so easily eradicated. This practice, known as 'gerrymandering', has to do with the mapping of electoral boundaries.[15] Evidently it is in the interests of any party to have a small majority in a great number of electorates (rather than a large majority in some electorates and a minority in others), or a majority in a small number of electorates (rather than a minority in many). Since it is usually well known where the strongholds of support for any given party are concentrated, electoral divisions can be made and electoral boundaries can be designed to favour one or another of the opposing parties, even if this implies that electorates of the oddest geographical shapes emerge.

Indeed, it is the strangeness of the electorates' shapes that gave this form of manipulation its name. This name originated in the United States at the beginning of the nineteenth century, when Governor Elbridge Gerry of Massachussets was in charge of the division of the State into senatorial districts. He managed to design these divisions in such a way that 50,164 voters of his own party elected as many as 29 State senators, while 51,766 voters of the opposing party elected only 11. To achieve this result Governor Gerry had to design electoral districts in the most contorted of shapes. When one observer remarked that these shapes reminded him of a salamander, another observer is supposed to have replied, 'This is not a salamander; this is a gerry-mander.' The name caught on and has been used to this very day to designate this manipulation, which apparently has occurred rather frequently in the Western world.

The only way to overcome this type of manipulation is to appoint non-partisan electoral distribution commissions, and it is not clear to what extent the various Western democracies have been successful in this feat. In Australia, for instance, major efforts are being made to safeguard the political neutrality of distribution commissions; but observers are not unanimous on the extent to which gerrymandering has, in fact, been eliminated.

A related practice is the creation of electoral seats of grossly unequal populations. Some instances of this were to be found in the United States before the 1962 Supreme Court decision curbed this practice. Other instances are to be found in Australia, where electoral boundaries are frequently weighted in favour of rural areas over urban ones, thus giving a disproportional advantage to the National Country Party. This type of practice is commonly considered as electoral manipulation since it violates the democratic principle of 'one vote one value'. But where the weighting is in favour of rural areas, some observers argue that it is merely a legitimate over-representation for a population group which contributes disproportionately to the country's economy while at the same time being widely dispersed and negligible in numbers.

In any case, the most important type of non-symbolic electoral manipulation concerns the handing out of material inducements in return for electoral, political support. This type of manipulation can take several forms. Some material inducements (for example, tax reductions) can be given (or promised) to the electorate as a whole. Alternatively, such benefits may be awarded to powerful interest groups whose political support is essential. Or else material benefits may be handed out to communities, or even to families and individuals. Material inducements of the later type may range all the way from cash bribery and treating (especially with alcoholic beverages) to the exercising of 'pull' with the authorities for the procurement of jobs, housing, subsidies, government contracts, tax reductions and any number of other benefits.

Ostensibly, this practice should have disappeared with the introduction of the secret ballot, which made it much more difficult for party representatives to ensure that they were getting a return for the good deeds they were doing for voters. Yet we know that this is not the case. This is due not only to various ways that were devised for dodging the secrecy of the ballot.[16] More importantly, it is due to the fact that the party handing out material inducements banks on building up a bond of gratitude and interests that ties the beneficiary to the party. The benefits anticipated may not materialize unless the given party is in power, or it may disappear or be reduced when the party is ousted. Benefits may entail the obligation of the beneficiary to be active on behalf of the party in persuading other voters. Voting for the party oneself is thus expected to ensue as a matter of course.

But, although this type of manipulation did not disappear with the introduction of the secret ballot, it has declined or diminished more recently all over the Western world. While benefits to the electorate as a whole or to powerful interest groups are apparently universal, benefits to families and individuals are not. The practice of extending such benefits was widespread in many Western democracies in the nineteenth century, but has become much less so today. In Britain, for instance, where such benefits were financed mainly by private wealthy candidates (who, despite their wealth, eventually succumbed under the soaring expenses), the practice was eliminated relatively early, towards the end of the nineteenth century. In Australia, where the practice was less widespread to begin with and where it was perpetrated mainly by individual candidates as well, it declined shortly afterwards.

In America, where the practice was bolstered up by powerful political machines, it was maintained much longer. It flourished at the beginning of the twentieth century, and was still in existence after the middle of the century. In 1960 Mayor Daley's political machine in Chicago was still a crucial factor in the close presidential contest, and even the most recent presidential election was not completely free of this type of manipulation. But even in the United States, political machines, and with them manipulation through material inducements, has substantially declined, and it no longer even remotely approaches its previous dimensions.

Symbolic manipulation
Some forms of non-symbolic manipulation thus persist and show no likelihood of disappearing, while others have declined significantly in recent years. This is more than can be said for symbolic manipulation which has benefited from technological advances as well as from market research in psychology and the social sciences, and thus, if anything, has been perfected in recent years. In Walter Lippman's (1961, p. 248) words:

That the manufacture of consent is capable of great refinement, no one, I think denies . . . . The creation of consent is not a new art. It has . . . improved enormously in technic because it is now based on analysis . . . . Within the life of the generation now in control of affairs, persuasion has become a self-conscious art and a regular organ of popular government.

Three interrelated sources for politically significant symbolic manipulation may be identified: political elites, commercial advertising and the mass media which, besides originating manipulation of their own, serve as a vehicle for the other two sources of manipulation.[17]

It is widely agreed among observers that present-day ruling elites in Western democracies (no less than in other regimes) promote consent for themselves by distributing information selectively, by emitting symbolic cues which define or interpret states of affairs for the public (Edelman, 1971), and by means of emotionally-laden linguistic symbols which in themselves contain predefinitions of the situation and create positive images of the system. Advertising, on its part, is said to act as a politically stabilizing agent by extolling the virtues of material goods, and thus by strengthening the definition of what is desirable, as embedded in the existing socio-political system (Marcuse, 1964; Mueller, 1973).

The development of the mass media and their increasing freedom from government intervention were earlier seen to increase the public's awareness of political processes. On the other hand, however, it cannot be denied that in many Western societies a large part of the media are run either by commercial interests, or by government instrumentalities — both of which have a clear stake in the maintenance of the system and therefore in manipulating the public into its acceptance. Although they may be legally and formally free, their place in the system motivates them to emphasize a moderate rather than a radical stand and this, even if it does not work explicitly in favour of one party rather than another, generally serves to perpetuate the *status quo*. [18]

Television, because of its visual impact, is held to be especially powerful. Its entertainment content, while ostensibly non-political, actually has a political impact in that it deflects attention from politics and furthers receptive passive, apathetic, rather than active, critical tendencies amongst the audience. Thus, it is claimed, media advertently or inadvertently tend to buttress prevailing institutions.

However, it must also be borne in mind that in Western democracies symbolic manipulation by ruling elites is usually counteracted through similar manipulation by counter-elites, including not only leaders of opposition parties, but leaders of anti-establishment groups as well. While established elites usually have a better access to the mass media of communication, this does not mean that alternative elites have no access at all. Besides direct access to the media (which for splinter groups may not be large), they have at their disposal rallies, marches and demonstrations. These have not only a direct impact on the public, but (if their magnitude is sufficient) are invariably reported in the media as well. While such anti-establishment splinter elites do not have the proverbial equal-time access to the media which established opposition leaders enjoy, they thus are not completely barred from bringing their views before the public.

There is also a limit to the biasing and pacifying effect of the media themselves. Some media display distinct radical affinities. But even those which do not work under certain constraints of the system. These, as we have seen, include the commercial and political interests of owners and controllers. But they also include professional ethics, and professional prestige rankings which increase not only with the uncovering of 'scoops', but with the general quality and quantity of the information supplied. Hence it is precisely the media which see to it that there is much that the ruling elites cannot get away with.

Conclusion

In the foregoing chapter it could be seen that in Western capitalist countries, the power of governments and through it the power of ruling elites has grown substantially. In this chapter it became evident that the growth of government and elite power has been countervailed by growing political participation of the public. Although there are no hard and fast measures to the efficacy of such participation, it seems evident that the public has recently had a greater impact on the political arena than was the case in pre-democratic regimes. Since governments and ruling elites have gained greater control over resources, there is now more at stake in the political arena. And since public participation has increased as well, this means that the change has been towards a more intense political process and that the potential for confrontation over political power has eminently increased.

However, the development of elections, which figures as a major avenue for growing participation of the public, may also be regarded as a certain pattern for the institutionalization of such political power conflict. By giving the public a say in the selection of elites, by making elites more responsive to public demands, and by furnishing the 'rules of the game' by which elites may vie with each other, elections may well have obviated other, more radical (and perhaps more violent) types of political conflict. Direct action, another growing avenue of public participation, has also turned into an increasingly institutionalized pattern of waging political conflict. This, in turn, has become possible through the development of freedom of speech and association.

It must be admitted that just as the growing power of ruling elites has been countervailed by the growing political participation of the public and by some institutionalized means by which the public can take part in political conflict, so have these developments on their part been counteracted – at least to some extent – by political manipulation of the public. Although some types of such manipulation have recently decreased, others have not, and some have even made further inroads in recent years. Paradoxically, however, it must also be asserted that the increasing reliance of ruling elites on political manipulation is in itself a mark of progress in public political participation.

In the first place, it shows that the consent of the public to the elites' rule has indeed grown in importance, or else why would the latter invest such major efforts in manipulating or 'manufacturing' such consent? Some theorists (it will be recalled) have belittled the importance of elections, and hence the increase in electoral participation. But if elections did not carry a major potential significance in selecting a ruling elite, elites and potential elites would not have bothered to invest such enormous resources and so much ingenuity in their manipulation.

Moreover, manipulation is rather a subtle means of control. It can be employed most effectively to the extent that the public is not fully aware of its occurrence. Therefore, there exists a potential means of resisting manipulation: the growing awareness and consciousness of the public. This holds especially for symbolic manipulation – the type of manipulation which has increased in importance in recent years.

Symbolic manipulation is one in which the ruling elites pre-define the situation for the public; but with the growing awareness of the public to such manipulation, there is a limit to the efficacy of such pre-definitions. Some situations cannot be defined away or defined into existence, especially as the public is likely to be exposed (albeit not as frequently and as forcefully) to alternative definitions. While the contradictory definitions may not be so well-balanced as to neutralize each other, they still detract from each other. The public thus has a certain independence of judgment (even if not unlimited freedom) in forming its opinion, and thus an effective means of resisting political manipulation.

There is thus great importance in the fact that manipulation has taken up a greater share of the elites' socio-political activity and that symbolic manipulation has asserted itself as over some other types of manipulation. Since the ruling elite's ability to maintain itself in power now rests increasingly on symbolic manipulation, and since there is much that such manipulation cannot define away, this means that in some respects the ruling elites must restrain their own (potential) exploitative actions in order to keep themselves in power.

Selected readings

Edelman, M. J. (1971), *Politics as Symbolic Action*, New York, Academic Press.

Etzioni, A. and Etzioni-Halevy, E. (eds) (1973), *Social Change* (2nd edn), New York, Basic Books, chs 25, 49, 50, 51.

Etzioni-Halevy, E. (1979), *Political Manipulation and Administrative Power*, London, Routledge & Kegan Paul.

Huntington, S. P. (1968), *Political Order in Changing Societies*, New Haven, Yale University Press.

Miliband, R. (1973), *The State in Capitalist Society*, London, Quartet Books.

8 · The advent and maturation of modern education

Education as a process through which children are inculcated with basic skills and values and trained for their future roles as adults — is universal. But the manner in which this process takes place in modern society is in many ways unique. To clarify the nature of this unique version of education and how it evolved, the following criteria of comparison and change are proposed:

(a) What is the structure of education? How are the educational agencies shaped, how do they function, and how has their structure changed with modernization and after?

(b) As a result of such structural changes, who benefits from what type of education?

(c) How have these structural changes affected the social role of education and what is this role in modern society?

Theoretical perspectives

Both the 'mainstream' and the Marxist schools of thought are in agreement on the crucial role of education, but they are diametrically opposed to each other as to how they conceive of this role in modern society. According to 'mainstream' sociology there has been an 'educational revolution' (parallel in its importance to the industrial revolution) whereby education has become a dynamic, equalizing force in society. According to the Marxist view, contemporary education is still designed to perpetuate the inequalities of the existent class system and to reinforce the capitalist *status quo*.

The 'mainstream' view

According to the first school of thought, the precursor to the educational revolution is the emergence of education as a distinct institution. In most pre-modern societies, education was a generalized, informal activity vested mainly in the family. With modernization, a major part of this task is severed from the family and vested in separate formal organizations in the form of schools, colleges, and universities. But at the beginning these organizations were few and far between. As Peter Drucker (1973) sees it, the educational revolution as such, therefore, is evident first in the subsequent explosive expansion of formal education; in the unprecedented proliferation of such organizations and in the unequalled growth in the numbers of those benefiting from them.

The educational revolution is evident in the second place in the close links that have developed with the economy: an abundant and increasing supply of highly educated people has become an absolute prerequisite for adequate economic performance. This is a complete reversal in man's history. Before the twentieth century no society could afford more than a handful of educated people, for it was the uneducated who through their manual labour produced society's sustenance, while the educated were unproductive. Since education prepared mainly for dignified leisure, educated persons were a luxury rather than a necessity; only a few could be spared from manual labour. To support more than the barest minimum would have required gross exploitation. Since the beginning of the century, however, 'We are undergoing an educational revolution because the work of knowledge is no longer unproductive . . . . In the new organization it becomes the specifically productive work. Productive work in today's society and economy is work that applies knowledge' (p. 235).

Education has thus become a crucial form of investment in the economy, and a major economic resource. And by the same token it has become a major military resource as well. ' "The Battle of Waterloo" it is said "was won on the playing fields of Eton." Perhaps, but no-one asserts that it was won in Eton's classrooms' (p. 237). Today, however, it is classroom education (and especially higher education) which gives a country its advantage in the struggle for military leadership and perhaps even for survival.

A further aspect of the revolution in education is its increased democratization and push for equality. According to A. H. Halsey (1962) and Burton Clark (1962a), what little education did take place in previous centuries was reserved almost exclusively for the upper classes. But with the education explosion has come a substantial increase in lower-class access to it. The function of education as confirming the position of the upper classes has been overlaid by its new function as a mass service in a technological society. Such a society has an insatiable appetite for educated talent and 'the extending and especially the equalizing of opportunity is a necessary part of a fuller use of talent for trained manpower' (Clark, 1962a, p. 77).

Technological change has thus led to the opening of educational opportunities for lower-class youngsters. 'What matters now . . . is that one travel the educational road; and access to this highway, despite the handicaps of dirt-road entrances for some, is increasingly open' (Clark, 1962a, p. 76). This does not imply that full equality of educational opportunity has been attained but this goal is now well within reach of Western education.

Another facet of the revolution is that education has ceased to be a conservative force in society and instead has become an active promoter of flexibility and change. For one thing, it has become an active agent of social mobility, of movement up the class hierarchy. In the past, education had little independent effect on class affiliation, it was merely a symbol of higher class. Today, however, education plays an active role in allocating people to occupations. As such, it defines their life chances and class affiliations. Increased access to education now fosters lower-class youngsters' chances of elevating themselves into the upper classes. Thus, while education previously merely lent a stamp of approval to existing class rigidities, it now spearheads class openness.

The dynamic role of contemporary education is further evident in the area of knowledge. In every society education fulfils the function of preserving the continuity of the cultural heritage — including knowledge — by transmitting it to succeeding generations. But in contemporary society the conservation and dissemination of knowledge is closely tied to its further development, through the mechanism of scientific research. Before the nineteenth century such research took place outside the system of formal education. The scientific, technological and industrial revolutions took place in spite of, and not because of, the universities, and only belatedly did these institutions adapt themselves to the demands of technological and economic change. Today, however, universities 'still serve as custodians of the intellectual capital of mankind' (Clark, 1962a, p. 27), but they have also come to serve as major centres of research in which invention, innovation, revision, expansion and application of knowledge to changing needs is taking place. Since scientific research is now increasingly harnessed to the service of technological and economic growth, and since the educated manpower produced by the universities is now increasingly in charge of monitoring that growth, education has also become an institutionalized source of economic change.

Finally, higher education has assumed a dynamic role in the political arena as well. Academic studies stimulate critical thought and innovative social ideas amongst both students and faculty. The institutions in which such studies take place have increasingly become centres of political ferment, and radical student movements tend to arise and flourish even where apathy prevails amongst the rest of the population. From being a mainly passive agent in previous epochs, education has thus turned into a propellor of change in the cultural, economic, political and class structure of modern society.

The Marxist view
Starting out from different premises, the Marxist school of thought comes up with a totally different view of modern education. As Louis Althusser (1971) sees it, the basic point of departure for the analysis of education is Marx's assertion that in order to survive, a social formation must reproduce itself at the same time as it produces. It follows that the ultimate condition of production is the reproduction of the forces of production and the relations of production. These in turn include not only material means (such as raw materials and machinery), but labour as well. The reproduction of the labour force is ensured by wages which enable the labourer to sustain himself, to reconstitute his labour power, and to raise the children in which he reproduces himself. This alone, however, is not sufficient, for these children, the newly reproduced labourers, must be suitable to be set to work in the complex system of production.

Under capitalism this is accomplished through the state apparatuses, of which two types may be distinguished: the Repressive State Apparatuses (RSA), and the Ideological State Apparatuses (ISA). The RSA secure by laws, administrative decrees and coercion the conditions for the effectiveness of the ISA, while the latter, in turn, secure the reproduction of the relations of production (see also chapter 3).

Dominant among the ISAs is the combination of family and education, which has replaced the previously dominant combination of family and church. The educational apparatus inculcates the competence necessary for production:schools teach children at their most impressionable age the skills necessary for production and the rules of good behaviour, that is, respect for the established order of private property. In this manner schools drum into children a certain amount of know-how wrapped up in the dominant ideology, whose absorption is a basic prerequisite for stabilizing the relations of production and the existent class structure.

In order to ensure the stabilization of the class structure even further, the schools also prepare children for the positions to which they are destined. Somewhere around the age of sixteen, a large mass of children are ejected from education into production, and these are destined to become workers or peasants. Others continue their education further and become middle-level technicians, lower white-collar workers and minor businessmen —in a word, the small bourgeoisie. A last portion reaches the summit and will become the agents of exploitation (capitalists, managers), the agents of repression (soldiers, policemen, politicians, administrators), and the professional ideologists (priests and intellectuals). Each of these groups is endowed with the attitudes that suit the role it has to fulfil in society. Workers are imbued with submissiveness and compliance, the agents of exploitation are provided with the disposition to dominate and to issue orders without antagonizing their subordinates (this being accomplished through 'human relations' techniques), while the agents of repression are endowed with the ability to rule through the manipulation of the masses.

The mechanisms which produce this vital result for the capitalist regime are naturally concealed from view by a universally reigning myth which represents the school as a neutral environment where teachers guide their pupils on the path to freedom, morality and responsibility. A few teachers do in fact turn the weapon of education against the system, but these are rare. Most teachers act out the roles assigned to them, do not even suspect the 'working' of the system in which they are entrapped, and are blissfully unaware of the fact that they are instrumental in the reproduction of the existent class structure.

By contributing to the persistence of this class structure, education works in the interests of the ruling class and therefore (not surprisingly) through its machinations. Given the fact that the ruling class ultimately holds state power, it also has hegemony over the ISA (including education) and ensures that its own ideology is perpetuated through it. Indeed, no ruling class could sustain its position for long without enlisting the services of the ISA and especially those of the educational system.

It does so not only by using this system to disseminate its ideology, but also by affording its own offspring a disproportionate advantage in it. The argument that education has become more egalitarian and that it now compensates for inequalities generated elsewhere is patently fallacious. And not only have inequalities in the school system not decreased, they have in fact become increasingly important in reproducing the class structure from one generation to the next (Bowles, 1976). These inequalities are manifested in the fact that upper-class children are much more likely than working-class children to be admitted into the academic-oriented streams of high-school education (which open the way for higher education) and, once admitted, to stay and be successful in them. 'The structure of the school system thus serves as a streaming system on a large scale, which sorts children in very large measure on class criteria' (Connell, 1977, p. 158). Universities, too, although they are not the exclusive pre-serves of the ruling class, are powerfully biased in its favour in both intake and output.

Why does this class bias in education occur? According to R. W. Connell, working-class children have been given (and have accepted) the answer: they haven't got the 'brains', and if you haven't got the 'brains', you can't do well. In reality, however, this reply is merely a device by which the children are led to blame themselves for what the system has done to them, and this self-legitimizing ideology is nothing but a mechanism by which the system, under the hegemony of the ruling class, leads to its own perpetuation.

Actual developments: structural changes

Actual developments, which have occurred with modernization and after, include as one outstanding feature the vast proliferation of formal education, and it is 'mainstream' rather than Marxist sociology which has conceptualized it. However, this proliferation has come about through a protracted process beset by major struggles, a fact to which the 'mainstream' school of thought has given little attention.

Modernization
Throughout most of recorded history, formal education (to the extent that it existed at all) touched only a few. In most societies, from the dawn of history to the onset of modernization, the masses of people received no education outside that provided as part of everyday life by their families and communities. Formalized knowledge (to the extent that it existed) was monopolized by a small minority. Ancient Greece, Judea and Rome are the first known societies in which large proportions of (free, male) youngsters obtained an education in separate organizations, that is, schools. This situation, however, did not last and, with the advent of the Middle Ages, school education shrank

to almost nil. The period's 'high' culture was transmitted by the education of a few, mainly through schools monopolized by the church and located in the monasteries and cathedrals, and through private tutors in the courts. But this education was so restricted that (outside the church hierarchy itself) illiteracy was almost universal. This situation persisted into the beginning of the modern era. At the time of the first colonial settlements in America, formal education (even of the most elementary level) still played a very limited role, and the situation was not much different in Europe.

This holds even more for higher education. Its beginnings, too, are to be found in antiquity – in the Greek and Roman schools of rhetoric, and in the Judean colleges of higher religious education. But in the early Middle Ages Europe was devoid of any system of higher education; it was not until the twelfth and early thirteenth centuries that the first European universities came into being. The numbers of these universities – which were also under the auspices of the church[1] – gradually grew and by the end of the fifteenth century there were seventy of them, dispersed from Sweden to Italy. However, by present standards these institutions were still small and sparse, and their size and number remained restricted even at the beginning of modernity.

It was only in subsequent centuries that the rapid expansion and growing complexity of knowledge necessitated the creation of increasing numbers of specialized agencies for its effective transmission. Further, the development of democratic values called for at least a minimum of knowledge on part of all citizens so as to make the democratic process feasible. Finally, the proliferation of educational institutions can be traced back to the growing pervasiveness of state intervention (see chapter 6) which came to include education as well.

However, every step to increase the state's initiative in and control over education involved a severe struggle. At least up to the French Revolution, education was held to be solely the domain of family and church. Their champions therefore opposed state intervention. Such intervention was opposed in particular by the representatives of the church, since the state usually claimed control of education on anti-clerical and even anti-religious grounds.

Eventually, however, as the state gained ascendancy over the church in other areas, it made headway in this respect as well. By the middle of the nineteenth century it was recognized almost everywhere that the state had the right as well as the duty to provide education for its citizens and the church was largely compelled to surrender its control of education. At the same time a compromise was reached in most countries whereby denominational and private schools were allowed side by side with the state-controlled school systems (Peterson, 1960).

Only in the United States did education develop under local control. The role of the states was minor and that of the federal government nonexistent until the middle of the twentieth century, when federal aid to education was translated into influence in educational policy as well. In Europe, the growing state control of education proceeded in three stages. The first was when the state assumed responsibility for the provision of schools; the second was when it made attendance at those schools compulsory, and the third and decisive stage was when the state took it upon itself to finance education and made attendance free.

Initially, and throughout the nineteenth century, the state was mainly concerned with the provision of primary education. In country after country, this resulted in a growing number of primary schools. To ensure that all citizens benefited from these schools, laws of compulsory education were introduced. In some instances (for example, in some German States) compulsory education came as early as the seventeenth century, but in most Western countries it was introduced only in the nineteenth and the beginning of the twentieth century. For instance, compulsory education was introduced in Britain in 1880; in America most States introduced it in the nineteenth century; but Mississippi, for one, did not do so until 1930.[2]

However, laws of compulsory universal (primary) education could not provide universal education in practice as long as the funds for financing it were not available. Thus, as Peterson points out, the Danish compulsory school attendance law of 1739 produced universal education in the statute book and nowhere else since the cost fell on the parishes, which had no funds to provide it. In practice, primary education thus became universal only when the state took it upon itself to finance it, and when it was made free of charge. This, too, occurred in most Western countries only during the nineteenth or the beginning of the twentieth century.

The establishment of an adequate, national system of primary education was therefore a protracted and, at times, painful process. Thus, in Britain, there was a marked shortage of primary schools at the beginning of the nineteenth century. The first half of that century saw an immense effort in voluntary school-building, especially by the Church of England. But despite the quantitative increase, the qualitative increase was less impressive, and by the middle of the century primary education in Britain was still 'a muddle and not far from being a disgrace' (Peterson, 1960, p. 15). More than half of the schools were private, neither assisted nor inspected by the government, and hence served mostly as places to which children were sent in order to keep them out of the way. By the standards of the times, the most successful schools were those which packed the largest numbers of children into the smallest space and managed to keep them quiet. Teachers' qualifications were poor or nonexistent; attendance was intermittent and most children received no more than one year's schooling. Only during the second half of the nineteenth century, as government funding and supervision were introduced, did a genuine national system of primary education come into being.

In the middle of the nineteenth century, France was the only European country with a national system of secular, state, primary schools. Even so, the conditions in these schools were no better than those in Britain: the classes were large and the ratio of teachers to students was often 1 to 100. Under such conditions studies could be no more than rudimentary and in fact consisted almost entirely of copying. Germany, Switzerland and the Netherlands also had well-established systems of primary education by the middle of the nineteenth century. But these were local systems rather than national, and were still under the control of the church. In the United States the control of schools was still too localized for any general system to be apparent.

General systems of secondary education took even longer to develop. In nineteenth-century Britain secondary education was even worse off than primary education. The network of so-called 'public schools', which were in fact private schools, catered only for a negligible minority of (upper class) youngsters. The supposed backbone of British secondary education was the grammar schools, but around the middle of the nineteenth century they numbered less than a thousand. Many had sunk to the level of inefficient primary schools; two-thirds of all localities had no secondary schools at all. During the second half of the nineteenth century the level of grammar schools improved considerably and at the first quarter of the twentieth century their numbers rose very rapidly, but even then they catered for only a minority of youngsters.

In most other Western European countries some rudimentary national systems of secondary education already existed by the middle of the nineteenth century but they too catered for only a very small number of youngsters; this situation continued into the twentieth century. In the United States in the early nineteenth century, secondary education was almost entirely concentrated in private schools (named academies). By the outbreak of the Civil War, most districts in the Eastern States had established public high schools. But, although free, these schools too were restricted to a minority, partly by economic exigencies that compelled poorer parents to send their children out to gainful employment and partly be entrance standards.

The development of higher education was even more protracted and intermittent. During the Middle Ages universities had been small and few in numbers; but in some areas of study (the humanities, law, medicine and theology) they had flourished, and this situation continued into the Renaissance. Later on, however, the universities declined, reaching their lowest point in the eighteenth century. Even at the beginning of the nineteenth century the number of universities was still comparatively small, their standards were questionable and they did not engage in scientific research. In Britain, for instance, because of the rudimentary state of high schools, the universities were forced to impart what amounted to no more than a secondary education. This situation improved during the second half of the nineteenth century and universities once more attained impressive academic standards. But it was only in the twentieth century that their numbers and sizes grew substantially, and it is only in recent years that their present dimensions have been attained.

Recent developments
Although in all Western countries state intervention eventually created national systems of education, it did not ensure more than a bare minimum of education for the 'masses'. Its result was the development, in practically all European countries, of dual, parallel systems of education: primary schools and terminal continuation classes (with varying lengths of attendance) attached to them for the bulk of the children, and secondary schools with special (mostly private) preparatory schools attached to them for a privileged minority. The former were designed to prepare their pupils for 'life', while the latter provided a preparation for academic studies, and for a long time there was in most countries practically no bridge to make transfer from the non-academic to the academic track feasible. Eventually, most countries made the transfer into academic secondary schools possible through an examination administered to all children somewhere between the ages of ten and twelve. But this system still afforded a substantial advantage to the graduates of the special schools who had received a better preparation for the examinations; so entry to the secondary schools was still relatively restricted.

In Britain, for instance, selection for academic secondary schools – the grammar schools – took place on the basis of the famous eleven-plus examination, so named because it was administered to most children between the age of 11 and 12. As a result of that examination some 20 to 25 per cent of the age group were singled out for education in the academic grammar schools; all others were enrolled in 'secondary modern schools' or in technical schools, which placed less emphasis on academic studies. Once classified into one or the other type of school most youngsters remained there. Most of those admitted to grammar schools were thus bound for higher education and for higher white-collar and professional occupations. Most of those channelled into the other schools were consigned to manual labour or low-ranking white-collar work.[3] The so-called public school system also persisted, but continued to cater to only a small group of privileged children.

The United States did not adopt the European-style dual system of education. During the nineteenth century, it will be recalled, secondary schools were still designed for only a small proportion of youngsters. But because of the phenomenal increase in wealth, and the prevalent ideology of equality of opportunity, there was a growing popular demand for high-school education. In response, a great expansion in high schools occurred from 1900 onwards. The curriculum, which previously had been devoted to academic subjects, was now altered to include almost any subject, and students could choose between the academic and non-academic ones according to their own preferences. Thus the first comprehensive high schools had come into being.

In Europe, the more selective high-school system persisted up to the middle of the twentieth century and beyond, but it eventually had to be modified as a result of the following trends:

(a) the growing complexity of modern technology, which caused a rapidly expanding demand for skilled and educated labour;

(b) economic growth and rising affluence, which made it possible to defer youngsters' entry into the labour market to a later age;

(c) increased expectations, and demands for extended education from all sections of society;

(d) increased pressure from labour parties and organizations to give working-class children a fairer share in education;

(e) growing criticism of the fact that children's futures were being decided at an age at which it was practically impossible to make a reliable appraisal of their capacities.

Accordingly, in practically all Western European countries, the last few decades (especially since the Second World War) have seen the introduction of structural changes and reforms geared towards the following objectives;

(a) increasing the numbers of youngsters who benefit from secondary and higher education;

(b) increasing equality of opportunity, and especially increasing the proportion of working-class youngsters in secondary and higher education;

(c) postponing the age of selection into the academic versus the non-academic educational tracks;

(d) facilitating the passage from one to the other — so that children who had been sifted out at an earlier stage could be given a second chance.

The structural changes that have accordingly been effected include:

(a) *The extension of compulsory education* Until the Second World War such education had usually been for eight years or less; since the mid-1970s it is almost without exception for nine years or more (see UNESCO, 1977, Table 3.1, pp. 126–41).

(b) *The extension of free education* In most Western-European countries secondary school fees were abolished by the end of the Second World War. In Britain, for instance, the abolition of fees came about through the Education Act of 1944. There is also a tendency towards the reduction of university fees. In Germany, for instance, tuition fees for higher education were abolished in the early 1970s; in Britain such tuition fees persist, but most students receive scholarships exempting them. This, by the way, does not hold for the United States where tuition fees for higher education are universal[4] and although there are many scholarships, the majority of students still have to pay.

(c) *Financial aid to students* In most Western European countries large numbers of students receive tertiary education allowances or other types of financial aid throughout their studies. This is again in contrast to the tendency prevalent in the United States where living grants are far less numerous.

(d) *Structural reforms* These reforms have been effected or tried out on a more or less extensive scale, and they lie in between two types: (1) combining the previous dual courses in a single, comprehensive type of school accessible to the whole school-age population; and (2) maintaining the previous parallel courses separately, but providing facilities for transfer between them.

One major example of the first type is to be found in Britain. Here the reform consists of the establishment of comprehensive secondary schools, offering different courses of study and accommodating students of different social background, with a counselling process taking the place of the previous abrupt selection by means of the eleven-plus examination. The reform encountered initial opposition from many authorities, intent on preserving the traditional system, but eventually made considerable headway. By 1975, 70 per cent of the school population attended comprehensive schools.

An example of the second type would be West Germany, where the main effort has been concentrated on facilitating transfer between non-academic and academic types of schooling, through the establishment of probationary periods of two years in the more academic schools (that is, the *Realschulen* and the *Gymnasien*). There was also an in-between type of reform, entailing the establishment of intermediary schools in which all children would be retained until anywhere between the ages of thirteen and sixteen, thus postponing the selection into different educational tracks (Poignant, 1969; Husén, 1972). In France, for instance, the reform which took effect in 1977 provides for access of all primary school-leavers to four-year colleges with mixed ability classes. These are intended to serve as frameworks for observation and orientation and thus to facilitate the subsequent selection into academic and non-academic schools.

The impact of structural changes: who benefits from what type of education

The impact on participation
The structural changes of the last few centuries, culminating in the reforms of the last few decades, have had their clearest impact on educational participation. As 'mainstream' sociologists have argued, these developments have indeed brought about a vast increase in the numbers of those benefiting from education. Around the year 1000 almost all the population of Europe was illiterate; in the seventeenth century, 55 to 65 per cent of the population in Protestant Europe and 70 to 80 per cent in Catholic Europe were still illiterate (Cipolla, 1969). Today close on 100 per cent of the adults in all these countries are literate, that is, are able to read at least on an elementary level. At the beginning of the nineteenth century in Britain only one child in twenty of the appropriate age groups frequented primary school; by the middle of the century, the proportion had risen to one in seven or eight. In recent years, in Britain as in other Western countries, practically all children of the appropriate age obtain a primary education. The

growth of secondary education has also been quite extensive, a process which has been continued even in recent years, as indicated in Table 8.1.

Clearly the growth has been most formidable in the United States. In 1870, only 2 per cent of all seventeen-year-olds were enrolled in high school; by 1910, the percentage had risen to 8·8 (Tyack, 1967, p. 468); in 1960, the table indicates, the proportion of youngsters of the appropriate age groups enrolled in high school reached 64 per cent; and in 1975, 91 per cent. The growth of secondary education in the various European countries, though less dramatic, has also been substantial. In recent years almost all have afforded secondary education to over 70 per cent of the appropriate age groups.

In most Western countries higher education is still reserved for a minority, but even in this area the increase has been far from negligible (Table 8.1). Once more, the growth has been most prominent in the United States: in 1870 only 1·68 per cent of the appropriate age groups were enrolled in institutions of higher education (Brookover and Gottlieb, 1964, p. 53); in 1975 the proportion had reached 54 per cent. But even in most of Western Europe close to one-fifth (or even more) of the appropriate cohorts have been enrolled in institutions of higher learning.[5]

The impact on scholastic standards
This raises the question of what impact the structural changes in Western education and the consequent explosive growth in educational participation have had on scholastic standards. One misgiving frequently expressed is that while these developments have led to an upward levelling of educational opportunities, they have also led to a downward levelling of educational standards. In other words, although more people benefit from education, they are benefiting from a lower quality of education.

To see whether these misgivings had any basis in reality, the International Association for the Evaluation of Educational Achievement (IEA), in its international study of achievement in science and reading comprehension, carried out a comparison between countries that had recently increased their secondary enrolments and countries that had not. This comparison showed that although for all countries combined the overall correlation between recent growth in secondary enrolments and aggregate achievements was negative, for the developed (mainly Western) countries, the correlation was *positive* even though small. This means that those Western countries which recently increased their secondary attendance had higher aggregate achievements than

Table 8.1 *Growth in secondary and higher education in Western countries, 1960–75*

Country	Percentage of age group enrolled in secondary schools		Percentage of population aged 20–4 enrolled in higher education	
	1960	1975	1960	1975
Australia	51	71	13	22
Austria	50	75	8	17
Belgium	69	84	9	22
Canada	50	94	16	35
Denmark	56	59	10	28
Federal Republic of Germany	53	70	6	20
Finland	75	107 (*sic*)	7	17
France	46	85	8	18
Ireland	35	65	9	16
Italy	34	71	7	24
Netherlands	58	86	13	24
New Zealand	73	83	13	27
Norway	53	90	7	21
Sweden	55	70	9	22
Switzerland	38	69	7	8
United Kingdom	67	76	9	16
United States	64	91	32	54

Source: World Bank (1978), p. 111.

those which did not (Passow *et al.*, 1976, ch. 3). On a preliminary basis, this result seems to dispel the misgiving that the expansion of Western education has had a negative effect on educational standards. However, it is possible that it is not the *recent* increase in secondary education, but rather the overall increase and the resulting rate of attendance which counts, and that the countries with highest attendance rates are the most likely to suffer from the lowering of standards.

This misgiving has been expressed in particular with regard to American secondary education where the schools are comprehensive, where massive increase in participation has advanced further, and where attendance rates are higher than in any other Western country. It has been expressed for instance by Peterson (1960, p. 175):

Its [secondary education's] disadvantages, in the retardation of the able pupil are admitted —it is, for instance, American educationists who point out that academically the American college entrant is two years behind his European counterpart and that 'pupils who have studied any given subject in the secondary school do not succeed any better in college than those who have not studied it'.

It seems that this misgiving has indeed been widely prevalent amongst American educationists. Torsten Husén (1972, p. 101) writes that at a conference on education which he attended in the United States in the late 1950s, one of the speakers compared American high schools unfavourably with their European counterparts, and that this implicit criticism did not elicit any hostile response from the audience since it fitted their own conceptions. Husén reports that he subsequently took the floor and pointed out that the comparison made was between American high-school graduates who comprised about 30 per cent of their age group at the time, and the small group of European academic secondary graduates who, in most countries, at that time, comprised no more than 5 per cent of theirs. This, he held, was obviously an unfair comparison; the question should rather be asked, whether the American comprehensive system is capable of bringing the top 5 per cent of its students up to the same level of performance as their European counterparts.

Husén goes on to report that the IEA in its international study on achievement in mathematics found that American students taking mathematics and science in the senior year of their high-school studies perform on the average far less well than British students in the same grade. However, when the average score of the top 4 or 5 per cent of the relevant cohorts in the various countries were compared, the American students did not score significantly worse than their equivalents in most European countries (Husén (ed.), 1967, vol. 2, pp. 122–3; 1972, pp. 115–6; 1977). The same holds for other subjects as well. The IEA study of achievement in science and reading comprehension shows that the United States and other countries offering mass schooling at the secondary level have not penalized their top achievers (Passow *et al.*, 1976, ch. 3).

Thus, on the face of it, it would seem that the American system has achieved a great educational breakthrough in recent years. It has succeeded in providing high-school education[6] for almost all youngsters, in preventing large-scale attrition, and at the same time in fostering an elite which does not fall significantly behind its counterpart in more selective systems. It thus seems to be getting the best of both worlds: the provision of education for the cohort as a whole and the advancement of the most talented as well. Yet, even by Husén's own testimony, the case seems more complex than that, for in Husén's book (1967, vol. 1, p. 106) it is also stated that:

> The corollary of lesser . . . selectivity is that much of the subject matter that in the first . . . types of systems is taught at the upper secondary school level has been moved up to the post-secondary level. Thus, the first two years of college in the United States, or in some places all four years, offer programs of study that are equivalent to the terminal classes at the French Lycée or the German Gymnasium.

Hence, although the top 4 or 5 per cent of the American cohort may not fall far behind their European equivalents, they are still obliged to enrol in a lower level of tertiary studies, at which they must spend at least two years before they catch up with European university entrants. It seems, then, that the advancement of the cohort as a whole still extorts a certain price in the retardation of the most able.

It is, therefore, not easy to evaluate the overall impact of the increase in education, especially secondary education, on scholastic standards. Once again, it seems that the best formulation of the problem is presented in Husén's book (1967, vol. 1, p. 111). According to this formulation, the crucial question (which unfortunately, is seldom made explicit) is: what criteria should be chosen as indicators for the scholastic standards of the different systems? Those in favour of a selective system tend to choose the attainment of the minority group that represents the end product of the academic program and disregard the rest. Those in favour of a comprehensive system offering wider participation prefer to consider the attainment of all who enter the system.

The impact on class representation

A further question would be how the structural changes and the dramatic growth in education have affected the representation of class in the education system. The 'mainstream' sociological view has been that more education results in more equal education, and it is this belief that has spurred the reforms undertaken in various Western countries. The Marxist school, however, denies this claim categorically. Actual developments in this respect have been rather complex, with some fluctuations over the centuries.

In the medieval period, formal and especially higher education was confined almost exclusively to the descendants of the upper classes. While some talented lower-class youngsters could gain admittance, their numbers were so minute as to be negligible. Subsequent industrialization rendered the inherited educational system inadequate, but after the initial opening up of the system a tighter pattern set in. In eighteenth-century Britain, for instance, lower-class representation in education was surprisingly large but by the nineteenth century this trend had patently been reversed. As Hans (1961) recounts:

> It is quite wrong to assume that [in the eighteenth century] only the upper class had the privilege of university education. The social composition of pupils in secondary schools and of students in the universities was more democratic than in the middle of the nineteenth century and even at the beginning of the twentieth century. About 50 per cent of the pupils in grammar schools, both public and private, were of lower social origin, as well as about 25 per cent of the students at Oxford and Cambridge. If we were to count the grandsons as well as the sons of farmers and craftsmen, the percentage would be much higher . . . [this] was facilitated by the peculiar organizations of grammar schools and universities. The majority of endowed schools . . . catered to the lower middle class, farmers and craftsmen. In many of them, special funds were established for free education of poor scholars chosen by local parishes. Private local grammar schools . . . were comparatively inexpensive and were attended by sons of farmers and artisans. Thus there was a constant supply of students for both universities from the lower groups. In the universities poor students could continue their education by working as 'servitors' (Oxford), or 'sizars' (Cambridge). (p. 141)

During the nineteenth century, however, the class structure changed considerably and

> secondary schools and universities changed their character accordingly. The grammar schools grew into expensive boarding institutions . . . available only to children of wealthy parents; and the universities in consequence became privileged institutions, closed to the sons of the lower classes as the practice of 'servitors' and 'sizars' was discontinued (p. 142).

The situation in nineteenth-century Germany was not much different. Only the upper echelons of the population had access to academic secondary and higher education and to the privileges which were its rewards. Data on the family background of university students suggest that the elite of the highly educated replenished itself to a remarkable extent from its own offspring. As the century progressed, new groups did increase their representation at the institutions of higher learning, and the rate of this increase was accelerated during the closing decades of the century. But even then the lower and working classes still added only an insignificant fraction to the university population. Of the students at Prussian universities between 1887 and 1890 little more than one in a thousand were the sons of workers and in 1902-3 only one in a hundred were of that origin (Ringer, 1967).

Germany apparently carried the exclusion of the working class from academic education to extremes unknown in other Western countries, but the general pattern of working-class disadvantage was common to all. In France, for instance, the results of a survey on secondary education in the 1860s (reviewed by Harrigan, 1976) indicate that because of high tuition fees and the division between primary and secondary education, the latter was not available to the working class. Less than 2 per cent of the students in French secondary schools at that time were sons of unskilled (rural or urban) workers and only 6 per cent were sons of skilled workers. But while few workers sent their children to secondary schools, this was not true of the lower middle class. Some 29 per cent of the students in secondary schools were sons of peasants, lower white-collar workers and shopkeepers.

Differences in education were thus one of the strongest social barriers between the working class and the more advantaged classes, a situation which was carried over to the middle of the twentieth century as well. For although working-class youngsters have gained a certain foothold in secondary and higher education, they have remained considerably under-represented as compared with their proportion of the population. Even the big increases in educational participation in the 1950s have brought only marginal advances in lower-class participation. One example of this phenomenon is illustrated by Table 8.2 which classifies the graduates of Denmark's *gymnasia* in 1951 and 1961 by parental occupation.

During this period the proportion of the age group obtaining the leaving certificate increased from 4·7 to 7 per cent, yet there was little change in leavers' origins. Indeed, a rather marked class bias persisted: almost 20 per cent of the pupils in the final grades of compulsory schooling came from agricultural homes and 32 per cent came from manual working-class homes. Together they constituted over half the population; but youngsters of such origins made up only 13-15 per cent of *gymnasium* graduates.

A similar stability existed in England and Wales during the same

Table 8.2 *Occupations of parents of certified* gymnasium *leavers in Denmark – 1951–61*

	1951	1961
Higher non-manual	36·4	37·0
Clerical	19·0	19·2
Tradesmen	28·9	25·4
Agriculture	7·5	6·9
Manual	5·6	8·0
Other	2·6	4·5
Total	100·0	101·0
Number of leavers	2,803	5,455

Source: OECD (1969), p. 79.

period. The percentage of youngsters admitted to academic secondary education increased considerably but class differences persisted: the proportion of youngsters from professional and managerial homes was from three to six times larger than that from the other occupational groups. In the Netherlands, although the number of certificate holders leaving general secondary education more than doubled between 1949 and 1960, the percentage of males from upper middle-class homes remained unchanged at 25 per cent, and that from lower-class homes increased only slightly from 21 to 23 per cent. In Italy, despite an increase in the number of secondary-school graduates between 1953 and 1959, students from professional and upper middle-class homes continued to comprise around two-thirds of them, falling only slightly from 67.5 to 65.9 per cent. Even in Sweden, where participation in upper-secondary and higher education expanded more rapidly, social inequalities continued. In 1960 manual workers made up more than half of the Swedish labour force but their children represented . less than a quarter of gymnasium admissions (OECD, 1969).

It seems that in recent years the representation of youngsters from working-class backgrounds – at least in higher education – has increased significantly as can be seen from Table 8.3. Even so it should be remembered that almost half the active male population in the late 1960s and early 1970s in most Western European countries were manual workers. Yet their sons and daughters constituted a quarter or

Table 8.3 *Distribution of university students by father's occupation in Western countries (in percentages)/a*

Country	Year	Students by category of father's occupation				
		Professionals, managers, higher-level administration	Clerical, sales-workers	Self-employed	Manual workers	Other
Austria	1965	32·4	31·8	17·3	5·5	13·0
	1970	27·1	35·2	17·2	10·8	9·7
Belgium	1962	30·0	15·0	23·2	22·8	9·0
	1966	32·3	18·3	21·0	22·8	5·6
Denmark	1964	24·3	24·9	34·6	15·5	0·7
Federal Republic of Germany	1952	38·3	22·9	34·1	4·4	0·3
	1970–1	26·2	35·7	24·9	12·6	0·6
France	1959	29·8	29·9	23·1	4·0	13·2
	1973	30·2	24·5	17·9	12·3	15·1
Italy	1953–4	19·0	44·3	23·9	11·4	1·4
	1967	9·4	39·5	23·9	19·6	7·6
Luxembourg	1964/5	27·3	37·9	23·3	3·2	8·3
	1972	26·2	37·7	21·3	9·4	5·4
Netherlands	1954–5	47·0	23·0	23·0	7·0	–
	1970	36·2	29·5	18·9	13·5	2·4
Norway	1964	33·6	11·1	12·7	23·9	18·7
	1970	40·8	15·9	8·5	17·9	16·9

Sweden	1960–1	31·1	29·5	21·1	14·3	4·0
Switzerland	1959–60	51·1	24·1	5·0	15·2	4·6
United Kingdom (England and Wales)	1960	62·9	9·9	–	27·2	–
	1971	28·5	19·2	–	48·4	3·9
United States	1958	52·4	9·6	10·6	26·6	0·8
	1965	37·0	20·0	8·0	34·0	1·0

Source: Busch (1975), pp. 164–5.

[a]The author notes that the comparability of the figures is too low to attach much significance to inter-country comparisons, but generally the figures permit comparisons over time, except for the United Kingdom, where the 1971 figures are based on a much wider coverage of education than those for 1960.

less of university students, with the United Kingdom and the United States as the only major exceptions.

A similar situation prevailed in Australia. Anderson and Western (1970) examined the social backgrounds of students entering four professional faculties of universities in all six Australian states and found that although industrial workers constituted about 60 per cent of the population their offspring comprised only 22·6 per cent of entering students. In a study of the social composition of 6,000 students entering the University of Melbourne in 1969 and 1970, Dow *et al.*, (1972), reported that the university still drew disproportionately from the upper strata of the population. Only in the United States have working-class youngsters made up over a third of university students and only in the United Kingdom have they approached one half of students and thus come close to reflecting their proportion in the population (see Table 8.3). Thus is would still be correct to say for most Western countries that despite the massive expansion of enrolments, and despite the changes in class representation, sons and daughters of the favoured have managed to hold on to a disproportionate percentage of university openings.

Explaining the bias in class representation
How can this continuing persistence of the class bias be explained? On the face of it, the most obvious explanation has to do with economic resources. Evidently, the parents who are worse off financially would be less able to afford tuition (where required) and to support their children through their high school and college studies. As it turns out, however, this is not the decisive factor. Recent surveys of existent research on attendance rates and scholastic achievements provide fairly consistent evidence that the introduction or expansion of free secondary and higher education for all have not changed the social structure of the enrolment to any great extent: children who take advantage of the increased opportunities for free education are already in a favoured or semi-favoured position (Husén, 1972, p. 33). The same is true of the provision of extensive scholarships. In George Bereday's (1973, p. 38) words: 'Many well-meaning and some astute egalitarian programs, such as scholarships for the poor, have been tried, only to end in the chagrin of the planners because they wind up in the hands of the rich.'

Even in Australia, where the abolition of university tuition and the introduction of a tertiary education allowance freed the less well-off parents from the burden of financial support, there was no substantial increase in the proportion of lower-class youngsters in higher education.

To be sure, these measures do not provide a solution for youngsters whose families are in dire straits and have no choice but to turn dependants into earners and family supporters. But the proportion of youngsters whose access to education is barred by such extreme duress is apparently not large.

A second and seemingly more important set of factors has to do with inter-class differences in child-rearing practices, and specifically with differences in the amount and quality of intellectual stimulation which parents of different classes are able to offer their children (and which is only partly connected with financial means). It has been reported, for instance, that working-class parents lag behind middle-class parents in their linguistic skills – including command of vocabulary and complexity of verbalization. They tend to engage in a lesser amount of verbal communication with their children, and the resulting verbal retardation affects these children's capacity of handling abstract symbols as well as their general mental development (Bernstein, 1962). It has also become evident that in comparison with middle-class parents, working-class parents have less financial ability and less awareness of the importance of supplying their children with toys, with books and newspapers, and with separate rooms and undisturbed time-spans in which to concentrate and prepare their homework. They are also less aware of the importance of limiting their children's television viewing and of encouraging them to read, and are less able to assist them in their school work.

A third and no less important set of factors has to do with parental attitudes and aspirations. Research has shown that the drive for achievement in general and for educational achievement in particular is weaker amongst working-class than amongst middle-class parents. For instance, working-class parents are more likely to be 'present oriented', that is, to stress the immediate gratification of needs. Middle-class parents, on the other hand, tend to be more 'future oriented', to put more stress on 'affective neutrality',[7] that is, on forgoing present satisfactions for the sake of greater gains in the future, an attitude which is crucial for the enhancement of educational (and other) achievements.

Middle-class parents also tend to have higher educational aspirations for their children. For instance, Douglas and his associates (1968), in a study of a sample of youngsters in England, found that 84 per cent of middle-class parents with higher education wished their children to obtain higher education, as compared to 21 per cent among manual workers with elementary education only. And even when working-class parents have high educational aspirations for their children, these aspirations tend to be on a generalized, abstract level, and they are less likely than middle-class parents to give their children the concrete encouragement and guidance that would make the realization of these aspirations possible (Havighurst, 1970; Goldthorpe *et al.*, 1969). It has also been shown that youngsters' own drive for educational achievement and their educational aspirations are strongly affected by parental attitudes and encouragement. In consequence, working-class children are less likely than their middle-class peers to embrace achievement-oriented values and high educational aspirations (Brookover and Gottlieb, 1964, pp. 153–92; Duncan *et al.*, 1972, p. 8; and Kahl, 1962).

A fourth set of factors has to do with school characteristics, teachers' competence and their attitudes towards different categories of students. Schools in lower-class neighbourhoods tend to be inferior in terms of facilities, equipment and teachers' competence. On the basis of his large nationwide survey of American education, Coleman reached the conclusion that these factors have only a negligible impact on youngsters' educational achievements (Coleman *et al.*, 1973). Not so with teachers' attitudes. Many observers, including Havighurst (1970), have claimed that teachers (who themselves are middle-class), tend to have less favourable attitudes towards, and lower expectations from, working-class children, and that these attitudes and expectations (no less than parental attitudes) exert considerable influence on the children's own educational expectations and aspirations. Concomitantly it has also been demonstrated (Coleman *et al.*, 1973) that the children's own self-images and aspirations have a considerable impact on their actual educational achievements.

Finally there is the problem of intelligence. Research has shown that there is a considerable stratification of measured intelligence[8] by social class (even though there is also much intra-class variability). The extent to which these class differences in intelligence are due to genetic factors (heredity) or to environmental factors (such as those enumerated above), is a matter of ongoing controversy. But whatever their source, these class differences in intelligence clearly account for some of the class differences in educational attainment. It is difficult to estimate, however, how decisive intelligence is in this respect.[9] It has been demonstrated, for instance, that even when class background is controlled, measured intelligence has a substantial, independent effect on educational attainments (Waller, 1973). But, by the same token, it has also been demonstrated that class background has an independent effect on educational attainments even when intelligence is controlled (Rogoff, 1962; Wolfle, 1962). This is another way of saying that middle-class children have a better chance of advancing in their studies than working-class children have, even when they do not surpass them in intelligence.

The impact on social mobility

How important are educational achievements as far as the youngsters' respective 'life chances' (that is, their future occupations and incomes) are concerned? Is education instrumental in providing social mobility as 'mainstream' sociologists have claimed, or does it merely translate class background into social position and thereby perpetuate the class structure, as Marxists have insisted? And have the developments in the structure of education effected any change in this respect?

Both schools of thought would probably concur that in the Middle Ages, school and university education was devoted exclusively to the task of preparing the descendants of the upper classes for elite positions. They would probably also not dispute that by the eighteenth century, in Britain at any rate, the situation had changed substantially. As Hans's (1961) historical analysis shows, the educational facilities then available greatly helped the social advancement of the abler members of the lower classes. At that time, the great majority of the lower clergy, teachers, and physicians, were people of humble origin who had worked their way upward through academic studies. In addition, poor boys of ability could and did rise through the educational facilities of apprenticeship. The great majority of surgeons, chemists, mathematics teachers, engineers, technicians and scientists, reached their positions in this manner. There was also the possibility of reaching such positions through self-instruction with the aid of public lectures and textbooks and there was a considerable group of autodidacts who had in fact done so.

The two schools of thought would probably also accept Hans's statement that by the nineteenth century the situation was quite different: since secondary and higher education, in Britain and elsewhere, was now more restricted to the privileged classes, it had less of a role in elevating the lower ones. They would similarly accept Harrigan's (1976) contention that secondary education in nineteenth-century France provided only limited mobility as the lower-class graduates came to occupy only slightly higher positions than those of their fathers. The question, however, is: how was the situation changed in the twentieth century? It is on this issue that the two schools of thought are at odds with each other.

A preliminary way to tackle this problem is to compare once more the selective systems of education with the comprehensive ones where rates of attendance are much higher, this time with regard to the social mobility they do (or do not) afford. Since the former systems are gradually giving way to the latter, such a comparison may help to establish some general trends with regard to social mobility through education. One such comparison has been made by Turner (1962), who argues that the two systems are based on different organizing principles: sponsored mobility and contest mobility.

Under the former system (most typically represented by pre-reform Britain) elite recruits are chosen by the established elites or their agents. Joining the elite is like entry into an exclusive club where candidates are sponsored by one or more members on the basis of their perceived qualities. Under the latter system (most typically represented by the United States), elite status is the prize in an open contest and is taken by the aspirants' own efforts. Under the former system there is early selection of the relatively small number of recruits necessary to fill anticipated vacancies. Under the latter system, the channels of advancement are kept open as long as possible, and everyone is kept in the running until the final stage.

Turner's comparison, however, points merely to the differences between the two systems in the *mode* of mobility rather than in its *extent*. The recently expanding comprehensive system does not obviate selection, but merely postpones it from the pre-secondary to the tertiary level. At this level, selection in the United States, for example, is quite stringent, even though in many cases rather subtle. Due to the large number of American universities and colleges, practically anyone who wants to can usually enrol at some kind of tertiary institution. Selection thus takes place not through rejection of applicants, but rather through the screening out of students during the course of their tertiary studies. Some, especially State universities, bow to the pressure for broad admission but then protect their standards by heavy attrition. This makes failure abrupt, public and fully visible.[10] Other, especially lower-ranking institutions of higher education, perform the same office in a more subtle manner, thus fulfilling what Clark (1962b) has termed a 'cooling out' function for the majority of their students. Continuing Turner's line of thought, Clark maintains that the American system is faced with the inconsistency between encouragement of all to participate in the race and the reality of limited opportunity to reach the finish line. For large numbers of aspirants, failure, the blocking of mobility, is thus inevitable. Since the system raises the aspirations of many but can grant fulfilment to only a few, it must also find a way to mollify the rest, in order to minimize frustration and deflect resentment.

Many colleges accordingly sidetrack unpromising students into easier fields of study, into extension divisions, remedial classes, or terminal programs which offer merely para-professional or vocational training. Diversion of students into such substitute programs reflects less unfavourably on their personal capacity than does dismissal, and much effort is invested in leading them to accept it as a satisfactory alternative. This 'cooling out' function can only be fulfilled as long as it remains hidden from the students themselves. Hence it is carried out through a variety of subtle procedures such as skilful counselling. Through these, students are made aware of their limitations and encouraged to scale down their ambitions; substitute avenues of achievement are made to appear similar to the original ones and failure is redefined as orientation to new goals and as the matching of a training program to one's individual ability. In this manner awareness of failure and the consequent stress on the individual (and the system) is minimized.

Following Turner's and Clark's analysis, then, it may be said that in the United States, with its comprehensive system of secondary education and its massive rates of attendance, selection is postponed and in many cases becomes less visible, and that the same may occur in other Western educational systems as their secondary schools become comprehensive and as their enrolment increases. However, they leave unanswered the questions of whether those selected for the completion of higher education thereby gain a substantial advantage in occupational achievement, whether education thus fosters occupational mobility, and whether its capacity to do so has increased in recent years.

A great variety of other studies, however, have addressed themselves to this issue. A re-analysis of some of these studies and of existent census data has led Anderson (1962) and Jencks (1972) to express scepticism as to the role of education in social mobility and to conclude that education accounts for only a small part of the variation in occupational rank, income and class position.

But the studies re-analysed by Anderson do not seem to support his scepticism. Thus, for instance, the national study on social class by Centers (1949), shows that only 23 per cent of the sons of manual workers obtained jobs superior to their fathers', if they had received less schooling than their fathers, whereas among those whose education exceeded their fathers', 53 per cent attained such jobs. Another study he re-analysed was that by Glass (1954). This study shows that

among British sons of unskilled and semi-skilled workers, 38 per cent of
those with more than a grammar school education achieved positions in
the top stratum — as against one in twenty among those with elementary education only. Glass's data also show that half of the people from
working-class backgrounds who moved into the top stratum had little
or no schooling. But, even so, the overall results seem to strengthen
rather than weaken the thesis on the connection between education
and mobility. As for Jencks, it has been claimed (e.g., Husén, 1975;
Psacharopoulos, 1975), that there are numerous deficiencies in his re-
analysis of data and that his conclusion on the feeble relation between
education and mobility is thus based on faulty methodology.

This claim is strengthened by the fact that practically all other
research done on this topic has established a substantial link between
education and occupational achievement or mobility. Thus, in an extensive research project on a cross-section of 20,000 American men, Blau
and Duncan (1967) established that the proportion of those who
experience intergenerational upward mobility increases steadily with
education from 12 per cent for those who had no schooling, to 76 per
cent for those who had gone beyond college. They also established that
the proportion of those who have moved up a large distance from their
social origins increased in the same regular fashion from under 8 per
cent for those with less than five years of schooling, to 53 per cent
for those with postgraduate education. Finally, they established that
there was a correlation of 0·60 between level of education and level
of occupational achievement, and that even when father's occupation
was controlled, there was still a correlation of 0·39 between the two.

Similarly, a survey and subsequent follow-up of all 1957 high-
school seniors in Wisconsin conducted by Sewell *et al.* (1970) indicated
that when social background factors were controlled, the path coefficient[11] between educational and occupational attainment was 0·55.
Similar results have been reported by Duncan *et al.* (1972); Alexander
et al. (1975), and Wilson and Portes (1975).

For Britain, a study of a national male sample conducted in 1972
by Halsey (1977) shows that when background factors are controlled,
the correlation between educational and occupational achievements
ranged between 0·32 and 0·34. Education thus has a far from negligible
independent effect on occupational achievement in Britain too. Even
stronger results in a wider perspective are presented by Psacharopoulos
(1975), who reviewed the major research in this area in the United
States as well as in other Western countries and came to the conclusion that when social background and even ability are controlled,

education is responsible for a major part of occupational earning differentials.

Moreover, it seems that the effect of education on occupational achievement and hence on mobility has intensified in recent years. Blau and Duncan (1967), for instance, found that among respondents' fathers, the correlation between education and occupation was 0·51, somewhat lower than the corresponding correlation of 0·59 observed for the respondents themselves. For Britain, the aforementioned study by Halsey shows that, when background factors are controlled, the correlation of education with occupational position is only slightly greater for younger cohorts (0·32 for those aged 40–59, as against 0·34 for those aged 25–39). But stronger differences are reported for Australia by Broom and Jones (1976), on the basis of a national survey conducted in the mid-1960s. They show that whereas the correlation between father's education and his last or present job is only 0·29, for sons the correlation is substantially higher at 0·43, and among sons themselves the correlation between education and occupation is higher for younger than for older men.[12] According to the various authors, these data, although sparse, suggest at least tentatively that the influence of education in promoting social mobility has somewhat increased within the last generation or so.

A question mark still remains, however, concerning the manner in which education has exerted this influence. Some observers claim that it has done so by imparting skills, through the content of what is being taught, and through the fostering of cognitive development. Others have claimed that education serves basically as a selection, labelling and accreditation agency whose main function is to put a stamp of approval on suitable recruits for jobs. But either way, or most likely through a combination of both, the effect of education can hardly be doubted.

Conclusion

All this leads to the question of whether the recent changes in education have resulted in increasing equality of educational opportunity for children of different classes. The answer probably depends largely on the manner in which equality of such opportunity is conceived. When conceived as equality of treatment, as the offering of equal education, it may certainly be seen to have increased. The revolutionary growth in the numbers of those benefiting from all levels of education, the trend towards the elimination of tuition fees for secondary education, the increase in scholarships and other financial aid for higher education, the trend towards the elimination of dual track educational systems and the introduction of comprehensive secondary schools, have all resulted in a more uniform and equal treatment of all children.

Recently, however, another conception of equality of educational opportunity has emerged which relates not to equal treatment but rather to equal outcome. According to Coleman (1966, pp. 71-2), 'equality of educational opportunity implies not merely "equal" schools but equally effective schools, whose influences will overcome the differences in starting point of children from different social groups'. As Husén (1972, p. 24) sees it, equality of opportunity in this sense implies not equal, but rather differential, educational treatment for children of different class origin. Accordingly, 'the issue can be stated in a paradoxical way, namely that every child should have equal opportunity to be treated unequally'.

When this conception is adopted, then the recent developments and reforms must be seen as less far-reaching where equality of educational opportunity is concerned. For although the representation of working-class youngsters at the higher levels of education has recently increased, they are in most countries still greatly under-represented in relation to their proportion in the population. This persistent under-representation has been accompanied by a certain (advertent or inadvertent) manipulation whereby equality of educational opportunity has been made to appear greater than it is in fact by 'cooling out' the low achievers and by inducing them to blame themselves rather than the system for their lack of success. This, in turn, has led to the deflection of potential criticism from the system and has thus contributed to its stability.

This does not imply, however, that education's *only* effect is to stabilize the system by perpetuating the existent forces and relations of production and the existent class structure. For one thing, the upper levels of education are increasingly linked to research, which in turn produces technological changes, that is, changes in the forces of production. According to Marx's theory such changes must eventually lead to changes in the relations of production and hence to changes in the class structure as well. Moreover, although Althusser has claimed that higher education produces the agents of exploitation and repression and inculcates them with the attitudes appropriate for their social roles, the opposite can also be seen to be the case. In recent years, many universities all over the Western world have become the centres of radicalism and protest. Although this trend has recently abated, and many former radicals have subsequently become conservatives, and although only a minority of students may have been actively involved, many have been affected. Many more have been exposed to the influences of radicalism and thus could, at least potentially, have been affected. This is another way of saying that higher education may teach not only to 'command' but also to revolt, at least to those who are open and receptive to this type of teaching. Finally, empirical data have shown that education has indeed had a substantial role in promoting social mobility and thereby the flexibility of the class structure.

Education in contemporary Western society thus contains within itself a paradox. On the one hand, working-class youngsters, even when they equal their middle-class peers in intelligence, are still under-represented in the educational system and thus have not been receiving an equitable share of one of society's major resources. On the other hand, the under-representation of lower-class youngsters in the upper echelons of the educational system has clearly been diminishing in recent years and education has had a significant and apparently increasing effect on social mobility. It thus still perpetuates class inequality for some, while at the same time making for greater equality and increased opportunities for others, and for greater flexibility in the system as a whole. At this present time, it is too early to tell whether the recent structural changes will eventually tip the scale towards even greater equality and flexibility or whether the remaining inequities and inequalities will be perpetuated into the future.

Selected readings

Althusser, L. (1971), 'Ideology and Ideological State Apparatuses', excerpt from his *Lenin and Philosophy and Other Essays* (trans. B. Brewster), London, New Left Books, pp. 123–73.

Connell, R. W. (1977), *Ruling Class Ruling Culture*, Cambridge University Press.

Etzioni, A., and Etzioni-Halevy, E. (eds) (1973), *Social Change* (2nd edn), New York, Basic Books, chs 24, 48.

Husén T. (1975), *Social Influences on Educational Attainments*, Centre for Educational Research and Innovation, Paris, OECD.

Karabel, J., and Halsey, A. H. (eds) (1977), *Power and Ideology in Education*, New York, Oxford University Press.

Peterson, A. D. C. (1960), *A Hundred Years of Education* (2nd edn), New York, Collier Books.

Part III

The previous chapters have brought out (among other things) some problematic features of Western capitalist societies. These and other problems have led some people to search for alternative social formations. We now turn to a discussion of the most important of these: communes and co-operatives.

9 · The search for alternatives

The problematic features of Western capitalist societies brought out in the previous chapters include, among other things, the alienation from work (as highlighted by Marx); the loss of traditional communities and common values (as analysed by Comte, Tönnies and Durkheim); the excessive rationalization (as dealt with by Weber); some persistent inequalities in the allocation of rewards, and the existence of an under-class of the unemployed, and the ethnically disadvantaged who do not share in society's growing affluence. To this, some contemporary critics have added the cog-like character of the individual's place in large-scale organizations and other impersonal settings, excessive materialism, the competitive struggle or the 'rat-race' into which individuals are forced, the confining and isolating nature of the nuclear family, the fragmented nature of all other relationships, and the consequent inability of the individual to form his identity and to express his individuality (Rigby, 1974a, ch. 3).

It has been claimed that most people take these and other problems in their stride because they view the social institutions in which they live as part of the natural order of things. In A. Rigby's words (1974a, p. 300): 'The real power lies in the fact that the values and the assumptions on which the system rests are never questioned by the mass of the people.' But in Western societies there is also a minority who view existent structures and institutions as mere human constructs which therefore can also be transformed through human action. Some of these people attempt to create social alternatives which (they hope), may eventually form the prototype for such a transformation. Remarkably, they attempt to do so on a peaceful, voluntary basis from below, in contrast to the seizure of central power and the introduction of reforms by coercive measures from above, the results of which have been so eminently evident in totalitarian regimes.

The question must be raised, however, whether the social formations thus established are indeed viable alternatives to the existent social

patterns in contemporary Western society. To answer this question the following criteria of evaluation are hereby suggested:
(a) Do these social formations solve a substantial part of the problems for which existent Western societies have been criticized?
(b) Do they not, through the very process of solving existing problems, create other and equally severe ones?
(c) Are they relatively stable social formations in which members can participate on a more or less permanent basis?
(d) Are they available and/or attractive to a sizeable proportion of the members of present-day Western societies?

In what follows, two major social alternatives are described and then evaluated according to these criteria.

Western communes

The most encompassing alternative social formation created in modern society is the commune. A commune may be defined as a group of three or more drawn from more than one family who are:
(a) associated with each other on a voluntary basis;
(b) living together on the same premises or the same entity of land;
(c) earning their livelihood through joint work at a project or projects owned collectively;
(d) and/or pooling their resources and incomes.

Communes, as here defined, are not a new phenomenon. The first known historical communes are those of the Essenes, established during the second century B.C., in Palestine. Since then, communes (both religious and secular) have become part of a long-standing tradition in the Western world. They have been set up by Christian heretical sects especially during the last 300 years; seventeenth-century Europe was full of such sects and when America was colonized, many emigrated there in search of religious freedom and set up their communes.

The nineteenth century

By the nineteenth century, religious communes had proliferated and were firmly established in the United States and secular communes were also coming into being. According to one estimate, over 100 religious communes with a total membership of 100,000 came into being in that country during the nineteenth century. They represented a great variety of sects including Shakers, Rappists, Zoarites, Amana Communists, Perfectionists, Separatists, Aurora Communists, Icarians, Inspirationists, and the communes they set up included Amana, Oneida, Zoar and many others.

The religious communes were established in order to enable their members to live according to their creeds. The creeds themselves were of great diversity but common to all communes was the very existence of the unifying faith as such. Also common to religious communes was the basic principle of the subordination of the individual will to the general interest of the collective — that is, their emphasis on collectivism — and the principle of subordination to the collective's leaders. The actual patterns of leadership varied from commune to commune, but most had strong leaders who established articles of faith and organization. Formally, leaders had to obtain the members' consent before making decisions but in practice members usually consented to any decisions the leaders might make.

The communes had clear rules and organizational patterns in which their emphasis on collectivism was institutionalized. Most required their members to sign over all their personal property, to live together in communally owned buildings, to eat together in common dining halls, and to share all group assets. Members were not paid salaries but were provided with all their needs regardless of their work. Some communes had general stores and gave their members allowances to make purchases, but there was no connection between the size of the allowances and the nature of employment. According to some observers this spelled absolute economic equality as leaders were accorded no special advantages over the rank-and-file. At the same time, hired labour was employed and some communes could not have existed without it.

Most communes were rural, with agriculture as their economic base, although some engaged in manufacturing as well. Work and work quality were greatly emphasized. For this reason, and also because members equated the collective interest with their own, they worked well even though their individual standard of living did not depend on it. Jobs were commonly rotated in order to prevent undue attachment to individual work at the expense of commitment to the collective.

Religious communes also went to some length to discourage exclusive bonds between members, and especially marriage partners, as these were considered detrimental to the collective. Most outstanding in this respect was the commune of Oneida where the nuclear family was abolished and replaced by 'complex marriage', which in effect meant that members could live with anyone they wished. In other communes marriage, though not discarded, was at least discouraged. Attachment to children was similarly attenuated though not eliminated. In Separatist communes, for instance, children were raised in special children's homes. This did not involve a total rupture of family ties, but it emphasized the primacy of the collective into whose care the children had been delivered.

To enhance their intense collective existence the religious communes encouraged common activities such as prayer, singing and reading aloud. For the same purpose, they attempted to dissociate themselves completely from the outside world by physical and psychological boundaries. Their colonies were usually located in isolated areas and dealing with visitors entailed special rituals, including sometimes a special house-cleaning following their departure.

Because of their predominant collectivism, solidarity, strong leadership and clear patterns of organization, many of the religious communes were rather stable and lasted for generations. Even so, many were eventually eroded by surrounding society although others continued to be founded and some survived into the twentieth century.

Religious communes were the most stable but not the only communes founded in nineteenth-century America. Their secular counterparts were fashioned according to the utopian socialist schemes following either Robert Owen's or Charles Fourier's vision. The characteristic features of the Owenite communes was their attempt to institute complete equality by sharing equally what little wealth was available and their rejection of formal belief systems, formal organizational structures and formal sanctions — in order not to infringe upon the individual liberties of their members. In sharp contrast to religious communes, they emphasized individualism and had no real binding force of common values or solidarity holding them together. Work was neglected, controversy and divisions began to develop and most therefore disintegrated shortly after their establishment. The first such commune, New Harmony, was created in the '1820s. By 1825 a thousand people had settled there, but inadequate production and social friction led to its dissolution in 1827. Similar groups which came into being during these years disintegrated quickly too, and by the 1840s the Owenite movement had ceased to exist.

At that time a large number of communes patterned on Fourier's ideas sprung up in various parts of the United States. These communes, known as phalanxes, were even looser in their patterns than their Owenite predecessors, and allowed far more diversity. Fourier did not believe in complete equality or the abolition of private property. Accordingly, community lands or enterprises were frequently owned by non-member shareholders; typically, members worked on these lands or enterprises and drew salaries commensurate with their work. Personal effort was thus clearly related to personal rewards, since this was held to be more conducive to hard work. At the same time profits (in the form of dividends), went to shareholders commensurate with their holdings.

Despite their similarity to capitalist enterprises, these communes too did not last. Members were diverse in their background and character and shared no common beliefs binding them together. Frequently the phalanxes were established on arid soil and were forced to subsist at a very low economic level. When financial or social crises arose, solidarity was inadequate to overcome them and the communities disintegrated. Similar groups established in the 1860s also disintegrated and by the end of the 1860s the American secular, utopian-socialist communitarian movement was over (Holloway, 1966; Nordhoff, 1966; French and French, 1975, chs 4 and 9).

Community schemes guided by the same general philosophies existed at that time in Europe as well but their record was even less impressive. In nineteenth-century Britain, for instance, some twenty-eight communes have been identified including communes of utopian socialism, communes of agrarian socialism (which reflected a belief in getting back to the land as a source of moral regeneration), religious communes and finally anarchist communes (established during the last decade of the century), which rejected the state and other forms of centralized control. All in all these communes were not only few in numbers but few in members as well and were mostly of short duration.

The twentieth century

Nevertheless, the communal idea lived on. During the first half of the present century anarcho-pacifists founded similar communal ventures in both Britain and the United States. Rejecting any attempt to create authority structures and blueprints of communal life, they insisted on the sovereignty of the individual conscience, on the right of the individual to shape his own life, and relied mainly on spontaneous living arrangements. These communes proliferated for some time. In Britain, for instance, they reached a peak in the 1930s. Estimates of their numbers at that time vary between thirty and several hundred. But by the end of the war the momentum subsided, and most of them folded up or turned into private settlements. Although it did not last, the anarchist tradition was important in that it served as a forerunner to the contemporary, secular commune movement.

The twentieth century has also seen the establishment of religious communes. In Britain, they too reached their peak in the 1930s. Some of them attempted to reconcile Christianity with socialism, most notably The Society of Brothers whose communes were known as Bruderhöfe. The members of this group came to England from Germany to escape Nazi prosecution but eventually most of them moved on to America, especially Canada and the United States, where they set up communities with a total population of about a thousand.

In the latter country the major religious communes have been those of the Hutterites. They usually live frugal and ascetic lives, dress plainly, and do not engage in amusements. They subsist on agriculture and various enterprises; families live in common buildings and utilize common dining halls, bakeries and laundries. No salaries are paid to members and all get an approximately equal share of goods. They extend little or no power to women and live under a quasi-patriarchal type of government. Important decisions are arrived at by a majority vote of all adult male members, with an executive of about half a dozen senior members. Because of their disciplined way of life, the Hutterites have been highly successful: in 1965 there were some 17,800 Hutterites in North America living in a hundred and sixty-four communes.

Most other twentieth-century American religious sects lacked the strong common faith and the dedication of the nineteenth-century religious settlers. Financial backing came easily from wealthy sponsors and some of them became part of the capitalist system, dispensing with communes altogether, while others set up communes that were small and short-lived (French and French, 1975, ch. 9; Rigby, 1974a, ch. 2).

In recent years: the United States
A few religious communes have been prospering in the United States in recent years too. These include, besides the Hutterites and the Bruder-hof society (described above), a commune adhering to Eastern mysticism (the Lama Foundation); some radical Christian communes, communes set up by the Catholic Workers' Movement; and a few Quaker quasi-communes. Several of them put great emphasis on work, on unanimity (rather than majority) in decision-making and on assistance to the under-privileged. They thus combine communal living with a sense of common purpose — which has apparently contributed much to their success (Roberts, 1971, ch. 6).

But numerically, at least, the emphasis has shifted to the secular communal movement which was revived once more in the 1960s by adherents to the 'hippie movement', or the 'counter culture'. One major centre, where many of the movement's ideas and communal experiments were started off, was Haight-Ashbury in San Francisco and in the Bay area, but hippie communes sprang up in other parts of the United States as well.

During those years — D. French and E. French (1975) report — thousands of students left their parents' middle-class suburban settings and turned their backs on existent society, in an attempt to set up a communal lifestyle that would be as great a contrast as possible to that society. They followed their Owenite and their anarchist predecessors in their rejection of dogmatic social blueprints and especially authority structures, in their insistence that nothing should be imposed on their members and in their emphasis upon the right of the individual to 'do his own thing'.

To this was added the rejection of materialism and the reduction of consumption, as well as the rejection of the conventional capitalist work ethic, and the consequent tendency to refrain from regular, full-time employment. Mostly the communes subsisted on grants, on money from home, on welfare, on sporadic odd jobs of their members and, for rural communes, on a bit of farming, while many were closely related to the drug culture.

For a time it seemed that the counter-culture adherents had found a new viable way of life and had devised a new form of human relations — until the communes started to fold up as abruptly as they had been created. And even when they survived, group membership was not stable. Such counter-culture communes as still persisted in the 1970s have tended to serve mainly as temporary refuges for people in transit.

The reasons for this speedy disintegration lie in the neglect of work and subsistence. Most could not survive without a steady flow of gifts from the outside; when these ceased the communes were no longer viable. A paradox thus developed whereby the new lifestyle, which communitarians had created in order to liberate them from the system, in fact created a total dependency on it.

Another factor which brought about the speedy disintegration of the counter-culture communes lay in human relations problems. Especially detrimental were the tensions created by the necessity to allocate tasks in a setting in which no formal rules, division of labour and authority prevailed. As close relations between members were generally discouraged, interpersonal ties were tenuous and hence could not survive such tensions.

Many of these problems were exemplified in 'The Group', an urban commune on the Pacific North-West of the United States. This unit was founded in the 1960s by students and faculty from the local college and at its peak it had no less than fifty members. It was also quite affluent because of a sizeable foundation grant and because many members received cheques from home, so only a minority had to do remunerative work. Intimate relations between couples were frowned on and personal commitments were avoided. Consequently, human relations became diluted and people were forever joining and leaving. Since work was minimized, members spent most of their time lying around on the floor and engaging in intense discussions on such issues as women's liberation and civil rights. At the same time, children were not properly cared for, many of them were disturbed and sickness abounded. Other communes of that time apparently did not fare much better and 'As the 1960s ended, the suspicion grew that the counter culture was ultimately far more concerned with escaping the old world than in building a new one' (French and French, 1975, p. 89).

From the beginning of the 1970s, a somewhat different type of communes has come into being in the United States; these are no longer steeped to the same extent in hippie culture, no longer tend to separate themselves so completely from existing society, and have a greater involvement in current social and political issues. They also show a greater tendency to accept work as an integral part of the communal way of life, to effect a balance between individuality and co-operation and to devise clearer organizational structures (Hardy, 1979, ch. 6).

One feature these communes have in common with their predecessors is their pattern of family living. In most American communes there is a great deal of sexual openness, but although there are some instances of 'group marriages', the most common sexual relatedness is that of pairing (even if only temporarily) (Seal, 1973, p. 7).

Like their predecessors, these communes are also based on egalitarian principles, but in most of them (as in other communes) the 'joiners' or the rank-and-file members, can generally be distinguished from the opinion leaders, whose voice is given most weight in group discussions.

The precise number of these communes is not known, and estimates vary between a hundred and several thousands.[1] But even by the most generous estimate they manage to attract only a negligible proportion of the American population. Those of them that have been observed and reported on seem to be more successful than their predecessors, but many still suffer the problem of high turnover, and it is too early as yet to predict the degree of their stability.

The general achievements and problems of these new communes are exemplified by 'Twin Oaks', a rural commune set up at the end of the

1960s which by the end of 1972 numbered close to fifty members. This commune was fashioned on B. F. Skinner's behaviourist model (as outlined in his utopia *Walden Two*). Accordingly, it adopted the principle of positive reinforcement for socially desirable behaviour, although it is not clear how this worked in practice. In addition, Twin Oaks has incorporated communal ownership of property, equal distribution of income and collective child care.

Twin Oaks's subsistence has been based on common enterprises (such as hammock making and home building) which have provided most of the group's income. Each of these enterprises has a branch manager and work in them is allocated as far as possible according to members' preferences. Those who are allocated to less desirable jobs work fewer hours, which is an additional way of equalizing rewards. But despite the fact that this commune has devised some original features to solve the problems that those of the 1960s were unable to cope with, it has still had a very high turnover. In 1973 alone, roughly one third of the members departed and were replaced by newcomers (French and French, 1975, ch. 9).

In recent years: Britain
Europe of the 1960s had a hippie movement of its own, with communes appearing especially in France, the Netherlands, West Germany and Britain. Like the communes of the American counter culture, the European communes have not put great emphasis on shared values, internal organization and durable commitments of members to each other. Hence it is not surprising that they have faced the same problems. However, due to a certain time-lag in the diffusion of the new culture, the growth of the communes occurred somewhat later in Europe. Thus in Britain, communes characteristic of America in the 1960s did not emerge until the end of that decade and did not gain momentum until the beginning of the 1970s. In 1970 there were approximately fifty such communes in existence and during the early 1970s their numbers apparently doubled. Most were rather small; membership ranged between five and twenty-five, but only in a few did it exceed a dozen.

According to Rigby (1974a and 1974b), the British communes may be classified into several sub-types such as self-actualizing communes, communes for mutual support, politically activist communes, practical communes (whose goal is greater efficiency in production and consumption) and therapeutic communes (designed to create the social environment conducive for psycho-therapy). They have also differed widely among themselves in the development of communal economic enterprises, in the degree to which property was shared and incomes were pooled, and hence in the degree of economic equality. Additionally, they differed widely in their patterns of leadership, in the degree of membership participation in the decision-making process and hence in the degree of power equality.

Despite these differences, most British communes display some common features. In contrast to their nineteenth-century forerunners whose members were mostly self-educated and of working-class background, their members are mostly well-educated and of middle-class background. They have followed the American counter culture in their leaning towards an anarchist type of philosophy involving the rejection of formal hierarchies and authority structures and the insistence on the right of members to 'do their own thing', so long as this does not impair the right of others to do theirs. Thus, the British communes have also been characterized by a lack of hard and fast rules about sharing property, and a lack of tight organization and explicit patterns of social control, so decisions have frequently been taken on an *ad hoc* basis.

Here, too, the majority of communes have subsisted on a very low level of income. A number of communitarians have obtained their main financial support from the state in the form of supplementary benefits, while others have refused to draw on this source. Some have earned money through dealing in (apparently 'soft') drugs, while others have not. But common to most was the unwillingness to take up regular, full-time employment.

One of the institutions from which many comunitarians have felt estranged is that of the nuclear family. They felt that the commune had an advantage over conventional society in that in it no two adults need be forced to spend time constantly and exclusively in each other's company. Some communes thus introduced the practice of group marriage; but most commune members were opposed to this practice on the grounds (among others) that children need to know who their parents are.

Like the American communes of the 1960s, British communes have been marked by their failure to continue for any length of time. None of them, so far, has approached the longevity and stability of religious communes. It has been estimated that the average life-span of a religious commune has been fifty years; that of a secular commune, no more than five. Indeed, in Britain only a fraction of the commune ventures have managed to get beyond the embryo stage of planning. According to Rigby this is due mainly to the economic problems involved in raising the capital necessary to finance the commune, and to the difficulty of gathering a sufficient number of like-minded and mutually committed people to carry out the venture.

Once established, many communes have failed through the collapse of their economic basis, but this itself has usually been brought about by the lack of formal procedures and responsibilities concerning financial matters, by the weakening commitment of members to the collective, and by factional divisions and interpersonal friction. Since communes have had no formal rules, there have been few splits on matters of principle. Instead, conflict has generally resulted from lack of selectivity and the consequent heterogeneity of membership and from the unwillingness of members to adhere to the demands of communal leaders or to accept communal discipline. This, in turn, has led to the problem of social control and especially that of the stance to be taken towards those who refused to do their fair share of work or to fulfil other communal duties, which thereby fell as an additional burden on others. The lack of formal financial rules formed an additional source of conflict in that people feared for their private possessions and in some cases even for their life savings. Additional dissent has developed over standards of cleanliness on the communal premises, space allocation and living arrangements, the relationship between the sexes, interpersonal jealousy and the lack of privacy.

The major problems confronting most British communes were thus neither ideological nor economic as such. What did threaten the existence of most of these communes as well as that of their overseas counterparts were rather those strains and stresses resulting from a group of people living in close proximity to each other. In Rigby's (1974a, p. 296) words: 'It is the petty vexations rather than the grand issues of communal living that threaten community experiments.'

It is difficult to appraise how far these threats have actually impaired the communes' longevity. Although their numbers continued to increase during the first half of the 1970s, it is less certain whether they were still continuing to do so during the second half of the decade or whether the peak is already past (Hardy, 1979, p. 226).

The Israeli kibbutz

The most successful venture in communes is without doubt the Israeli kibbutz movement. The first kibbutz dates from 1910, so the movement is now in its eighth decade. It has thus outlasted even the more successful contemporary communes in Western countries. Although some of the early kibbutzim disintegrated, the movement as a whole has had a relatively high level of stability. Kibbutzim are also larger than the average secular Western communes. They vary in size from forty to fifty members in newly founded settlements to a thousand in longer established ones; the average kibbutz includes roughly four hundred people, of which about half are adult members. Altogether some 100,000 Israelis live in kibbutzim, which is probably a greater number than that of all commune residents in the West taken together.

General background
The kibbutz is a rural settlement, organized on communal principles of common ownership of the means of production and property (except for a few personal belongings) and communal organization of production through common enterprises, including agriculture and industry. Consumption is also communal, members may take meals collectively in the communal dining hall or use the kibbutz's supplies to prepare their own meals. All incomes are pooled and go into the common treasury; there are no salaries, the members' material needs are provided for by communal institutions, and allowances are paid for the fulfilment of special requirements, such as vacations or cigarettes.

As the kibbutz venture grew and became more established, there appeared a certain movement towards the loosening of communal ties — collective commitment has levelled off, and less time is spent in communal activities (see below). Some observers have therefore prophesied that the kibbutz movement is apt to turn itself from a communal into a less compact co-operative movement. But so far this has not occurred and the communal patterns are still very much in evidence.

It would seem then that the kibbutz movement is a highly stable enterprise. And yet it shares with all Western voluntary communes the problem of high turnover of membership. Although the rate of that turnover is by far lower in the kibbutz, and although in each kibbutz a stable, veteran membership exists, attrition is nevertheless a severe problem. As in Western communes, it frequently results from personal frictions and incompatibilities, or else from the special exigencies facing the kibbutz's second or third generation. Upon the completion of their military service,[2] these young people frequently opt for other outside activities such as tertiary education, and after having lived outside the kibbutz for a substantial number of years, they thus do not face the problem of whether they wish to leave the kibbutz, but rather the reverse one of whether they wish to return to it.

Also, while 100,000 residents form a very substantial population, they still comprise only less than 4 per cent of the Jewish population in Israel. Furthermore, half of that population is now composed of people from Middle Eastern origin, most of whom reached the country after the establishment of the state in 1948. Of these, only a negligible fraction have joined kibbutzim.[3] This means that the kibbutz way of life is potentially attractive to only a special type of people: Jews from European or Western origin, and even here it attracts only a small minority.

One reason for this lies in the fact that the kibbutz was initially created by young people from Eastern Europe as a kind of rebellion against the traditional way of life of Jews in that part of the world (whence most Jews in Western countries have originated). Part of this rebellion was to be expressed in an abandonment of the various 'airy' and 'unproductive' occupations and in a return to the soil and to manual labour. Another part of that rebellion was to be expressed in the adoption of a socialist way of life where each was to work according to his ability and to receive according to his needs. It was thus to be expressed in the institution of complete equality, including equality between the sexes, and also in a minimization of traditional family ties.

In a sense, the kibbutz movement was therefore a venture in utopia, although contrary to the classical utopia it was neither static nor isolated from the wider society. On the contrary, the kibbutz was always characterized by a high level of commitment to the values of Israeli society (including Zionism and Jewish national identification) and a high level of integration in Israel's broader social and political structures, and especially the labour movement.

The kibbutz movement was not only a venture in utopia but also (and perhaps through this very fact) a massive social experiment of a magnitude that no social scientist could ever have devised. Not surprisingly, it has aroused an unusual amount of interest amongst such scholars all over the world, and many of them have utilized its observations to test their theories. Indeed, volumes upon volumes of writings have resulted from these observations and although the kibbutz movement encompasses only such a small portion of Israeli society, far more has been written about it than about the rest of that society.

The sociological questions posed by the kibbutz experiment are basically three: first, has the kibbutz indeed solved the general problem of inequality of Western capitalist society, or in more general terms, is complete equality possible? Second, has the kibbutz solved the problem of the nuclear family and can that institution be eliminated or minimized? And finally, has the kibbutz indeed solved the problem of 'sexism' and is equality between the sexes possible?

The problem of equality

As far as equality in general is concerned, the kibbutz incorporates a certain contradiction: an elitist and an egalitarian principle at one and the same time. The elitist principle applies as far as the surrounding society is concerned, while the egalitarian principle (at least in the economic realm) applies internally. At the onset, the elitist principle was expressed in the kibbutz members' utmost dedication to national objectives, in accordance with the maxim of *noblesse oblige*. In other words, kibbutz members saw themselves as an elite of pioneers, willing to advance into outlying, arid regions, to live in extreme austerity while at the same time acting as first-line frontier outposts and coping with the heavy burden of self-defence in a hostile environment. At present, some kibbutzim are still frontier settlements and the principle of *noblesse oblige* is still evident in the exceptional dedication of kibbutz youngsters to defence: they make up a disproportionate percentage of officers, pilots and volunteers in the special (and most dangerous) elite corps.

At the same time, the elitist principle is now working in the opposite direction as well. High productivity in kibbutz enterprises, combined with various favourable developments have gradually led to increasing affluence — especially in the veteran and well-established kibbutzim — and the average standard of living of kibbutzim now seems to be higher than that for the country as a whole. Also, there is the differential created by hired labour. In principle, the hiring of labour is contrary to kibbutz ideology and for many years there has been fierce resistance to this practice on the ground that it is necessarily exploitative. Intense ideological debates were waged, but eventually those in favour of hiring labour won out, opposition was slowly eroded and by the later 1960s outside workers accounted for some 9 per cent of overall kibbutz employment and for some 50 per cent of employment in kibbutz industry. Whether or not kibbutzim have thus become capitalist-like employers who expropriate the surplus value of others' labour is a matter of opinion. But it is at any rate beyond doubt that inequality has been introduced by the very fact that kibbutzim tend to mete out the less skilled and more menial tasks to outside (and frequently less qualified) labourers and to retain the skilled, the clerical and especially the managerial tasks for their own members.

This elitism in confronting the outside world is in marked contrast to economic egalitarianism on the inside, which is undisputedly the kibbutz's greatest achievement. Basically, all members share equally in the kibbutz's resources and rewards. Since there are no salaries, food supplies are not restricted, and monetary allowances are equal, practically no economic differentiation is generated by the kibbutz structure. Some sons and daughters of kibbutzim are sent to institutions of higher education while others are not, but the latter are then compensated in different ways, for example, by being sent for trips abroad — so that here, too, near-equality is maintained. When new and more spacious dwelling units are built, it is customary for old-timers to get precedence over their younger comrades, but it is presumed that eventually, the latter will obtain new and equally spacious accommodations, so that differentiation is temporary (Shepher, 1977, pp. 121-3). All kibbutzim used to adhere to the injunction that their members must turn over to the collective all private property (and even privately received presents). However, the necessity of giving up one's life savings upon joining a kibbutz has acted as a deterrent and decreased the induction of the new members that the kibbutz so directly needed. Consequently, it is no longer adhered to in as orthodox a way as formerly.

Also, there is a tendency in some kibbutzim to substitute general allowances for itemized allowances. Traditionally, each member has been entitled to an equal sum of money for each expense item (e.g., cigarettes, clothing, sound systems) and unused money in one category could not be used to procure items of another sort. In place of this, some kibbutzim are considering, or have introduced, comprehensive allowances for all the individuals' consumption with freedom to spend these as they choose. Some observers consider this innovation to hold the danger of more individual differences and therefore inequality in consumption. But only the future can tell whether this danger will actually materialize. As far as the present is concerned, at any rate, it is clear that the kibbutz comes as close to domestic material equality as is humanly possible.

Material equality, however, must not be equated with overall equality, and the problem of the distribution of power and influence is by far more complex. Formally the sovereign body of the kibbutz is the general assembly, which is made up of all kibbutz members and meets weekly. The kibbutz's various committees (including the committees of economics, labour, education, culture, housing, social welfare, etc.), are all elected by and responsible to the general assembly. The kibbutz's central office holders, the secretary and the treasurer, are also elected by and responsible to the assembly, and so is the kibbutz's central executive body, the secretariat, which includes these central office holders, as well as the chairpersons of the major committees (such as that of economics and labour).

On the face of it this is a perfect model of direct, participatory democracy, where each member may have a say in the decision-making process and an opportunity to be elected to one or another of the policy-devising bodies. And indeed, the kibbutz probably comes closer to participatory democracy than most other existent socio-political structures. Nevertheless, there are certain barriers to participation, created by the members' personal needs and characteristics no less than by the kibbutz's structure. For one thing, in recent decades general assemblies have not been well attended and with the introduction of television, attendance has shrunk even further. Also, in many kibbutzim items to be discussed are posted on the notice board only a short while before the convening of the assembly, so that there is little time for these items to be aired informally and for public opinion to be formed. Members are thus ill-prepared for assembly discussions and more often than not, central position holders are able to carry their proposals.

Central positions and committee participation are usually rotated, and research has shown that a relatively large percentage of all kibbutz members have at one time or another served on committees. But the central and most powerful positions are sometimes rotated within a more limited group of people[4] and others are only rarely included. Whether such an elite emerges because its members are popular and influential, because they are best organized or because others shirk the responsibility is a moot point. What is important is the emergence of the elite as such. Moreover, it has been found that some members of this elite tend to exert a substantial influence on decision-making, even when they are not formal office-holders at that particular time or, for that matter, at any time.

Finally, there is the power and authority created through the work process. Work must be co-ordinated and each of the kibbutz's many work-branches and enterprises is headed by a branch manager. While branch managers shoulder heavy responsibilities without enjoying any substantial additional material rewards (Yuchtman, 1972), they do have authority over others. Work branches are supposed to be organized according to the principles of industrial democracy, but this does not always work out in practice. For instance Rosner (n.d.) found in a research project on thirty-four kibbutz plants, that only in fourteen have branch meetings taken place as frequently as once a month, and in the rest, meetings were less frequent.

The problem of the family

Whilst power equality is problematic, sexual equality is even more so, especially in recent years. This, in turn, is closely related to developments in the kibbutz's family structure. According to Talmon (1972), when the kibbutz movement was first established, it was widely considered that there was an inherent contradiction between the family and the collective. For this, as well as for other reasons, the role of the family was restricted:

(a) The first kibbutz members were young new immigrants who, through the very act of immigration, had severed their ties with parents and relatives remaining abroad. Extended family ties were thus practically non-existent.

(b) Because of the austere and hazardous conditions in which the kibbutzim had to survive there was a severe limitation of the family in the sphere of procreation — birthrates were restricted and maintained below the replacement level.

(c) Since the kibbutz as a whole acted as a unit of consumption and because of the need to economize through increased efficiency, the family's role in this sphere was practically eliminated. Meals were taken in the communal dining hall and clothing was cared for by the kibbutz laundry. The family premises were rather simple and there were few household chores attached to them — most household duties were thus taken over by the kibbutz.

(d) To enable women to work, the role of the family in the sphere of socialization was also severely restricted: children were cared for, and slept in a communal children's house. Parents and children were able to spend their leisure time together but the main socialization agents were the professional personnel and the peer groups.

(e) Social life and leisure time activities were also organized on communal rather than on family lines. Spouses' work schedules were not generally co-ordinated so they could not have their leisure hours, rest days and vacations simultaneously; and in any case, couples' tendencies to spend time privately in their family units were strongly discouraged; there was hardly any family entertaining and visiting — members spent most of their leisure time together on communal premises engaging in collective activities such as singing and dancing.

(f) The sexual ethic was unfavourable to the family. The kibbutz ideology called for sexual equality, for the abolition of the bourgeois double standard and of requirements for life-long fidelity, maintaining instead that sexuality should be anchored in spontaneous feelings of both sexes. Premarital relations were thus permissible, even though the ideology of 'free love' was counteracted by an ethic of puritan asceticism, so that promiscuity was frowned on and only rarely prevailed. In line with the tendency towards spontaneity in sexual relations, however, the role of marriage and its attendant ceremony was minimized. It was customary for a couple to signal its intention of establishing a family by merely moving into common premises (a 'family room') without rabbinical blessing. Marriage itself was usually deferred until pregnancy or after, and then it was treated as an afterthought, a mere formality resorted to in order to lend legitimacy to the union's offspring.

Thus, although the family persisted as an identifiable unit with especially intimate ties among its members, its functions and rituals were severely curtailed.

Since then, however, the situation has changed fundamentally. Gradual stabilization of the kibbutz movement, routinization of life in it and the levelling of collective commitments have brought about a greater tolerance towards the family which is no longer considered as a threat. The improved economic conditions have enabled the kibbutz to allocate more resources to family needs and diminished the pressure for a non-familistic division of labour. Thus, the family in the kibbutz has regained legitimacy and has become increasingly pervasive:

(a) As the kibbutz moved from first to second and third generation and as parents of grown-up children began living together on the same kibbutz in close proximity to each other, extended family ties were re-established.

(b) As economic and security conditions improved, the family's role in the area of procreation increased as well, and today the birthrate in kibbutzim is significantly higher than it is among people of similar socio-economic positions in the rest of the country.

(c) The role of the family in the sphere of socialization has also reasserted itself. In some kibbutzim, children now reside with their parents and although most have maintained the communal arrangements, parents now demand and receive a greater say in the education of their children.

(d) With economic improvement, the family has regained some of its functions in the sphere of consumption: meals are more frequently prepared and consumed in separate family settings; larger flats and more attractive furnishings demand more care and serve as an encouragement to families to spend more time in their family dwellings rather than on communal premises.

(e) Social life and leisure time activities are now increasingly focused around the family unit. Husbands' and wives' work and leisure schedules are more frequently co-ordinated, social invitations are usually extended by couples to couples (rather than individually). Social networks usually include families as wholes and collective leisure time activities have declined to make way for private, family centered ones.

(f) The sexual ethic has changed as well: non-marital sex has not been ruled out but it is now expected that when a couple has established a permanent relationship and has decided to found a family, they will enter the state of matrimony. In line with this, the marriage ceremony has been restored and endowed with unprecedented splendour and lavish festivities. As marriage has gained in importance, informal pressures against divorce have increased and the divorce rate has declined: until the 1960s this rate was higher in the kibbutz than it was in the country as a whole, but now the reverse is true (Talmon, 1972; Tiger and Shepher, 1975, ch. 9).

The attempt to minimize the role of the family has thus been successful only temporarily. For reasons that have not been wholly clarified, the kibbutz family has made a dramatic comeback and today it is no less pervasive than the family in any other modern setting.

The problem of sexual equality

Nevertheless, the kibbutz family differs from other modern families in that it has liberated women from economic dependence on men (husbands or otherwise) and has provided them with the structural framework in which they could also be liberated, to a much greater extent than other women, from household chores and child care. In addition, the kibbutz ideology was especially adamant in its call for equality between the sexes. And so, both a structural and an ideological framework was created in which women could be equal to men.

And indeed, in the initial period, the division of labour between the sexes, although it did not disappear, was minimal. Women participated in all kinds of 'production' work, and men participated in 'service' work.[5] Men tended to work in the services less than women did in production, and frequently they did so on a temporary basis. But because of the extreme austerity, meals were of the utmost simplicity and household chores, that is, service work, was generally minimized.

So, although it was mostly the women's realm, a very significant proportion of women could be spared from it and employed in production. It has been estimated that at the early stage, in the 1920s and 1930s, 50–60 per cent of women were so employed.

Household chores within the family (or rather those few that persisted), were shared equally between the spouses; and in the sphere of power the differentiation between the sexes was also minimal. The collectives were small, decisions were arrived at through informal processes in which women participated as a matter of course. The near-equality between the sexes was also expressed in outward appearance: women's attire was austere and consisted mainly of plain slacks, skirts, and blouses; feminine embellishment was practically eliminated and the differences between the sexes in presentation of self were thus minimized.

Subsequently, however, the rising standard of living and the reinstatement of the kibbutz family have gone hand in hand with certain transformations in the role and status of women. Sexual equality is still a basic kibbutz principle and much of the structural basis for such equality persists, but nevertheless the practices are not quite as they were before. With growing prosperity and declining asceticism, a new emphasis is being put on feminine adornment (including styling of dresses, hairstyles and cosmetics) and on feminine sex appeal. Women have thus come to be increasingly differentiated from men in their self-presentation and presumably in their self-images as well.

The rising living standard has had an additional implication: the higher quality dwellings, and the increasingly family centered patterns of consumption require more numerous household chores to be performed during leisure hours and those now fall predominantly to the lot of women, allthough men tend to do most of the gardening around the family unit. Women have thus re-emerged as the families' main housekeepers. The tendency of women to re-assume household duties have been evident in the kibbutz's overall division of labour as well. As the standard of living rose, more effort came to be invested in communal cooking and other communal household chores as well and more staff had to be allocated to them. As the birthrate rose, more and more people had to be allocated to child care and teaching – and all these expanding services were predominantly 'manned' by women, a lesser percentage of whom could thus be spared for production work. Whereas in the early days some 50 to 60 per cent of women worked in production branches, in the 1970s only 30 to 35 per cent have been doing so.

Moreover, the polarization is even greater than these numbers suggest, for within the broad category of 'production' women tend to specialize in certain sub-categories. In agriculture, they tend to concentrate on hothouse farming, vegetable and flower gardening and poultry; and in industry they tend to specialize in plastics, printing, textiles, arts and crafts and clerical work while they are greatly under-represented in other types of industrial work and especially in industrial management. To the extent that men work in services, they gravitate towards special occupations as well, especially general maintenance and the education of older children. Men comprise 40 per cent of high school teachers, 18 per cent of elementary school teachers, but as a rule cannot be induced to care for pre-schoolers or infants. They participate in kitchen and dining hall duties on a temporary roster (especially on the Sabbath and the holidays), but are usually absent from the permanent staff of these institutions. There is also some research evidence that men's occupations enjoy higher prestige than women's work, so the differentiation is not only horizontal but vertical as well (Tiger and Shepher, 1975, ch. 5).

A similar tendency for sex-differentiation is evident in the political sphere. At the outset, women were no less active than their male comrades. But by the 1940s there were already clear signs of decreased political alertness; at that time, only some 29 per cent of all committee members were women. Research has shown that in the 1950s women were likely to participate fully in the less important committees (for example, social welfare and culture) and especially in the child related committees, but they were under-represented in the most important bodies (for example, the secretariat and the economic committee) as well as in the central positions (such as that of secretary and treasurer).

At this present time, women are clearly less active than men on all levels of the political arena. Women attend the general assembly much less than men, and when they do attend, are much less apt to participate in the discussions. According to Tiger and Shepher, in a typical kibbutz, six times as many men as women were found to be active in assembly meetings (although women tended to be quite vocal in expressing their opinions informally afterwards). Also, as in the 1950s, women still tend to find their way most frequently into the less important committees while men tend to be over-represented in the more important ones. Furthermore, men tend to be over-represented among chairmen of committees more than among committee members, and even more so among central office holders. Thus, the higher the level of power and authority, the greater the tendency for male over-representation (Tiger and Shepher, 1975, ch. 6).

This raises the question of why sex-equality did not eventuate, despite such favourable conditions, and why women have reverted to more traditional sex roles precisely at a time when women's liberation movements have become more vocal and more influential all over the Western world. One explanation would be that they have been overtly or covertly pressured to do so. Tiger and Shepher (ch. 10) however, have cited research which shows that kibbutz women tend to be no less satisfied with their work than men and that most of them feel that they do have full opportunities for political participation, if only they wished to take advantage of them. Another explanation is that women have been socialized to re-embrace their traditional roles just as they have in other societies. This makes sense to the extent that such socialization originates from the media and from Israeli society at large. At the same time it ought to be remembered that, for second generation kibbutz women, the main (kibbutz) agents of socialization have been members of a generation adhering to sexual equality more than they do.

It has also been suggested (Tiger and Shepher, ch. 11) that this newly emerging sex differentiation is due to some biologically ingrained, natural, dispositions that cannot be disregarded for long without reasserting themselves, including women's special affinity to their young and their power inferiority *vis-à-vis* males. Hence women's tendency to choose service occupations allowing them to work in proximity to the children's houses and so to nurse and/or visit their offspring during the day. Hence also their tendency to minimize political activity which would expose them to power competition with men and also detract from the leisure time which they prefer to devote to husbands and children. Yet another, and perhaps more plausible, explanation would be that kibbutz women choose to do what other women are forced to do by external constraints precisely because they do not feel inferior to their male counterparts; that contrary to women's liberationists they feel so secure in their equality to men that they do not feel the need to prove it. Hence they can afford to choose the occupations that are truly congenial to them without losing self-respect. But whatever the explanation the fact remains that after an attempt to eliminate or restrict them, the kibbutz has reverted to traditional patterns in both the family and the differentiation between the sexes.

Co-operatives

Because of their encompassing nature the kibbutz and other communes are undoubtedly the most far-reaching attempt to devise an alternative to existent social patterns. But they are not the only such attempt. Another, albeit less radical alternative, is the co-operative movement, which at present has a membership of many millions around the world.

A co-operative may be defined as a voluntary association carrying out some services for the mutual benefit of its members through an enterprise which is collectively owned by them. The major types of modern co-operatives include farmers' co-operatives, consumers' co-operatives (such as co-operative stores, housing co-operatives), credit unions and mutual savings and loans associations, mutual insurance groups, cultural-educational co-operatives, business-industrial co-operatives and workers' productive associations. Many co-operatives are limited to a single purpose — such as farmers' marketing co-operatives, but some are multi-purpose groups, such as the Israeli moshav shitufi, a type of settlement where the ownership of the means of production, work and marketing are co-operative while consumption is private and based on the individual family farm.

General background

Co-operative or quasi-co-operative structures were in existence from the inception of the ancient Egyptian empire (approximately 3000 BC), and can subsequently be found in various societies in antiquity, the Middle Ages, and early modernity. According to E. P. Roy, the modern co-operative movement, however, has its antecedents in the co-operative ventures that sprang up in Britain in the wake of the industrial revolution in the second half of the eighteenth century and the beginning of the nineteenth century. Some four to five hundred such ventures came into existence but they were not greatly successful and by the 1830s and early 1840s they had reached a low ebb.

The founding of the Rochdale Equitable Pioneers Society in 1844 is usually thought to have signalled the beginning of the modern co-operative movement itself. This was a group of twenty-eight craftsmen who came together for the co-operative purchase of supplies and consumer goods. It was highly successful and in fifty years it had grown to 12,000 members and had an annual turnover of $1,5000,000. The venture was successful in another way as well, for it established the co-operative principles which, with some modifications, have remained at the core of the co-operative movement to this day.

In the United States too, the co-operative movement had its modest antecedents during the second half of the eighteenth and the first part of the nineteenth century. In the 1860s many new Rochdale-type co-operatives were founded, and while most were short-lived they served as forerunners to existent co-operatives, and a few survived to this day. Between 1890 and 1920, the number of active, local co-operatives increased to more than 12,000; such co-operatives came to be established in all States and several regional and national co-operative federations came into being. New Deal legislation in the 1930s was mostly supportive to the development of co-operatives, which steadily continued to grow and proliferate. Since 1955 there has been substantial growth, especially in farmer and consumer co-operatives. Also, these bodies have become more pervasive in their activities: farmers' marketing co-operatives are processing farm products more completely and purchasing co-operatives are going into manufacturing as well.

In some European countries (for example, France, Germany, Italy) co-operatives suffered a setback during the two world wars and the period of fascism and nazism, but after the Second World War much of the previous achievements were recovered and there and in other Western countries the co-operative movement was strengthened even further. It has been estimated that in the 1970s co-operative membership reached 38·14 per cent in Canada and the United States, 25·3 in Europe and 10·14 in Oceania. Assuming that most of the members were heads of households, each of which represented several persons, the total participation in co-operatives must be reckoned to have been even higher than that (Roy, 1976, pp. 83–90).

Northern Europe (including the Scandinavian countries, Finland and Iceland) is probably the most developed from the point of view of co-operation of any area in the world. In the 1970s it has had a co-operative membership of 63·1 per cent and practically every type of co-operative organization has been utilized there at one time or another. But co-operatives have been very prominent in Western Europe as well. In Britain, for instance, consumer co-operatives have recently been most prominent. Since the Rochdale Society of 1844, such co-operatives have increased in numbers to a thousand, with a membership of 12 million. Local societies are federated into two national societies, which together own a total of two hundred and thirty factories, employing 750,000 people. Another strong aspect of the British movement has been the agricultural supply co-operatives of which several have performed marketing functions.

In France the emphasis has been on agriculture (including dairy and wine marketing and processing association) and on consumer, trade, craftsmen, workers' and educational co-operatives. In West Germany, agricultural and credit co-operatives have been most important. In the Netherlands, cheese-making co-operatives have been- prominent. In Israel the co-operative sector has conducted a large part of the country's agriculture, a third of its public works, nearly a quarter of industry and crafts and equally large proportions of transport.

In the United States there have recently been some 108,000 co-operatives, including farming co-operatives, consumer co-operatives, credit unions, mutual savings and loans associations, mutual (including medical) insurance groups, workers' co-operatives, housing associations and cultural-educational co-operatives. In addition, there have been some 7,720 business-industrial groups with hundreds of thousands of firms belonging to them.

The limitations of co-operatives

Co-operations have thus proliferated and prospered all over the Western world. However, as potential social alternatives, they have had some severe limitations. Some of these have been related to their tendency to grow in size — especially in the United States.

By the beginning of the 1970s, five American co-operatives were listed among *Fortune*'s 'top 500'. One of these, Farmland Industries, has had 400,000 members and $400 million in assets. In the late 1960s and early 1970s a new and distinctive co-operative movement seemed to emerge, which has put special emphasis not only on the economic aspects of life but on cultural activities as well. The Genessee co-operative in Rochester, New York for instance, has included a free university and an underground paper. The Oakland co-operative in Pittsburgh, Pennsylvania, has developed a market information service and co-operative study groups. Other recently founded co-operatives have come together around the provision of land, agricultural tools, food purchasing or child care. But as the new co-operatives matured some of them have begun to grow as well: the Boston Food Co-operative, for instance, admitted more than 4,000 members within two years of its establishment. Accompanying these co-operatives' growth has been their tendency to put greater emphasis on profits. Contrary to the original spirit of the movement, many co-operatives have thus come to resemble regular commercial enterprises.

Also, contemporary co-operatives have been diverging to some extent from their avowed principles. As noted, these principles have been based on the code of the Rochdale Equitable Pioneers Society.

According to this code, ownership of capital is to be the source of neither profit nor power. Instead, profits are to be refunded to consumers-members; control is to be in the hand of these members as well and is to be shared equally by all of them on the basis of one member one vote. (Some elements have since been added to the canon but the fundamentals remain the same.) In practice, however, many co-operatives have only partially implemented these principles. For instance, the principle of control by members is formally implemented in general elections for the association's board of directors (which usually appoints the management) and frequently for other councils or committees as well. This board and these councils, in turn, are formally responsible to the association's membership. However, as co-operatives grew, actual control has tended to move further and further away from the rank-and-file and come to be vested more and more firmly in the various elected and appointed bodies.

Whatever control is retained by members is not necessarily distributed equally. In many co-operatives, the Rochdale principle of 'one member — one vote' has been replaced by voting according to shares or according to patronage. Shares and patronage are not necessarily equal (although there is a certain limit on numbers of shares that may be owned). Thus equity rather than equality is the principle which has in practice come to permeate many co-operatives.

Finally, co-operatives are fairly restricted in the type of sociability they provide. As a rule they furnish more social affinity than the regular settings of modern life, but they tend to be specialized around a particular service with little overlap between them. They are thus fairly restricted in the facets of daily life which they encompass, they make only limited demands on their members and usually require little in terms of interpersonal involvement, group solidarity and collective commitment (French and French, 1975, ch. 6; Roy, 1964; 1976).

Conclusion

The continuous search for different social formations especially (but not exclusively) in Western societies indicates a certain dissatisfaction with existent patterns at least among some sections of the population. The question has been raised, however, whether this search has led to social formations which may indeed form viable alternatives to these patterns. Following the criteria set up at the opening of the chapter it might be said that Western communes, at any rate, have gone a certain length in solving existent social problems. They have addressed themselves in particular to the loss of common values and community, and the consequent isolation of the modern individual and the nuclear family, to the excessive competitiveness of capitalist society, and to economic inequality. But besides being attractive to only a few, they have left many problems unsolved, and created new ones as they went along.

Religious communes for instance have been among the most stable social alternatives in Western society, and have supplied an anchorage in common values and commitments. But their very success has depended largely on conformity to fairly authoritarian patterns of organization — a sort of inequality which many critics of existent society have made a special point of denigrating. Moreover, with the general trends towards secularization in the West, it is unlikely that such communes will hold attraction for sizeable parts of the population. Even with the proliferation of new, esoteric religious sects, they cannot hope to be more than a marginal social phenomenon at best.

The secular communes, on their part, may have solved problems of isolation, inequality and materialism but they have either ignored or created an array of other problems. As French and French (1975, p. 228), put it, with regard to counter-culture communes:

In ignoring 'hard questions' like the organization of work and instead letting the large society pay the bills, the counter culture expressed its ultimate dependence on that society. In so doing it closed off any hope that all could join in its postrevolutionary revels.

Moreover, secular communes in general have been caught up in the problems of the small tensions and petty irritations and jealousies of people living in close proximity to each other. For these reasons as well as others, they have not attracted large numbers and have suffered from high turnover and instability. In Rigby's (1974a, p. 302) words:

The simple fact is that in Britain there are not many communes in existence and many of them seem to be continuously on the verge of collapse . . . . Thus it can be argued that while communes do represent alternative structures and life projects based on the counter values, they are as yet too limited in number and size to have much influence on society.

The Israeli kibbutzim — the most successful venture in communal living in any Western-style democracy — have had great achievements in the attainment of internal economic equality; but they have not solved the problem of elitism in relation to the surrounding society, and neither have they solved the problem of the differential distribution of

254 *The search for alternatives*

power and authority. Because of their relatively large membership, their tenacious persistence and their approximation to domestic economic equality, they probably come closer to presenting a social alternative than any other type of commune. But they, too, are limited to a small percentage of the Israeli population, they are attractive to only a special segment of that population, and they are certainly far from presenting a commodity for export to other societies.

The fact that despite all these problems and shortcomings communes are still being created is evidence of the vitality of the communal idea. But although communes may be well suited, and present legitimate social alternatives for certain individuals (and even when these persons eventually leave, their communal experience may have been an important phase of their personal development) they do not seem to fulfil the requirements of large segments of the population and therefore do not present a true challenge to the existing order.

The same, albeit for different reasons, may be said of the co-operative movement. Because of its egalitarian principles and vast membership it was at one time considered as the beginning of a peaceful revolution which would supplant the exploitative capitalist system. But by now it has become evident that the co-operatives have made but a limited contribution to the elimination of either economic or power inequality. Also, many of them are commercialized, they usually encompass only a small fragment of their members' lives, hence tend to be viewed more in terms of the services they provide rather than as a new way of life; they easily accommodate to and are easily accommodated within the existent capitalist system and hence do not form a true challenge to it either.

Selected readings

French, D., and French, E. (1975), *Working Communally*, New York, Russel Sage Foundation.
Rigby, A. (1974), *Alternative Realities*, London, Routledge & Kegan Paul.
Rigby, A. (1974), *Communes in Britain*, London, Routledge & Kegan Paul.
Roy, E. P. (1976), *Cooperatives* (3rd edn), Danville, Ill., Interstate Printers & Publishers.
Talmon, Y. (1972), *Family and Community in the Kibbutz*, Cambridge, Mass., Harvard University Press.
Tiger, L., and Shepher, J. (1975), *Women in the Kibbutz*, New York, Harcourt Brace Jovanovich.

Conclusion

Drawing together the threads of the foregoing theoretical and empirical analyses, it may be said that Western capitalist societies have been characterized by the paradox of persistence through change. They have been able to maintain some basic continuities, first and foremost that of capitalism itself, through their ability to generate and absorb major transformations. In this manner they have coped with some of the most severe problems created by modernization and the rise of capitalism which have beset them in their most acute form during the eighteenth and the nineteenth centuries. These include recurring economic crises, the dismal working and living conditions especially of the urban working classes, gross economic and political inequalities between the classes and the resultant, violent class conflicts. Western dominant classes and ruling elites, have thus safeguarded their basic power and interest structures, by getting a better hold of their countries' economies and by a certain responsiveness to pressures for change.

This, however, has benefited the lower classes as well. It has ensured that technological and economic development brought about increasing affluence, as well as better working conditions and greater economic security for them. It has secured a more equitable distribution of resources and rewards, and enhanced possibilities for social advancement. It has further resulted in the balancing of enhanced government power by broader avenues of political participation. Finally, it has brought about a dramatic increase in formal education and a somewhat greater representation of working-class youngsters in it. These are formidable achievements, and some of them are unprecedented. These changes, on their part, have led to the mitigation of working-class consciousness, to the shrinking vehemence and violence of class conflict and hence to a greater stabilization of the system.

Keynes is supposed to have said[1] that 'Capitalism is the extra-ordinary belief that the nastiest of men, for the nastiest of motives, will somehow work for the benefit of us all'. Absurd as it sounds, it seems that they have in fact done so — not (as the philosopher of

255

capitalism, Adam Smith, held) because they were guided by an invisible hand — but because this was the only way in which they could preserve the system and their position in it. The stabilizing effects of the substantive changes have in turn been bolstered by various types of manipulation whose effect it was to make these achievements seem even greater than they have in fact been.

Such manipulations have been evident in all spheres of social life. In the economic realm they have manifested themselves in the disproportionate emphasis put by the media and especially by commercial advertising on consumer goods, thus encouraging people to strive for, and be satisfied with the type of rewards which the system has the ability to offer. In the area of stratification, this manipulation has taken the form of making inequalities less visible than they had previously been, thus causing the semblance of equality to be greater than equality as such. It has also taken the form of perpetrating the belief in the embourgeoisement of the working class, and that of the American (or perhaps the Western) dream of the almost limitless possibilities of success and advancement for all those who really try. In the political arena it has, in recent years, taken predominantly the form of symbolic devices by which the political elites have moulded the public's consent for themselves, and by which they have made the semblance of public political power and participation even greater than the public's power and participation have actually come to be. And in education, the manipulation has taken the form of 'cooling out' the low achievers and inducing them to believe that failure attests only to their own shortcomings rather than to those of the system.

This is not to say that such manipulations are necessarily the result of a conspiracy on part of the dominant classes or elites to hoodwink the public. Rather, it seems that most of them are built into the system. This is also the case with some other related modern phenomena, those that result from the loss of traditional communities and their unifying values and from excessive rationalization. Those are the phenomena that sociologists refer to as alienation and anomie, or the prevalent sense of estrangement, meaninglessness, powerlessness and isolation attached to many types of work settings, to the confrontation of individuals with over-sized organizations, and to many urban settings. While these phenomena have been a salient source of modern discontent, it seems that they have at the same time induced a sense of political apathy, and to this extent they may have had a stabilizing effect on the system.

All this, however, would not have worked if, in a way, the system had not also 'delivered the goods' in the form of growing prosperity, greater equality and mobility, and wider avenues for participation. In addition, these 'goods' include certain codes of ethics, norms of behaviour or 'rules of the game' which have been adopted by, or foisted on Western elites and publics. Most prominent amongst these rules of the game have been those governing the institutionalization of conflict. This refers first to the institutionalization of industrial conflict through the organization of the parties involved, processes of arbitration, strikes and lockouts. It further includes the institutionalization of political conflict through the introduction of universal suffrage, greater freedom of organization and the press and unharassed elections, enabling the public to choose between competing elites and power centres. Finally it includes the institutionalization of legal conflict through certain judicial procedures and especially the relative independence of the judiciary from political intervention.

The normative patterns developed in modern Western societies also include the relative prominence of universalistic (objective) criteria for the distribution of rewards. This is not to say that particularistic criteria (for example, 'connections', 'favouritism'), no longer count, but merely that they count less than in most pre-modern and in many non-Western societies. Last but not least, these codes of ethics include the safeguarding of certain basic human rights − the right to life, to a substantial degree of personal liberty, privacy and immunity from arbitrary harassment. Critics may well point to the limitations of such rights, for instance to the potential incursion of privacy thorugh computerized storing of personal information by nosy authorities. But even a cursory glance into some non-Western countries which shall remain unnamed should serve to increase even these critics' appreciation of the Western human rights as far as they go. These codes and rules are the outgrowth of previous struggles, but by now they have crystallized into certain traditions which, so far, have only rarely been duplicated outside the West. Are the members of the dominant classes and elites themselves committed to these codes and rules? Or are they thrust upon them by public opinion and the leaders of public opinion? Do they fear, therefore, that their defiance of such codes could be used by their adversaries to discredit them? And what about the public? What proportions of its members have internalized those rules and are truly committed to them? These are moot points. What is crucial is the willingness of both the elites and the public to abide by them to a reasonable extent in their patterns of interaction.

At the same time this willingness may be rather fragile. Quite possibly, the continued adherence of all parties to the rules of the game hinges, among other things, on their perceived prospects of reaping at least some benefits from that game. Hence the continued persistence of the rules – one of the most distinctive features of Western social systems – depends, among other things, on these systems' ability to go on delivering the 'goods' which, by now, people have come to expect as their right. Moreover, because of the recent trends of increasing prosperity and mobility, people have come to expect not merely a steady but an *increasing* level of goods from the system. Any halting of these trends may thus result in a formidable gap between constantly rising expectations and the reality of what is actually attainable. As sociological observers have long recognized, the resulting frustration may well be channelled into political resentment.

Hence it is disquieting to some (and perhaps encouraging to others) that the Western system's continued ability to hand out successively higher levels of benefits to successively larger proportions of the population, is by no means ensured for the future. Leaving aside armed conflicts in which Western countries may become involved and whose occurrence and outcomes are largely unpredictable – Western prosperity is still closely related to the stability and good will of non-Western countries. Whether the West depends for its further development on the availability of third world countries as general suppliers of raw materials and cheap labour or as 'dumping grounds' for Western surplus goods, is still a matter of ongoing controversy. But it is no longer in doubt that the West increasingly depends for its prosperity on the policies of oil-producing countries, no less than it depends on its own ability to conserve energy and/or to develop energy sources of its own. A certain 'dependency in reverse' has thus developed and the trend whereby Western countries have recently gained a fuller control of their economies is thus suffering a severe setback.

As a consequence, the statistics show, in the most recent years (that is from 1973 onwards) Western economic growth has slowed. And although average real wages have continued to grow, it is possible that eventually there may be a slow-down, or a halt of this trend commensurable with the general economic trends. The people's rising expectations for a continuously rising standard of living may thus be patently frustrated.

Western capitalism has been able to maintain itself, among other things, because too many people have had too much at stake to risk its demise. If the slowdown of economic growth is translated into limitations of individual income – many people will still have much at stake, but less so than before. This is so especially since the recent economic recession (in combination with other factors) has resulted in higher levels of unemployment. Which means that small but growing proportions of the population — the long-term unemployed — have been gaining no, or only marginal benefits from the system and thus have only a marginal stake in it.

It has been argued that the growing frustration of the unemployed has been alleviated to some extent by growing unemployment benefits. Also, it has been claimed that a certain proportion of the unemployed no longer accept the Western 'work ethic' and are quite content to trade in material rewards for leisure and autonomy. And yet, no one has demonstrated that the majority of the long-term unemployed are content to subsist at the level accorded to them by the dole, that is, at the threshold of poverty or below.

Since certain categories of people (such as racial and ethnic minorities and/or those with low levels of education) are especially prone to be among the recently increased numbers of the perpetually unemployed, it must be concluded that a division is developing between this under-class (whose benefits from the system are minimal or non-existent), and all others (whose benefits from the system are more substantial), and that this division rivals traditional class divisions in its importance. Given the appropriate leadership it is not inconceivable that members of the underclass will become increasingly conscious of this fact, that they will become organized and (to paraphrase Marx) turn from an 'underclass in itself' into an 'underclass for itself' and translate in-dividual frustration into collective action.

In addition, working-class and other lower-class people, though they gain more substantial benefits from the system, may become increasingly dissatisfied as well. This is so because class inequalities which had been decreasing for some time — have (by and large) ceased to do so for the last three decades or so, while the remaining inequalities are still sub-stantial. Despite the partial concealment of this reality, there may eventually be growing awareness thereof among those who are negatively affected. In addition, to the extent that mobility has been increasing in recent years, this has been due not to the greater openness of the occupational structure but rather to the upgrading of that structure — a process which may well exhaust itself in the near future.

The fact that inequalities may thus be becoming more stable and rigid is especially significant since Western societies have increasingly adhered to ideologies of equality or of equality of opportunity and have thus promoted egalitarian expectations. As Aron (1968, p. xv) put it: 'Modern industrial societies are both egalitarian in aspiration and hierarchical in organization.' Here too, then, a discrepancy may be developing between aspirations and expectations, on the one hand, and actual developments, on the other. This is not to say that the frustration created by this discrepancy must necessarily be converted into political resentment, but it certainly has the potential of doing so.

One manner in which resentment toward the existing Western regime has already become evident is in the sizeable communist parties in France and Italy. It may be argued that these countries have been prone to authoritarian regimes and to relatively great church power and have not developed stable democratic traditions. But similar pronouncements may well be made about West Germany and in any case, who is to say that countries with more stable democratic traditions are necessarily immune.

Another manifestation of resentment towards the existing Western systems is to be found in the student, New Left, and other protests which have been evident in several Western countries in the 1960s. Although these protests were carried by only small minorities of the population, the support they marshalled was much wider and they were widely regarded as seismographic. However, these protests were hampered by the lack of a positive vision for an alternative society by which the system of Western capitalism could be replaced, or in favour of which the Western political elites could be called upon (or be forced) to abdicate. Thus, they turned into just another form of direct action, with which the Western system could cope by the introduction of limited reforms. In any event, they subsided shortly after their appearance. At the moment, neither Euro-communism nor yet the New Left loom as major threats to the stability of Western societies. But if economic setbacks, growing unemployment and large gaps between those at the top and those at the bottom continue to prevail there is no certainty that this will continue to be so.

Yet another indicator of dissatisfaction with existing Western systems is to be found in the continuous and recently accelerated search for social alternatives in the form of communes and co-operatives. Each of these, however, has developed its own intrinsic drawbacks. Communes, despite their considerable achievements in combating isolation and promoting economic equality have been hampered by self-created problems of inter-personal friction. For this, as well as for other reasons, they have been attractive to only small minorities of Western populations and have tended to be rather unstable. Co-operatives on their part have been rather fragmentary besides being beset by a tendency to accommodate to the existent system, thus strengthening rather than replacing it. Neither of them have thus posed a real challenge to the existent establishments, and indeed from the viewpoint of these establishments they have been rather innocuous. This is not to say that the search for alternatives will be (or should be) abandoned forthwith. It does not mean that persons so inclined will not (or should not) continue to seek self-fulfilment by joining innovative social formations or by working to create the society of their dreams. But it is hereby suggested that until a large-scale alternative materializes, there is still the legitimate task of improving what we have. It is further suggested that this must, in the first place, take the form of stepped-up public vigilance for the dominant classes and ruling elites' meticulous observance of the existent codes and rules.

Some observers have argued that the rules of the game by which the system operates, and especially those governing strikes and elections, do not present the public with true alternatives. Hence, they merely lend an illusion of power rather than power itself. This argument may be countered by the claim that the codes and rules of the game, although they do not present the public with the option of replacing the system, may serve as rather effective tools for more limited social improvements. Existent rules of waging conflict — especially strikes and elections — may serve as instruments of pressure for policies that will decrease unemployment and socio-economic inequalities. Rules safeguarding freedom of expression (however imperfect) may serve as instruments for exposing and increasing awareness concerning the manipulation of the public by dominant classes and elites and thereby diminish its effect.

Some observers would claim that all this is of little significance, since the advantage of the ruling classes over the exploited classes and/or of the ruling elites over the masses are maintained in any event. It could be retorted, however, that it is the degree of advantage that counts as well. To be sure, adherence to Western rules and regulations is not about to result in a totally egalitarian, classless or eliteless society. But not all forms of inequality or domination — as long as they exist — are equivalent. Some dominant classes are more exploitative than others and some elites are more despotic than others. So even if one holds the view that exploitation and domination can eventually be *abolished* it is important that in the meantime they can quite definitely be *restricted*.

Immunity from replacement is one of the major devices for the enhancement of elite power. Elections thus restrict the elites' power by confronting them with the periodical threat of being ousted and thus making them more accountable for their actions while in office. Manipulation is one of the major ways in which elites attempt to prevent their replacement and hence is one of the most eminent ways in which they enhance their power. Exposing manipulation is thus one of the foremost ways of restricting that power. Arbitrariness is one of the marks of despotism. Existing codes of universalism (or objectivity), if meticulously enforced, make it more difficult for the elites to exercise their power in an arbitrary fashion and hence form another way of restricting that power. Western codes, if truly institutionalized, are thus among the most effective restraints to the dominant classes and elites' power. They will not bring about a classless or an eliteless society. But they have already done a lot and they may still do a lot more towards making life in a class- and elite-dominated society more tolerable.

Once more, some observers would claim that making life in the existent system more bearable is not a goal worth striving for, as it merely retards the replacement of the system by a totally different and better one. But so far, all visions for a wholly egalitarian society in which classes and elites will be nonexistent and exploitation and manipulation will vanish from the face of the earth have been rather deficient. They have either been fragmentary and suitable for only a small part of the population, and even here have been only partly successful, or else have been addressed to society as a whole but have focused on a more distant (and indefinite) future, that is, on the long, rather than on the short run. But as Keynes has aptly remarked,[2] in the long run we are all dead, and the task at hand seems to be to make social life more liveable while we are still alive.

Notes

Preface

1 Quoted from Toffler (1970, p. 4).

Introduction

1 Other 'mainstream' groups of theories include symbolic interaction-
  ism and exchange theory. Also, there are some newer perspectives
  which claim to be alternatives to 'mainstream' sociology – phenom-
  enology and ethnomethodology. But they have not made a substantial contribution to the analysis of modernization – and hence
  will not be discussed here.
2 Whose leading figures were A. R. Radcliffe-Brown and Bronislaw
  Malinowski.
3 Marx was also the only one whose influence reached far beyond
  sociology. Here we shall be concerned with his sociological influence
  only.
4 That is, societies which feature predominantly capitalist economies
  in conjunction with Western-style democracies. They include most
  of non-communist Europe, the United States, Canada and Australia.
  Israel may be designated as a Western democracy too, but its historical development is totally different. Hence, little could be gained
  by including it in an analysis designed to bring out the general con-
  tours of development in the Western world. This country has been
  included only in the discussion of the search for alternatives (chapter
  9) – an area in which it has played an especially prominent role.

1 The advent of modern society in classical sociology

1 The beginning of effective food production by men was made possible
  by the domestication of plants and animals. This food-producing
  revolution marked the transition from hunting and gathering to
  agricultural societies and paved the way for the subsequent development of more complex civilizations.
2 Modernization is the current term for the transformation that took
  place in the Western world from the sixteenth century onward,

culminating in the industrial revolution in the eighteenth and the beginning of the nineteenth century. In the contemporary world it has been defined as the process whereby less developed societies acquire characteristics common to more developed societies (Lerner, 1968, p. 386). This definition is rather controversial and there probably is no definition that would be acceptable to all scholars in the field. For the more concrete features of modernization, see chapter 2.

3 Other evolutionist thinkers of that time include L. H. Morgan (1818–81), E. B. Tylor (1832–1917) and L. T. Hobhouse (1864–1929).

4 Comte's main works include *Cours de Philosophie Positive* (1830–42) and *Systéme de Politique Positive* (1851–4).

5 Many of Comte's ideas were developed in co-operation with Henri de Saint-Simon and some may even have been originated by Saint-Simon.

6 Spencer's main works include: *Social Statics* (1850), *The Study of Sociology* (1874) and *Principles of Sociology* (1876–96).

7 Marx's main works include: *The German Ideology* (1846), *The Communist Manifesto* (1848), *Capital* (1867–94), and many others. The dates refer to the original publications; newer publications will be cited below.

8 Note that Comte, for instance, included science in the realm of ideas rather than in the economic area.

9 Current accumulation of capital is to be distinguished from primitive (initial) accumulation of capital, which preceded the full development of capitalism and will be dealt with below.

10 Defined as the exchange value of a commodity in excess of wages and raw materials.

11 Defined as dependency on an entity which was originally one's own and now confronts one as something external.

12 Tönnies' main work is *Gemeinschaft und Gesellschaft* (1878).

13 Durkheim's main works include: *The Division of Labour in Society* (1893), *Suicide* (1897), and *The Elementary Forms of the Religious Life* (1912).

14 Although Durkheim's argument on this topic is constructed as a refutation of Spencer's theory, he actually accepts some of Spencer's most basic tenets.

15 Weber's main works include: *The Protestant Ethic and the Spirit of Capitalism* (1904–06), and *The Theory of Social and Economic Organization* (1922). Here, too, the dates cited refer to the original publications. A more recent publication of the *The Protestant Ethic* will be cited below.

16 According to Weber, rationality is also evident in Western music and architecture, although these areas are less central to his argument.

17 Weber admitted that later this emphasis declined.

18 Another classical theorist who perceived society in terms of an elitist model is Roberto Michels (1876–1936). However, in contrast

to Pareto and Mosca, he did not emphasize the cyclical character of elite replacement and social change to the same extent.

19 On the other hand, his explanations and prophecies for the demise of capitalism, have been widely criticized.

20 Among the most outstanding Enlightenment thinkers who expounded these ideas were Voltaire (1694–1778), and J.-J. Rousseau (1712–78).

21 Utilitarianism was most prominently represented by J. Bentham (1748–1832), and J. S. Mill (1806–73).

22 The most famous nineteenth-century conservative thinkers were L. G. A. Bonald (1754–1840), and J. Maistre (1753–1821).

23 A series of laws were enacted by which the family and religion were subordinated to the state, which was thus enhanced at the expense of traditional associations. In the nineteenth century, alternative associations were created (including trade unions, benevolent societies and mutual aid associations), but these lacked the intimate character of traditional associations.

24 He was militantly opposed to state control and intervention.

25 Even though he, like many other sociologists, was not conservative in his political allegiance.

26 In Weber's case, as we saw, such criticism was not warranted.

27 These criticisms were not fully justified as far as Comte and Durkheim are concerned for, as we saw, these thinkers were ambivalent with regard to the past.

2 The advent of modern society in contemporary sociology (A): 'mainstream' and modernization theory

1 Social strain must be distinguished from psychological strain. Although the two may be interrelated they are not identical.

2 Another possible reaction is ritualism – i.e., the adoption of the legitimate means for success, but the abandonment of the success goal itself. This reaction, however, is only on the verge of deviance.

3 A similar view on traditional institutions has been expressed by Myrdal (1968).

4 Note that the first and fifth dilemmas derive from Weber's distinction between the traditional ethic and the spirit of capitalism, while the others grow out of Tönnies's distinction between *Gemeinschaft* and *Gesellschaft*.

5 Although it has been pointed out that it now has the provision of companionship and psychological security as one of its major tasks.

6 For more details on these features see Parsons (1951); Hoselitz (1964); Lerner (1965); Black (1966); Rostow (1973); and many others. Some of these dimensions of modernization, as featured in Western countries, are taken up in greater detail in the second part of this book.

7 Alternatively, the convergence towards an end state of development

is predicated, the latter being conceived of as a combination of at least the following traits: self-sustained economic growth, the redistribution of assets and income on a more egalitarian basis and a new change-oriented national self-image (see Portes, 1973). Since the concepts of modernization and development are so closely akin, no systematic distinction between the two is being made in this book.

8   In traditional society, time is thought to be divided by the rhythm of day and night and the passage of the seasons. Only in modern society is time thought to be precisely calculated by hours, minutes, and seconds.

9   Other writers in the power and conflict perspective include Lewis Coser, who became famous for his attempt to combine this perspective with the structural-functional view (Coser, 1973). Mention should also be made of David Lockwood and John Goldthorpe, who have presented a power and conflict perspective in their writings, and whose research has dispelled the view that the modern working class tends to converge with the middle class (Goldthorpe *et al.*, 1969). The conflict perspective has been well summarized by Rex (1961).

10 Similar ideas on the diminution of alienation have also been expressed by Blauner (1964).

11 Other authors who have expressed various versions of the idea of a post-industrial society include Boulding (1964) and Brzezinski (1970).

12 For another theory that explains modernization through psychological factors, see Hagen (1962).

13 Note that in some conceptions this drive for achievement is regarded as part of modernity, while in others it is considered as a force propelling towards modernity. These two roles are not necessarily mutually exclusive.

14 As established by certain indicators in popular literature and school readers.

15 This last critique is of special importance because it forms the basic tenet around which the rival of modernization theory — dependency theory — builds its case (see chapter 3).

3   The advent of modern society in contemporary sociology (B): Marxist, neo-Marxist and dependency theory

1   This part of the chapter has benefited from the analyses of Anderson (1976); Baldock (1978) and Burawoy (1978).

2   Other well-known figures are Theodor Adorno, Max Horkheimer, Erich Fromm, Leo Lowenthal and Jurgen Habermas — of whom more will be said below.

3   Economic surplus may be defined as that which remains from economic output after consumption has been subtracted.

4   Identity is commonly defined as the answer the individual gives

to the question: who am I?

5   Monopoly refers to a situation where the market is controlled by one enterprise; oligopoly — to a situation where the market is controlled by a small number of enterprises.

6   Marx's ideas on the topic are to be found for instance in *Capital*, vol. 3, and in some articles which he wrote for the *New York Daily Tribune* in 1853.

7   For a concise summary of this argument see Alexander (1979).

8   Except in Latin America, where exploitation was backed by territorial conquest right from the beginning.

9   As is well known, there are several shortcomings to growth in GNP as a measure of economic growth: the problem of equating different currencies through exchange rates; the incomparability of national accounts; and the fact that economic development is a multivariate concept which also includes productive capacity and infrastructure. Nevertheless, most studies employ this as a shorthand measure because it seems to be the best available.

10 That the poorer countries do indeed have a lesser chance of economic growth is conclusively substantiated in Table 3.1.

4   The advent and maturation of the modern economy

1   The idea of setting up criteria for the comparison of social spheres in different societies has been adopted from the lectures of Professor S. N. Eisenstadt, The Hebrew University, Jerusalem. However, the criteria used here are not necessarily identical to the ones employed in these lectures.

2   Other 'mainstream' sociologists (for example, Levy, 1966) have pushed the notion of convergence between the West and the Soviet bloc even further. Their central argument is that both types of society have become centralized, bureaucratized and increasingly ruled by technology.

3   It must be borne in mind, however, that prices fell at the time, so that in real terms GNP declined only to around three-quarters of what it was before.

4   That is, contractual agreements between companies to co-ordinate prices, divide the market, etc.

5   That is, tacit agreements to co-ordinate prices.

6   Some historians have even here emphasized the gains of the working class — for example, working-class clubs, friendly societies, etc., that did not exist in the 'idiocy of rural life'. It is doubtful, however, that these gains outweighed the slum conditions.

7   Although children were in the labour force, and working hours were long, in rural areas as well.

8   Figures have been adjusted to take account of inflation.

9   For more detailed data see Mitchell (1975, pp. 166–8); US Bureau of the Census (1975, p. 135).

10 Due to variations in the sources of the data, in the definition of

unemployment, and even in the definition of the workforce, as a percentage of which unemployment is calculated.

11   The Chartist movement had no explicit, official, social program, but the reforms it advocated were evidently designed to improve the lot of the lower classes.

12   For instance, in Britain, unions gained full legal recognition in 1871; in Austria in 1870; and in France in 1884.

13   The question of whether equality has increased as well is deferred to the next chapter.

5   The advent and maturation of the modern class structure

1   Strictly speaking, mobility does not increase equality. But it increases equality of opportunity and many observers would argue that this is itself a dimension of equality.

2   Although distinct social strata or classes may be confined to the more complex societies.

3   Some 'mainstream' sociologists subdivide these into a lower-lower, an upper-lower, a lower-middle, an upper-middle, a lower-upper, and an upper-upper class.

4   Only through the Black Death of 1348–9 were the rewards of the surviving peasantry raised.

5   There is a major school of historians who claim that the standard of living of the working class (especially the British working class) rose during the first half of the nineteenth century. But many historians agree that the *quality* of their life deteriorated (see chapter 4). Since the rewards of the capitalist class apparently increased considerably, it is, at any rate, safe to assume that the gap between the classes widened.

6   It has been claimed that the empirical evidence on which this statement is based — derived mainly from tax returns — has some obvious defects and that it tends to underestimate the income of those in the upper income brackets. It seems, however, that although those defects may well distort the picture to a certain extent at a given point in time, they are much less likely to bias the analysis of trends, since it may be assumed that they remain roughly constant over time.

7   A measure of inequality ranging from 0 to 1.

8   As Lenski and Lenski point out, however, when one takes into account the accumulated equities which workers have built up in governmental and private pension systems, this inequality is somewhat mitigated: when pension rights are included, the proportion of Britain's wealth owned by the top 5 per cent of the population is reduced to 35 per cent.

9   Statistics on wealth distribution suffer from defects similar to those of income distribution, hence should be regarded as an approximation only.

10   The poverty threshold for a non-farm family of four in 1974 was

an annual income of less than $5,038.

11 The measure of poverty adopted was the standard of living by which people were entitled to the aid of the National Assistance Board.

12 The dividing line was drawn at $A62.70 per week for a household of four. As can be seen, it is exceedingly difficult to compare levels of poverty for different countries and to trace poverty over time. Presumably, the poverty line is drawn in such a manner that those underneath it are seriously short of basic needs such as minimal food and shelter. But basic needs vary and concepts of what is minimal may well change. It is therefore quite possible that today's poor in most Western countries would not have been considered as such a hundred years ago. Nevertheless, the fact remains that by present standards, a considerable portion of the population of the West lives in poverty.

13 Although at the bottom of the scale there are clerical workers who are paid less than skilled manual workers.

14 Most mobility studies focus on men. This is so, probably, not so much because of sexist discrimination, but because of the complicating factors besetting the analysis of women's mobility: many women do not work outside their own homes and these women's class positions are basically determined by those of their husbands.

15 It must be remembered, however, that in this case, the time and generation effect may be confounded with possible age effects.

16 In circulatory mobility, someone must move downwards for every person moving upwards; this is not the case for structural mobility.

17 This variance can apparently be traced back to differences in the samples studied.

18 The author distinguishes between elite I − the most exclusive occupational group, and elite II − a still exclusive but somewhat wider group. He also gives the combined data for both elites. It is these data that are reported here.

6 The advent and maturation of the modern polity (A): the power of governments and ruling elites

1 Political power may be defined as the ability to control or influence the allocation of resources (including material goods, services, positions or anything that may affect people's life chances) through the political process. The ruling elite is that group of people who, in a given society, exercise the greatest amount of such power over the greatest numbers. The public is that category of people over which such power is exercised.

2 Much of the debate and research on the pluralist and the elitist models has been at the level of the local community. This is not directly relevant to the present discussion and will not be dealt with here.

3 For other examples of pluralist analyses see Polsby (1963);

Rose (1967); and Hewitt (1974).

4   For similar analyses see Almond and Verba (1965) and Huntington (1968).

5   For excerpts of these theorists' works see Etzioni and Etzioni-Halevy (1973), ch 4, 14, 22.

6   However, Keller does not accept many other assumptions of the elitist model.

7   For a similar view, see Galbraith in his later writings (1967, p. 197). For additional elitist analyses see Prewitt and Stone (1973) and Etzioni-Halevy (1979).

8   For other Marxist interpretations see Domhoff (1967, 1970); Playford and Kirsner (1972).

9   While the weakened, largely nominal empire of the early feudal period was also superseded by the territorially more limited but much more effective state.

10   Including federal military, federal civilian, State and local government employees.

7   The advent and maturation of the modern polity (B): public participation and political manipulation

1   Cited by Crossman (1939, p. 39).

2   Adopted by the French National Assembly in 1789.

3   It has been estimated that the number of newspapers published in Europe doubled during the last two decades of the nineteenth century.

4   For instance, the Belgian of 1831, the Dutch of 1848, the Swiss of 1874.

5   A prominent example is the recent no-confidence vote against the Clark government in Canada, which precipitated the 1980 elections.

6   Unless there is a disparity between the two houses in a bi-cameral legislature.

7   By 1859, five colonies had the ballot; Western Australia followed in 1877.

8   Before the introduction of the Australian ballot another system of voting was tried out, which supposedly was secret, but actually was not: ballots were printed by parties or candidates and were sometimes in different colours or otherwise recognizable. Eventually it was recognized that the only truly secret ballot was the Australian one. It used standardized government-printed ballot papers, combined with physical arrangements designed to safeguard the privacy of the voting procedure.

9   But some States lagged behind and adopted it only during the first half of the twentieth century.

10   For instance, in Belgium manhood suffrage was introduced in 1893, universal suffrage in 1948; in Canada manhood suffrage was introduced in 1917, universal suffrage in 1920; in Denmark manhood

suffrage came in 1901, universal suffrage in 1915; in France manhood suffrage was granted in 1848, but voting took place in an
authoritarian environment which was not abolished until 1875;
universal suffrage was adopted in 1944; in the Netherlands all men
were enfranchised in 1917 and universal suffrage followed in 1919;
in Norway almost all men got the vote in 1898, women in 1913,
but universal suffrage came only in 1919 when persons on public
assistance were given the vote; in Sweden manhood suffrage was
introduced in 1909, universal suffrage in 1921; Switzerland granted
manhood suffrage as early as 1848 but universal suffrage was not
obtained until 1971 (Mackie and Rose, 1974).
11 However, in Australia all Aborigines only attained the vote in 1962
and in Switzerland, as noted, women did not attain the vote until
1971.
12 For instance, in Belgium in 1971 voting turnout was 91·5 per cent;
in Canada in 1972 the percentage was 77·2; in Denmark in 1971 —
87.2; in Finland in 1972 — 81·4; in France in 1968 — 80·0; in the
Netherlands in 1972 — 83·5; in New Zealand in 1972 — 89·9; in
Norway in 1969 — 83·8; in Sweden in 1970 — 88·3; and only in
Switzerland in 1971 was voting turnout lower than in the United
States — with 56·8 per cent of the electorate turning up at the polls
(possibly because of the new enfranchisement of women) (Mackie
and Rose, 1974).
13 Political manipulation may be defined as an attempt to control or
influence people's political behaviour — of which those subject to
it are not meant to be aware.
14 Although not all these theorists explicitly use the term.
15 Hence cannot be applied where there is proportional representation.
16 Such as the Tasmanian Dodge, which originated in Tasmania,
Australia, in the nineteenth century (see Etzioni-Halevy, 1979,
ch 4).
17 Some observers see education as yet another source of such manipulation (see next chapter).
18 Some of the media controlled by government instrumentalities (for
example, the British and the Australian Broadcasting Corporations)
are said to be left-wing in their political orientations. But Marxists
usually retort that they are never radical to the extent of questioning the system.

8 The advent and maturation of modern education

1 At least, their charters were granted by the church. But their
teachers (even though mostly priests) struggled for independence
from the mother institution.
2 Subsequently some Southern States abolished compulsory education
because of the 'problem' of desegregation.
3 There was considerable dropout from the grammar schools and
some secondary modern school children succeeded in trans-

ferring to them. But most children remained in the tracks in which they were initially placed.

4   In the prestigious private universities fees are very high indeed, but in the State universities and colleges fees are much lower.

5   It must be borne in mind that much of what is termed higher education in the United States is not defined as such in Europe. In the United States almost all post-secondary education takes place in a college framework while in many European countries certain professional and para-professional courses (such as nursing) are studied in other types of institutions.

6   Albeit not necessarily academic high school education.

7   This concept (coined by Parsons) is discussed at greater length in chapter 2.

8   As measured by a variety of verbal and non-verbal tests.

9   It has been claimed that intelligence tests themselves are class biased. But even if this is so, it still remains a fact (and it is commonly agreed upon) that they do measure the potential, or the mental capacity for scholastic achievement and that this potential is positively correlated with social class.

10   It has been suggested that it is precisely for this reason that students' unrest in the 1960s had its beginnings in these universities.

11   The path coefficient is a measure for the amount of variation in the dependent variable per unit change in the independent variable, when the other independent variables are controlled.

12   However, most of the latter differences may be an artifact of the brevity of the younger men's careers.

9   The search for alternatives

1   These differences in estimates are to be explained by the adoption of different definitions of communes, by the fact that there is no actual central registration of communes and by the fluidity of the situation whereby communes quickly disintegrate.

2   Lasting three years for men and one and a half years for women.

3   Arab Israelis have neither joined kibbutzim nor set up their own.

4   Sometimes this is a group of old-timers or a group of people from a certain country of origin.

5   In the Kibbutz the basic distinction is between 'production' work, that is, agriculture, construction and industry, and 'service' work, that is, the various communal household and childcare chores.

Conclusion

1   As quoted by Hoogvelt (1976, p. 156).

2   As quoted by Lipset *et al.* (1956, p. 401).

Bibliography

Abel-Smith, B., and Townsend, P. (1965), *The Poor and the Poorest*, Occasional Papers on Social Administration, no. 17, London, Bell.

Ahluwalia, M. S. (1974), 'Income inequalities', in Chenery, H., Ahluwalia, M. S., Bell, C. L. G., Duloy, J. H., and Jolly, R., *Redistribution with Growth*, Oxford University Press, pp. 3–37.

Alexander, K. L., Eckland, B. K., and Griffin, J. L. (1975), 'The Wisconsin model of socio-economic achievement: a replication', *American Journal of Sociology*, 81, pp. 324–42.

Alexander, M. (1979), 'The political economy of semi-industrial capitalism', Ph.D. thesis, McGill University, Montreal.

Almond, G., and Verba, S. (1965), *The Civic Culture*, Boston, Little Brown.

Althusser, L. (1971), 'Ideology and Ideological State Apparatuses', excerpt from his *Lenin and Philosophy and Other Essays* (trans. B. Brewster), London, New Left Books, pp. 123–73.

Amin, S. (1974), *Accumulation on a World Scale* (trans. B. Pearce), New York, Monthly Review Press.

Amin, S. (1976), *Unequal Development* (trans. B. Pearce), Hassocks, Sussex, Harvester Press.

Anderson, C. A. (1962), 'A skeptical note on education and mobility', in Halsey *et al.* (eds), (1962), *Education, Economy and Society*, pp. 164–79.

Anderson, D. S., and Western, J. S. (1970), 'Social profiles of students in four professions', *Quarterly Review of Australian Education*, 3, pp. 3–28.

Anderson, P. (1976), *Considerations on Western Marxism*, London, New Left Books.

Andreski, S. (1965), *The Uses of Comparative Sociology*, Berkeley, University of California Press.

Aron, R. (1968), *Progress and Disillusion*, London, Pall Mall Press.

Aron, R. (1978), *Politics and History* (trans. and ed. M. Bernheim-Conant), New York, Free Press.

Ashenfelter, O. (1978), 'What is involuntary unemployment', *Proceedings of the American Philosophical Society*, 122, pp. 135–8.

Australian Commonwealth Bureau of Census and Statistics (1971), *Official Yearbook of the Commonwealth of Australia*, no. 57, Canberra.

Australian Council of Social Service (1979), 'Who wins who loses',

Australian Social Welfare: Impact, 9.

Bagwell, P. S., and Mingay, G. E. (1970), *Britain and America 1850–1939*, London, Routledge & Kegan Paul.

Baldock, C. V. (1978), *Australia and Social Change Theory*, Sydney, Ian Novak.

Baran, P. A. (1957), *The Political Economy of Growth*, New York, Monthly Review Press.

Baran, P. A., and Sweezy, P. M. (1966), *Monopoly Capital*, New York, Monthly Review Press.

Barber, B. (1957), *Social Stratification*, New York, Harcourt Brace.

Barber, B. (1973), 'Change and stratification systems', in Etzioni and Etzioni-Halevy (eds) (1973), *Social Change*, pp. 199–209.

Bell, D. (1973), *The Coming of the Post-Industrial Society*, New York, Basic Books.

Bereday, G. Z. F. (1973), *Universities for All*, San Francisco, Jossey-Bass.

Berger, B. (1971), *Societies in Change*, New York, Basic Books.

Bernstein, B. (1962), 'Social class and linguistic development', in Halsey *et al.* (eds) (1962), *Education, Economy and Society*, pp. 288–314.

Berthoud, R. (1976), *The Disadvantages of Inequality*, London, Macdonald & James.

Black, C. K. (1966), *The Dynamics of Modernization*, New York, Harper & Row.

Blau, P. M., and Duncan, O. T. (1967), *The American Occupational Structure*, New York, John Wiley.

Blauner, R. (1964), *Alienation and Freedom*, University of Chicago Press.

Bornschier, V., Chase-Dunn, C., and Rubinson, R. (1978), 'Cross-national evidence of the effects of foreign investment and aid on economic growth and inequality', *American Journal of Sociology*, 84, pp. 651–83.

Boulding, K. E. (1964), *The Meaning of the Twentieth Century*, New York, Harper & Row.

Bowles, S. (1976), 'Unequal education and the reproduction of the social division of labour', in Dale, R., Esland, G., and MacDonald, M. (eds) (1976), *Schooling and Capitalism*, London, Routledge & Kegan Paul, pp. 32–41.

Bowman, M. J., and Anderson, C. A. (1963), 'Concerning the role of education in development', in Geertz, C. (ed.) (1963), *Old Societies and New States*, New York, Free Press, pp. 247–79.

Braverman, H. (1975), *Labor and Monopoly Capital*, New York, Monthly Review Press.

Brookover, W. B., and Gottlieb, D. (1964), *A Sociology of Education*, (2nd edn), New York, American Book Company.

Broom, L., and Jones, F. L. (1969), 'Father to son mobility', *American Journal of Sociology*, 74, pp. 333–42.

Broom, L., Jones, F. L. (with the collaboration of Zubrzycki, J.) (1976), *Opportunity and Attainment in Australia*, Canberra,

Australian National University Press (6th edn).

Broom, L. and Selznick, P. (1977), *Sociology*, New York, Harper & Row.

Burawoy, M. (1978), 'Contemporary currents in Marxist Theory', *The American Sociologist*, 13, pp. 50–64.

Burnham, J. (1944), *The Managerial Revolution*, New York, Putnam.

Busch, G. (1975), 'Inequality of educational opportunity by social origin in higher education', *Education, Inequality and Life Chances*, 1, Paris, OECD, pp. 159–81.

Butler, D. E., and Pinto-Duschinsky, M. (1971), *The British General Election of 1970*, London, Macmillan.

Brzezinski, Z. (1970), *Between Two Ages*, New York, Viking Press.

Cabral, A. (1969), *Revolution in Guinea*, London, Stage One.

Caldwell, M. (1970), *The Imperialism of Energy and the Energy of Imperialism* (pamphlet) London.

Centers, R. (1949), 'Education and occupational mobility', *American Sociological Review*, 14, pp. 143–4.

Chirot, D. (1977), *Social Change in the Twentieth Century*, New York, Harcourt Brace Jovanovich.

Cipolla, C. M. (1969), *Literacy and Development in the West*, Harmondsworth, Penguin.

Clark, B. R. (1962a), *Educating the Expert Society*, San Francisco, Chandler Publishing Co.

Clark, B. R. (1962b), 'The "cooling out" function in higher education', in Halsey *et al.* (eds), (1962), *Education, Economy and Society*, pp. 513–23.

Cohn, S. H. (1970), *Economic Development in the Soviet Union*, Lexington, Mass., Heath Lexington.

Coleman, J. S. (1966), 'Equal schools or equal students?', *The Public Interest*, no. 4, pp. 70–5.

Coleman, J. S., *et al.* (1973), 'Enhancing equality of educational opportunity', in Etzioni and Etzioni-Halevy (eds) (1973), *Social Change*, pp. 505–13.

Connell, R. W. (1977), *Ruling Class Ruling Culture*, Cambridge University Press.

Coser, L. A. (1973), 'Social conflict and the theory of social change', in Etzioni and Etzioni-Halevy (eds) (1973), *Social Change*, pp. 114–23.

Crossman, R. H. S. (1939), *Government and the Governed*, London, Christophers.

Dahl, R. A. (1956), *A Preface to Democratic Theory*, University of Chicago Press.

Dahrendorf, R. (1959), *Class and Class Conflict in Industrial Society*, Stanford University Press.

Davis, K., and Moore, W. E. (1945), 'Some principles of stratification', *American Sociological Review*, 10, pp. 242–9.

Domhoff, G. W. (1967), *Who Rules America?*, Englewood Cliffs, NJ, Prentice-Hall.

Domhoff, G. W. (1970), *The Higher Circles*, New York, Random House.

Douglas, J. W. B., Ross, J. M., and Simpson, H. R. (1968), *All Our Future*, London, P. Davies.

Dow, K. L., Jones, L. D., and Osman, L. M. (1972), 'The social composition of students entering the University of Melbourne in 1969 and 1970', *Melbourne Studies in Education*, 1972, pp. 77–95.

Drucker, P. F. (1973), 'The educational revolution', in Etzioni and Etzioni-Halevy (eds) (1973), *Social Change*, pp. 232–8.

Duncan, O. D. (1965), 'The trend of occupational mobility in the United States', *American Sociological Review*, 30, pp. 491–8.

Duncan, O. D., Featherman, D. L., and Duncan, B. (1972), *Socioeconomic Background and Achievement*, New York, Seminar Press.

Dye, T. R., and Zeigler, L. H. (1975), *The Irony of Democracy* (3rd edn), North Scituate, Mass., Duxbury Press.

Edding, F. (1966), 'Expenditure on education', in E. A. G. Robinson and J. E. Vaizey (eds) (1966), *The Economics of Education*, London, Macmillan, pp. 24–5.

Edelman, M. J. (1971), *Politics as Symbolic Action*, New York, Academic Press.

Eisenstadt, S. N. (1966), *Modernization, Protest and Change*, Englewood Cliffs, NJ, Prentice-Hall.

Eisenstadt, S. N. (1973a), 'Breakdowns of political modernization', in Etzioni and Etzioni-Halevy (eds) (1973), *Social Change*, pp. 320–32.

Eisenstadt, S. N. (1973b), *Tradition, Change and Modernity*, New York, John Wiley.

Etzioni, A., and Etzioni-Halevy, E. (eds) (1973), *Social Change*, (2nd edn), New York, Basic Books.

Etzioni-Halevy, E. (1979), *Political Manipulation and Administrative Power*, London, Routledge & Kegan Paul.

European Economic Community Commission (1977), *Report on the Development of the Social Situation in the Communities in 1976*, Brussels and Luxembourg.

Farrell, J. P. (1975), 'A reaction to the macroplanning of education', *Comparative Education Review*, 19, pp. 202–9.

Field, G. L. and Higley, J. (1979), 'Elites, insiders and outsiders', in Denitch, B. (ed) (1979), *Legitimation of Regimes*, Sage Studies in International Sociology, no. 17, pp. 141–59.

Field, G. L. and Higley, J. (1980), *Elitism*, London, Routledge & Kegan Paul.

Foster-Carter, A. (1974), 'Neo-Marxist approaches to development and underdevelopment', in de Kadt, E., and Williams, G., *Sociology and Development*, London, Tavistock Publications.

Frank, A. G. (1967), *Capitalism and Underdevelopment in Latin America*, New York, Monthly Review Press.

Frank, A. G. (1970), 'The development of underdevelopment', in Rhodes, R. I. (ed) (1970), *Imperialism and Underdevelopment*, New York, Random House, pp. 4–17.

Frank, A. G. (1971), *Sociology of Development and Underdevelopment of Sociology*, London, Pluto Press.

French, D., and French, E. (1975), *Working Communally*, New York,

Russel Sage Foundation.

Galbraith, J. K. (1952), *American Capitalism*, Boston, Houghton Mifflin.

Galbraith, J. K. (1958), *The Affluent Society*, Boston, Houghton Mifflin.

Galbraith, J. K. (1967), *The New Industrial State*, Boston, Houghton Mifflin.

Giddens, A. (1973), *The Class Structure of Advanced Societies*, London, Hutchinson.

Ginsberg, M. (1930), 'Class consciousness', in Seligman, E. R. A. (ed) (1930), *Encyclopedia of the Social Sciences*, 3, New York, Macmillan, pp. 536–8.

Glass, D. V. (ed) (1954), *Social Mobility in Britain*, London, Routledge & Kegan Paul.

Goldthorpe, J. H. (1969), 'Social stratification in industrial society', in Heller (ed) (1969), *Structured Social Inequality*, pp. 452–65.

Goldthorpe, J. H., Lockwood, D., Bechhofer, F., and Platt, J. (1969), *The Affluent Worker in the Class Structure*, Cambridge University Press.

Griffin, L. J., and Alexander, K. L. (1978), 'Schooling and socioeconomic attainments', *American Journal of Sociology*, 84, pp. 319–47.

Gusfield, J. (1973), 'Tradition and modernity', in Etzioni and Etzioni-Halevy (eds) (1973), *Social Change*, pp. 333–41.

Guttsman, W. L. (1963), *The British Political Elite*, London, MacGibbon & Kee.

Habermas, J. (1975), *Legitimation Crisis*, Boston, Beacon Press.

Hagen, E. E. (1962), *On the Theory of Social Change*, Homewood, Dorsey Press.

Halsey, A. H. (1962), 'The changing functions of universities', in Halsey *et al.* (eds) (1962), *Education, Economy and Society*, pp. 156–65.

Halsey, A. H. (1975), 'Education and social mobility in Britain since World War II', in *Education, Inequality and Life Chances*, 1, Paris, OECD, pp. 501–59.

Halsey, A. H. (1977), 'Towards meritocracy? The case of Britain', in Karabel and Halsey, (eds) (1977), *Power and Ideology in Education*, pp. 173–86.

Halsey, A. H., Floud, J., and Anderson, C. A. (eds) (1962), *Education, Economy and Society*, Chicago, Free Press.

Hans, N. (1961), 'Class, caste and intellectual elite in comparative perspective', *Comparative Education Review*, 4, pp. 140–6.

Hardy, D. (1979), *Alternative Communities in Nineteenth-Century England*, London, Longman.

Harrigan, P. J. (1976), 'The social origins, ambitions and occupations of secondary students in France during the Second Empire', in Stone, L. (ed), *Schooling and Society*, Baltimore, Johns Hopkins University Press, pp. 206–35.

Hauser, R. M., and Featherman, D. C. (1973), 'Trends in the occupational mobility of U.S. men, 1962–1970', *American Sociological*

Review, 38, pp. 302–10.
Hauser, R. M., Koffel, J. N., Travis, H. P., and Dickinson, P. J. (1975a), 'Temporal changes in occupational mobility', *American Sociological Review*, 40, pp. 279–97.
Hauser, R. M., Dickinson, P. J., Travis, H. P., and Koffel, J. N. (1975b), 'Structural changes in occupational mobility among men in the United States', *American Sociological Review*, 40, pp. 585–98.
Havighurst, R. J. (1970), 'Social class and education', in Dropkin, S., Full, H., and Schwarcz, E. (eds) (1970), *Contemporary American Education* (2nd edn), London, Collier-Macmillan, pp. 466–82.
Havighurst, R. J. (1971), 'Education, social mobility and social change in four societies', in Gezi, K. I. (ed) (1971), *Education in Comparative and International Perspectives*, New York, Holt Rinehart & Winston, pp. 262–79.
Heilbroner, R. L. (1962), *The Making of Economic Society*, Englewood Cliffs, NJ, Prentice-Hall.
Heller, C. S. (ed) (1969), *Structured Social Inequality*, New York, Macmillan.
Henderson, R. F. (1975), Chairman, Commission of Inquiry into Poverty, *Poverty in Australia: An Outline*, Canberra, Australian Government Publishing Service.
Hewitt, C. J. (1974), 'Policy making in postwar Britain', *British Journal of Political Science*, 4, Part 2, pp. 187–216.
Hollander, P. (1973), *Soviet and American Society*, Oxford University Press.
Holloway, M. (1966), *Heavens on Earth* (2nd edn), New York, Dover Publications.
Hoogvelt, A. M. M. (1976), *The Sociology of Developing Societies*, London, Macmillan.
Hope, K. (n.d.), 'Trends in the openness of British society in the present century', (unpublished).
Hoselitz, B. F. (1964), 'Social stratification and economic development', *International Social Science Journal*, 16, pp. 237–51.
Huntington, S. P. (1968), *Social Order in Changing Societies*, New Haven, Yale University Press.
Husén, T. (ed) (1967), *International Study of Achievement in Mathematics* (2 vols), Stockholm, Almquist & Wiksell International.
Husén, T. (1972), *Social Background and Educational Career*, Paris, OECD.
Husén, T. (1975), *Social Influences on Educational Attainments*, Centre for Educational Research and Innovation, Paris, OECD.
Husén, T. (1977), 'Academic performance in selective and comprehensive schools', in Karabel, J. and Halsey, A. H. (eds) (1977), *Power and Ideology in Education*, pp. 275–82.
Inkeles, A. (1960), 'Social stratification in the modernization of Russia', in Black, C. E. (ed), *The Transformation of Russian Society*, Cambridge, Mass., Harvard University Press.
Inkeles, A. (1973), 'Making men modern', in Etzioni and Etzioni-Halevy (eds) (1973), *Social Change*, pp. 342–61.

Inkeles, A., and Smith, D. H. (1974), *Becoming Modern*, London, Heinemann.

International Labour Office (1976; 1978), *Yearbook of Labour Statistics*, Geneva.

James, J. L. (1974), *American Political Parties in Transition*, New York, Harper & Row.

Jencks, C. (1972), *Inequality*, New York, Basic Books.

Jones, F. L. (1974), 'Social inequalities in industrial societies', (unpublished).

Jouvenel, B. de (1952), *Power: The Natural History of its Growth* (rev. edn), London, Batchworth Press.

Kahl, J. A. (1962), 'Common man boys', in Halsey *et al.* (eds) (1962), *Education, Economy and Society*, pp. 348–66.

Karabel, J., and Halsey, A. H. (eds) (1977), *Power and Ideology in Education*, New York, Oxford University Press.

Kaufman, R. Chernotsky, H., and Geller, D. (1975), 'A preliminary test of the theory of dependency', in *Comparative Politics* (Chicago), 7, pp. 303–30.

Keller, S. (1963), *Beyond the Ruling Class*, New York, Random House.

Key, V. O. Jr (1958), *Politics, Parties and Pressure Groups* (4th edn), New York, Crowell.

Knowles, L. C. A. (1932), *Economic Development in the Nineteenth Century*, London, Routledge & Kegan Paul.

Lane, R. E. (1959), *Political Life*, Chicago, Free Press.

Lenski, G. (1954), 'Status crystallization', *American Sociological Review*, 19, pp. 405–13.

Lenski, G., and Lenski, J. (1978), *Human Societies* (3rd edn), New York, McGraw Hill.

Leonard, R. L. (1968), *Elections in Britain*, London, Van Nostrand.

Lerner, D. (1965), *The Passing of Traditional Society*, New York, Free Press.

Lerner, D. (1968), 'Modernization – social aspects', in Sills, D. (ed) (1968), *International Encyclopedia of the Social Sciences*, 10, New York, Macmillan and Free Press, pp. 386–94.

Levy, M. Jr (1966), *Modernization and the Structure of Societies* (2 vols), Princeton University Press.

Lippman, W. (1961), *Public Opinion*, New York, Macmillan.

Lipset, S. M. (1967), 'Party systems and the representation of social groups', in Macridis, R. C. (ed) (1967), *Political Parties*, pp. 40–74.

Lipset, S. M., and Bendix,R. (1964), *Social Mobility in Industrial Society*, Berkeley, University of California Press.

Lipset, S. M., Trow, M. A., and Coleman, J. S. (1956), *Union Democracy*, Chicago, Free Press.

Little, A. and Westergard, J. (1964), 'The trends of class differentials in educational opportunity in England and Wales', *British Journal of Sociology*, 15, pp. 301–16.

Lydall, H. (1968), *The Structure of Earnings*, Oxford, Clarendon Press.

McConnell, G. (1967), *Private Power and American Democracy*, New York, Knopf.

McClelland, D. C. (1973), 'Business drive and national achievement', in Etzioni and Etzioni-Halevy (eds) (1973), *Social Change*, pp. 161–74.
McGowan, P. J. (1976), 'Economic dependence and economic performance in Black Africa', *The Journal of Modern African Studies* (Cambridge), 14, pp. 25–40.
Mackie, T. T., and Rose, R. (1974), *The International Almanac of Electoral History*, London, Macmillan.
Macridis, R. C. (ed) (1967), *Political Parties*, New York, Harper & Row.
Macridis, R. C. (1967), 'Introduction', in Macridis, R. C. (ed) (1967), *Political Parties*, pp. 9–23.
Mandel, E. (1975), *Late Capitalism* (trans. J. de Bres), London, New Left Books.
Mann, M. (1973), *Consciousness and Action Among the Western Working Class*, London, Macmillan.
Mannheim, K. (1946), *Man and Society in an Age of Reconstruction* (trans. E. Shils) (rev. edn), London, Kegan Paul Trench Trubner.
Mannheim, K. (1950), *Diagnosis of Our Time*, London, Routledge & Kegan Paul.
Marcuse, H. (1964), *One-Dimensional Man*, Boston, Beacon Press.
Marx, K. (1976), *Capital* (trans. B. Fowkes), Harmondsworth, Penguin.
Marx, K., and Engels, F. (1848), 'The class struggle' (from the *Communist Manifesto*), in Etzioni and Etzioni-Halevy (eds) (1973), *Social Change*, pp. 32–9.
Merton, R. K. (1957), *Social Theory and Social Structure* (rev. edn), New York, Free Press.
Merton, R. K. (1957a), 'Manifest and latent functions', in his *Social Theory and Social Structure*, pp. 19–84.
Merton, R. K. (1957b), 'Social structure and anomie', in his *Social Theory and Social Structure*, pp. 131–60.
Michels, R. (1949), *Political Parties*, Chicago, Free Press.
Miliband, R. (1965), 'Marx and the state', *The Socialist Register*, pp. 278–96.
Miliband, R. (1973), *The State in Capitalist Society*, London, Quartet Books.
Miller, H. P. (1969), 'What's happening to our income revolution?' in Heller (ed), *Structured Social Inequality*, pp. 133–8.
Miller, S. M. (1969), 'Comparative social mobility', in Heller (ed.), *Structured Social Inequality*, pp. 325–40.
Mills, C. W. (1951), *White Collar*, New York, Oxford University Press.
Mills, C. W. (1959a), *The Power Elite*, New York, Oxford University Press.
Mills, C. W. (1959b), *The Sociological Imagination*, New York, Grove Press.
Mills, C. W. (1973), 'The sources of societal power', in Etzioni and Etzioni-Halevy (eds) (1973), *Social Change*, pp. 123–30.
Mitchell, B. R. (1975), *European Historical Statistics 1750-1970*, London, Macmillan.
Moore, W. E. (1973), 'Motivational aspects of development', in Etzioni and Etzioni-Halevy (eds) (1973), *Social Change*, pp. 301–9.

Mountford, J. (1966), *British Universities*, London, Oxford University Press.

Mueller, C. (1973), *The Politics of Communication*, New York, Oxford University Press.

Musgrave,R. A. (1969), *Fiscal Systems*, New Haven, Yale University Press.

Myrdal, G. (1968), *Asian Drama* (3 vols), Harmondsworth, Penguin.

Myrdal, G. (1969), 'Challenge to affluence', in Heller (ed), *Structured Social Inequality*, pp. 138–43.

Nash, M. (1963), 'Introduction: approaches to the study of economic growth', *The Journal of Social Issues*, 19, pp. 1–5.

Nettl, J. P., and Robertson, R. (1968), *International Systems and the Modernization of Societies*, New York, Basic Books.

Nisbet, R. A. (1953), *The Quest for Community*, New York, Oxford University Press.

Nisbet, R. A. (1967), *The Sociological Tradition*, London, Heinemann.

Nordhoff, C. (1966), *The Communistic Societies of the United States*, New York, Dover Publications (first published in 1875).

O'Brien, P. J. (1975), 'A critique of Latin American theories of dependency', in Oxaal, I., Barnett, T., and Booth, D. (eds) (1975), *Beyond the Sociology of Development*, London, Routledge & Kegan Paul, pp. 7–27.

O'Connor, J. (1973), *The Fiscal Crisis of the State*, New York, St Martin's Press.

OECD (1969), *Development of Secondary Education*, Paris.

Parsons, T. (1949), *The Structure of Social Action*, (2nd edn), Chicago, Free Press.

Parsons, T. (1951), *The Social System*, Chicago, Free Press.

Parsons, T. (1954), *Essays in Sociological Theory*, (rev. edn), Chicago, Free Press.

Parsons, T. (1966), *Societies: Evolutionary and Comparative Perspectives*, Englewood Cliffs, NJ, Prentice-Hall.

Parsons, T. (1973), 'A functional theory of change', in Etzioni and Etzioni-Halevy (eds) (1973), *Social Change*, pp. 72–86.

Passow, H., Noah, H. J., Eckstein, M. A., and Mallea, J. R. (1976), *The National Case Study, International Studies in Evaluation*, 7, Stockholm, Almquist & Wiksell International.

Peaslee, A. C. (1967), 'Primary, school enrolments and economic growth', *Comparative Education Review*, 11, pp. 57–67.

Peterson, A. D. C. (1960), *A Hundred Years of Education* (2nd edn), New York, Collier Books.

Pirenne, H. (1939), *A History of Europe*, London, Allen & Unwin.

Playford, J., and Kirsner, D. (eds) (1972), *Australian Capitalism*, Penguin, Australia.

Poignant, R. (1969), *Education and Development in Western Europe, the United States, and the USSR*, New York, Teachers College Press.

Polsby, N. W. (1963), *Community Power and Democratic Theory*, New Haven, Yale University Press.

Portes, A. (1973), 'Modernity and development: a critique', *Studies in Comparative International Development*, 8, pp. 247–79.

Poulantzas, N. (1975), *Political Power and Social Classes* (trans. T. O'Hagen), London, New Left Books.

Prewitt, K., and Stone, A. (1973), *The Ruling Elites*, New York, Harper & Row.

Projector, D. S., and Weiss, G. S. (1966), *Survey of Financial Characteristics of Consumers*, Federal Reserve Technical Papers, Washington DC, Federal Reserve Board.

Psacharopoulos, G. (1975), *Earnings and Education in OECD Countries*, Paris, OECD.

Putnam, R. D. (1976), *The Comparative Study of Political Elites*, Englewood Cliffs, NJ, Prentice-Hall.

Reid, I. (1978), *Sociological Perspectives on School and Education*, London, Open Books.

Rex, J. (1961), *Key Problems of Sociological Theory*, London, Routledge & Kegan Paul.

Riesman, D. (1961), *The Lonely Crowd*, New Haven, Yale University Press.

Rigby, A. (1974a), *Alternative Realities*, London, Routledge & Kegan Paul.

Rigby, A. (1974b), *Communes in Britain*, London, Routledge & Kegan Paul.

Riggs, F. (1966), *Thailand*, Honolulu, East-West Center Press.

Ringer, F. K. (1967), 'Higher education in Germany in the nineteenth century', in Laquer, W., and Mosse, G. L. (eds) (1967), *Education and Social Structure in the Twentieth Century*, New York, Harper & Row, pp. 123–38.

Roberts, R. E. (1971), *The New Communes*, Englewood Cliffs, NJ, Prentice-Hall.

Rogoff, N. (1962), 'American public schools and equality of opportunity', in Halsey *et al.* (eds) (1962), *Education, Economy and Society*, pp. 140–7.

Rose, A. (1967), *The Power Structure*, New York, Oxford University Press.

Rosner, M. (n.d.), *Worker Participation in Kibbutz Industry*, Ruppin Institute.

Rostow, W. W. (1973), 'The takeoff into self-sustained growth', in Etzioni and Etzioni-Halevy (eds) (1973), *Social change*, pp. 285-300.

Roy, E. P. (1964), *Co-operatives: Today and Tomorrow*, Danville, Ill., Interstate Printers and Publishers.

Roy, E. P. (1976), *Co-operatives: Development, Principles and Management* (3rd edn), Danville, Ill., Interstate Printers & Publishers.

Rubinstein, W. D. (n.d.), 'Perspectives on I. Wallerstein's, *The Modern World System*', (unpublished).

Sartori, G. (1962), *Democratic Theory*, Detroit, Wayne State University Press.

Sartori, G. (1971), 'Technological forecasting and politics', *Survey*, 16, pp. 60-8.

Schumpeter, J. A. (1962), *Capitalism, Socialism and Democracy* (3rd edn), New York, Harper & Row.

Seal, H. (1973), *Alternative Life Styles*, Hamilton, Waikato University.

Sewell, W. H., Haller, A. O., and Ohlendorf, G. W. (1970), 'The educational and early occupational status attainment process', *American Sociological Review*, 35, pp. 1014–27.

Shanon, R. (1975), 'Inequality in the distribution of personal income', in *Education, Inequality and Life Chances*, 1, Paris, OECD, pp. 109–58.

Shepher, J. (1977), *Introduction to the Sociology of the Kibbutz*, Rupin, Institute (Hebrew).

Skinner, B. F. (1948), *Walden Two*, New York, Macmillan.

Skocpol, T. (1977), 'Wallerstein's world capitalist system', *American Journal of Sociology*, 82, pp. 1075–90.

Smelser, N. J. (1973), 'Toward a theory of modernization', in Etzioni and Etzioni-Halevy (eds) (1973), *Social Change*, pp. 268–84.

Smith, A. (1973), *The Concept of Social Change*, London, Routledge & Kegan Paul.

Steinberg, A. (1972), *The Bosses*, New York, New American Library.

Talmon, Y. (1972), *Family and Community in the Kibbutz*, Cambridge, Mass., Harvard University Press.

Thernstrom, S. (1966), 'Class and mobility in a nineteenth century city', in Bendix, R., and Lipset, S. M. (eds) (1966), *Class, Status and Power*, (2nd edn), New York, Free Press, pp. 602–15.

Thernstrom, S. (1973), *The Other Bostonians*, Cambridge, Mass., Harvard University Press.

Thomson, D. (1967), *Europe Since Napoleon*, (rev. edn), Harmondsworth, Penguin.

Tiger, L., and Shepher, J. (1975), *Women in the Kibbutz*, New York, Harcourt Brace Jovanovich.

Toffler, A. (1970), *Future Shock*, New York, Random House.

Touraine, A. (1971), *The Post Industrial Society* (trans. L. F. X. Mayhew), New York, Random House.

Truman, D. (1959), 'The American system in crisis', *Political Science Quarterly*, 74, pp. 481–97.

Turner, R. H. (1962), 'Modes of social ascent through education', in Halsey *et al.* (eds) (1962), *Education, Economy and Society*, pp. 121–39.

Tyack, D. B. (1967), *Turning Points in American Educational History*, Waltham, Mass., Blaisdell.

UNESCO (1968), *Access to Higher Education in Europe*, Paris.

UNESCO (1977), *Statistical Yearbook 1976*, Paris.

United Nations (1967), *Incomes in Postwar Europe*, Geneva.

United Nations (1978), *Statistical Yearbook 1977*, New York.

United States Bureau of the Census (1960), *Historical Statistics of the United States – Colonial Times to 1957*, Washington, DC.

United States Bureau of the Census (1975), *Historical Statistics of the United States – Colonial Times to 1970*, Washington, DC.

United States Bureau of the Census (1977), *Statistical Abstract of the*

United States: 1977, Washington, DC.

Walker, D. A. (1976), *The IEA Six Subject Survey, International Studies in Evaluation*, 9, Stockholm, Almquist & Wiksell International.

Waller, J. H. (1973), 'Achievement and social mobility', in Eysenck, H. J. (ed) (1973), *The Measurement of Intelligence*, Lancaster, Medical and Technical Publishing Co., pp. 384–91.

Wallerstein, I. (1974a), *The Modern World System*, New York, Academic Press.

Wallerstein, I. (1974b), 'The rise and future demise of the world capitalist system', *Comparative Studies in Society and History*, 16, pp. 387–415.

Weber, M. (1958), *The Protestant Ethic and the Spirit of Capitalism* (trans. T. Parsons), New York, Charles Scribner's Sons.

Weber, M. (1961), *General Economic History* (trans. F.H. Knight), New York, Collier.

Wilson, K. L., and Portes, A. (1975), 'The educational attainment process', *American Journal of Sociology*, 81, pp. 343–62.

Wolfle, D. (1962), 'Educational opportunity, measured intelligence, and social background', in Halsey *et al.* (eds), (1962), *Education, Economy and Society*, pp. 216–40.

World Bank (1978), *The World Development Report*, Washington, DC.

Young, M. (1958), *The Rise of Meritocracy, 1870–2033*, London, Thames & Hudson.

Yuchtman, E. (1972), 'Reward distribution and work role attractiveness in the Kibbutz', *American Sociological Review*, 37, pp. 581–95.

Zeitlin, I. M. (1968), *Ideology and the Development of Sociological Theory*, Englewood Cliffs, N.J., Prentice-Hall.

Index

Abel-Smith, B., 134
Absolutism, as political stage, 144,
  145, 151, 152, 156; divine
  right, 167; and parliament,
  171, 172
Accountability, political, 48
Achievement: and class, 35;
  class bias, 214–17; educational,
  205–6, 207, 215; and expectations, 216; need for, 47–8,
  53–4, 79, 215–16; as pattern
  variable, 37–9, 40; and
  Protestant ethic, 23–4; and
  strain, 35
Administration, state, see
  Bureaucracy
Advertising: and consumption,
  59, 60, 88, 91, 105; and
  control, 59, 60; and political
  manipulation, 187–9
Affectivity, as pattern variable,
  37, 38
Affluence: and education, 215–16;
  and income, 133–4; and inequality, 142; relative, 114,
  129, 130, 131–5; rising,
  99–105, 112, 123, 134; and
  status, 123
Africa: aid to, 82; dependency
  theory, 67
Agriculture: in developing countries, 67; growth, 94; labour
  in, 67, 99; and recession,
  94; revolution, and capitalism,
  21
Aid, to developing countries, 46,
  48, 49, 55–6, 65, 72–3, 82
Alexander, K. L., 220
Alexander, M., 83

Alienation: in capitalism, 13, 29,
  45, 59, 61, 227; and modernization, 50; in post-industrial
  society, 46, 256
Alternatives, social, 227–54,
  260–1; communes, 228–37,
  260–1; co-operatives, 249–52,
  260–1; kibbutz movement,
  237–48; viability, 227–8,
  252–4
Althusser, Louis, 60, 195, 222
America, see United States
Amin, Samir, 67, 70
Anarchism, and communes, 231,
  236
Anderson, C. A., 219
Anderson, D. S., 214
Andreski, Stanislav, 127, 130
Anomie, 16, 29, 31, 44–6, 50,
  257; definition, 29, 35
Antiquity: in Marxist theory, 12;
  as theological stage, 10
Apprenticeship, 217
Arab countries, in world system,
  78
Argentina, in world system, 71
Aristocracy, power, 128, 129,
  149, 151–2, 162; see also
  Ruling class
Armies, see Military power
Aron, Raymond, 43–4, 148, 259
Asceticism, and capitalism, 18,
  23, 24
Ascription, as pattern variable, 37,
  38
Aspirations: educational, and class,
  215–16; egalitarian, and
  achievement, 260
Assemblies, seeParliament

285

Guilds, 160; and individualism, 26-7
Gusfield, J., 52
Guttsman, W. L., 163

Habermas, Jurgen, 62
Hague, Frank, 185
Halevy, E. Etzioni-, *see* Etzioni-Halevy
Halsey, A. H., 193, 220, 221
Hans, N., 209, 217
Hardy, D., 234, 237
Harrigan, P. J., 210, 217
Hauser, R. M., 137, 138, 142
Havighurst, R. J., 216
Hegemony of Western capitalism, 58-60, 124
Heilbroner, R. L., 93, 94, 95, 97, 131, 133
Henderson, R. F., 135
Hierarchy, social, *see* Stratification
Higher education: and class, 209, 214-17; development, 198, 201, 205; free, 203, 214-15; role, 193, 195; selection in, 218-19
High schools, 201, 202
Higley, J., 99, 147
Hinduism and capitalism, 25
Hippie communes, 233-4
Hitler, Adolf, 59
Holding companies, 96
Holland, *see* Netherlands
Hollander, P., 105
Holloway, M., 231
Hoogvelt, A. M. M., 50, 53, 56, 73, 78, 80
Hope, K., 138
Hoselitz, B. F., 37, 51
House of Commons, *see* Parliament
Huntington, S. P., 144, 171, 172, 175
Husén, Torsten, 204, 207-8, 214, 220, 222
Hutterite communes, 232

Identity, problem of, 62, 227

Ideological State Apparatuses (ISA), 195-6
Ideology: of class 'system, 114, 128-9; and control, 60; of democracy, 158-9; and education, 195-6; and government power, 158-60; nationalism, 158-9
IEA, *see* International Association for the Evaluation of Educational Achievement
IFTU, *see* International Federation of Trade Unions
Illiteracy, *see* Literacy
Immediate gratification, 38, 215
Imperialism, and modernization, 55, 56, 64; and stability, 68
Imports, protection, 72
Income: and class, 131-5; and fertility, 136; inequality of, 131-5, 141; and wealth, 133-4
India: capitalism in, 25; in world system, 71
Individualism: in communes, 230, 231, 233; in contemporary society, 227; doctrines, 26-7, 28-9, 45; as pattern variables, 37, 38
Individual representation, 175
Individual traits, and modernization, 40
Industrial conflict, institutionalization, 89, 109-11, 120
Industrial injury, legislation, 106
Industrialization: definition, 98; and occupational change, 99; phases, 98-9
Industrial revolution: and class, 128; and conflict, 109-10; effects, 9; and global theories, 10-13; living conditions, 101-2; phases, 98-9
Industrial societies: bases, 11; labour force, 99; ruling class, 117
Inequality: basis of, 116, 121; changes in, 114, 122-3, 141, 143, 144, 259; definition, 115-16; global, 67; of power,

Monarchy, *see* Crown
Monopoly: and mega-corporations, 90, 91, 96-8; processes, 96; tendency towards, 63, 96
Moore, W. E., 47, 115
Moral code, and capitalism, 24, 257
Mosca, Gaetano, 18-19, 41, 147
Mueller, C., 188
Multi-national corporations, economic colonialism, 72-3
Musgrave, R. A., 154, 159
Myrdal, G., 134, 135

Naples, Kingdom of, parliament, 171
Napoleon Bonaparte, 156
Nash, M., 49
National Commission, Enquiry into Poverty, 135
Nationalism, 34-5, 159
Nationalization, 184
Nation-state, development, 158-9
Nazism, 28, 33, 34-5, 109
Needs: immediacy of, 251; relative, 114, 142
Neo-colonialism, 70, 72-3, 77; and under-development, 80-3
Neo-evolutionism, 38-9
Neo-marxism: alienation, 46; change in capitalism, 62; dependency theory, 63-4; development, peaceful, 73
Netherlands: capitalism, 24; communes, 235; co-operatives, 251; as core country, 67; education, 200, 206, 211, 212; elites, origins, 139; GDP, 104; GNP, 102; income distribution, 132, 134; industrialization, 98; occupations, 101; unemployment, 107; wages, 104; welfare expenditure, 108
Nettl, J. P., 57
Neutrality, affective, 37, 38, 215
New Deal policy, 94, 95; and co-operatives, 250; and welfare, 106; and worker organization, 111

New England, capitalism, 24-5
New Harmony commune, 230
New Zealand: education, 206; income, inequality, 134; welfare expenditure, 108; in world system, 70, 76-7
Nisbet, R. A., 26, 27
Non-symbolic manipulation, 183-7
Nordhoff, C., 231
Norms, collective, 15-16, 257; individual, 16; and integration, 15-16; in modernization, 47
Norway: education, 206, 212; income, relative, 132, 133; unemployment, 107, 109; welfare, expenditure, 108

Oakland co-operative, 251
O'Brien, P. J., 73
Occupation: and birth rate, 136; change, 89-90, 99, 100, 101, 136; and education, 219-21; and social mobility, 130, 136-7, 138, 139, 141-2
Oceania, co-operatives in, 250
O'Connor, J., 62
Oil, prices, 100, 112
Oil-producing countries: economic growth, 81; in world system, 78, 258
Oligopoly, tendency towards, 63, 96
Oneida, commune, 229
Open society, 123, 138, 168-9
Opportunity, equality of, 63, 93, 120, 129, 142; in education, 221-2
Opposition, institutionalization, 173; *see also* Conflict
Organization, freedom, 167, 169-70
Oriental society, capitalism, 25; marxist view, 12
Overlords, 125, 127
Owen, Robert, 230, 233
Ownership: and class conflict, 41-2; communal, 12, 229-30, 238, 241, 243-4; and power,

Ownership: (*cont.*)
41–2, 63, 88–9, 116–17, 121,
122, 125

Parents, and status, 118, 123
Pareto, Vilfredo, 18–19, 41, 47
Parliament: composition, 163;
development of, 171–2;
individual representation, 175;
power, 172, 175
Parsons, Talcott: criticism of,
51; and history, 49–50; multi-
causal analysis, 46–7; neo-
evolutionism, 38–9; pattern
variables, 37–8, 51; strain, 34–5
Participatory democracy, 166–81;
and consent, 166–7; elections,
174–81; increase in, 145, 189;
information, freedom of,
167–9; manipulation, political,
181–9; in modernization, 40,
50, 144, 145; organization,
freedom, 167, 169–70;
parliament, 171–2; political
parties, 173–4; and protest,
170; representative institutions,
170–4
Particularism: as pattern variable,
37, 38; in Western society,
51–2
Parties, political: in capitalism,
150; evolution, 173–4
Passow, H., 206, 207
Patriotism, 159
Pattern variables, 37–8, 51
Peace Corps, 55
Peaslee, A. C., 79
Pensions, state, 107
Periphery in world system, 68–70
Permissive society, 59–60
Pervasiveness of government acti-
vity, 154–5, 159, 198
Peterson, A. D. C., 199, 207
Phalanxes, communes, 230–1
Pinto-Duschinsky, M., 163
Pirenne, H., 129
Pluralist model of polity develop-
ment, 145–7, 160, 181, 182
Poignant, R., 204

Polar dichotomies, 9, 14–18; and
contemporary theory, 36, 38;
criticism of, 51–3
Political organization, 169–70
Politicians, and knowledge
class, 118
Polity, modern: democracy,
emergence, 144; develop-
ment, 145–9; elitist model,
147–9, 162, 181–2; empi-
rical developments, 150–6;
government power, 150–62;
marxist view, 149–50, 161–2,
181–2; participation, *see*
Participatory democracy;
pluralist model, 145–7, 160,
181, 182
Population growth, *see* Fertility
rates
Portes, A., 50, 52, 56, 220
Portugal, capitalism, 24, 25
Postivist stage of evolution, 10,
28
Post-industrial society, 44–6, 56,
89–90, 99, 117, 118; alienation,
46, 256; community in, 45
Poulantzas, Nicos, 149, 150
Poverty, increasing, 134–5
Power: bases of, 125; capitalist
control, 59–60; centralization
of, 151–2; and consent, 166–7;
countervailing, 145, 146, 161,
166; and cyclical theorists, 19;
definition, 151; dynamics of, 1
19; elitist view, 147–9; of
governments, 144, 150–62; illusion of, 261; and inequality,
116; and land, 116, 121, 125,
128; and manipulation, 190;
monopoly of, 145; parliamentary, 172; participatory, *see*
Participatory democracy;
pluralist view, 145–7; political, 144, 145, 151; and pressure groups, 145–6, 148,
160–2, 166; and wealth,
ownership, 134
Power and conflict school: and
change, 56; class conflict, 41–2;